Commemorating and Forgetting

Commemorating and Forgetting

Challenges for the New South Africa

MARTIN J. MURRAY

MINNESOTA

UNIVERSITY OF MINNESOTA PRESS

MINNEAPOLIS • LONDON

The University of Minnesota Press gratefully acknowledges financial assistance provided for the publication of this book from the Office of the Vice President for Research, the Taubman College of Architecture and Urban Planning, and the Department of Afroamerican and African Studies at the University of Michigan.

Published by the University of Minnesota Press
111 Third Avenue South, Suite 290
Minneapolis, MN 55401-2520
http://www.upress.umn.edu

ISBN 978-0-8166-8299-7 (hc)
ISBN 978-0-8166-8300-0 (pb)
A Cataloging-in-Publication record for this book is available from the Library of Congress

Printed in the United States of America on acid-free paper

20 19 18 17 16 15 14 13 10 9 8 7 6 5 4 3 2 1

CONTENTS

PREFACE

Faced with the challenge in the "new South Africa" of forging a shared national identity out of a fragmented past, citizens from across the divides of race and class have been asked to set aside differences in the name of reconciliation and forgiveness as a way of moving forward into the future. Close to two decades after the end of apartheid and the transition to parliamentary democracy, the ongoing tension between what to remember and what to forget has remained unresolved. On the one side, those who emphasize the need to hold onto the painful memories of the past contend that mourning loss requires "working through" these disturbing memories as a necessary step for letting go of the past. On the other side, those who stress "letting go" of the past argue that reconciliation and forgiveness, as the core elements of the nation-building project, require a kind of willful and selective forgetting.[1]

Yet the lingering legacy of white minority rule is everywhere: in the spatial form of cities, in the enduring inequalities in life chances, in the mistrust, fears, and hostilities that saturate daily life across the lines of race and class. These traces of the past do not allow for any easy exit from history, standing in the way to the rush toward "normalization." The proximity of the apartheid past and the post-transition present renders the future uncertain.

This book is an engagement—provisional, selective, tentative—with the vexing question about how various modes of collective remembrance become embedded in the social fabric of everyday life in the "new South Africa." I am interested in questions of spatialized time and temporalized space, the mutually reinforcing dynamics of memory and amnesia, and the power of various modes of remembrance to influence the present. The mnemonic devices that I have chosen to investigate are diverse sites of memory, such as monuments and memorials and the conflicting meanings attached to them over time, museums and the work of curatorial construction, wall murals and graffiti, photographic images, pageants and parades, autobiographies, fiction writing, and theatrical performance. The particular memory-markers that I have selected certainly do not exhaust what would be possible to investigate, but I do think they represent the broad field of how collective memory is produced and reproduced. These cultural forms are not innocent iconographic representations of the historical past. They are the real embodiments, both actually and symbolically, of what is new (and old) about the "new South Africa."

Looking at the making and meaning of collective memory in the "new South Africa" can provide important insights into the stability of the new political order, the vibrancy of civic life and public culture, and the strength of the commitment to constitutional rights. As the cultural critic Andreas Huyssen has argued, "Remembrance shapes our links to the past, and the ways we remember define us in the present."[2] For those overwhelmed by painful memories, the past appears as a vast, almost endless reservoir of trauma, suffering, and loss. For others, the past (no matter how traumatic) is a collective resource that can be mobilized as a shared source of inspiration, empowerment, and redemption.[3] For still others, the overabundance of shared memory seems to hold the present hostage to the past. After all, as Huyssen has suggested, "The desire to forget always seem to grow in proportion to the desire to remember," especially when problematic questions of responsibility, culpability, and guilt are at stake.[4]

The primary aim of this book is to trace the production, contestation, interpretation, and redefinition of memory-carriers in the "new South Africa" over time and across space. It seeks to lay bare the complex interplay between collective memory, national identity, and place-making. To accomplish this goal, I focus on three separate yet overlapping dynamics: first, to show how memory-markers serve as devices both for recalling the past and for representing an imagined future; second, to expose the ongoing tension between collective memory and selective amnesia; and third, to demonstrate that forging a new national identity does not take place in a vacuum but instead emerges out of struggles over the recovery and suppression of past memories.

The basic argument I present here is that commemorative practices, and especially those that mark the end of autocratic rule and that usher in a new era of inclusionary politics, are a specific kind of history-making exercise that aims to promote and secure particular interpretations of past events while at the same time impeding or erasing potentially divergent or rival readings. The official commemorative culture that has taken root in (post-apartheid) South Africa has played a fundamental role constructing a particular understanding of the past and in legitimating a specific vision of the imagined future. Not only has this official culture of commemoration generated an uplifting narrative that interprets the transition from white minority rule to nonracial parliamentary democracy in a particular way, but it also defines the meaning of "freedom," "liberation," and "reconciliation" to conform to specific aims.[5]

The key question I address is the role that myth and memory play in the formation of collective identities. Myth and memory are not separated from history. Properly understood, history is an interpretation of the past, not the past as it really was. Myth and memory constitute the ceaseless transformation and reconstruction of history. The image of the past is subjected to constant reconsideration and reconstitution in the light of the ever-changing present.

I also seek to explore how collective memory works, that is, how particular versions of the historical past are made to matter in the "new South Africa." Framing events, persons, and places worthy of remembrance and honor entails a selective appropriation of the usable past, and not necessarily an empirically reliable mastery of history.[6] While history and memory overlap and intersect, they are certainly not identical. A central concern is the question of representation: how the historical past is made to appear in the present. How is the history of white minority rule represented, and thereby mediated, after the end of apartheid and the transition to parliamentary democracy? How are past events and major figures reconfigured and reinterpreted to fit with new national narratives and the forging of a new national identity? Addressing these questions requires a critical examination of how the practice of commemoration inscribes collective memory in places, objects, and words, and conversely, how the stories attached to these mnemonic devices selectively recount the past in ways that sometimes sanitize, distort, embellish, compress, and even fabricate history in the service of "nation-building." Transformed into cultural heritage, the practice of commemoration runs the risk of becoming escapist nostalgia or invented tradition.

I focus on the centrality of place as an anchoring device in the making and meaning of collective memory, beginning with the premise that seemingly disconnected objects as monuments and memorials, cultural-heritage sites, museums and exhibitions, public art and architecture, building typologies, landscape design, street names, public testimonials, celebrations and rituals, and autobiographical writings are all vehicles for the storage and dissemination of collective memory. Far from operating as passive receptacles or neutral storehouses for holding onto the remembered past, these mnemonic devices are active agents in shaping the construction of a tenuous collective identity and shared meaning in the everyday lives of South African citizens.[7] In short, to uncover the making and meaning of a shared collective identity, as Svetlana Boym has argued, "one needs a dual archaeology of memory and place, and a dual history of illusions and actual practices."[8]

This book gestures more to the (imagined) future than to the deep historical past. Writing contemporary history—the history of the present—forces one to confront a conundrum: Where to start the story of the often bitter and contested struggles over collective memory? The memory crisis that accompanied the end of apartheid and the transition to parliamentary democracy did not emerge full blown, born in the exuberance of the "liberation moment" and its immediate aftermath. On the contrary, contemporary disputes over remembering and forgetting can trace their deep historical roots to earlier times and places. From the seventeenth century to the present, the story of South Africa has been more or less about the continuous making and remaking of "memoryscapes." Unpacking the layered, inosculated tapestry of myths, beliefs, and cultural sensibilities that have defined white South Africa and its multiple Others requires the kind of rigorous, systematic, and critical investigation of the history of remembering and forgetting that is beyond the scope of what I can accomplish here. Rather than surveying a full spectrum of the "memoryscapes" that accompanied the long, complicated, and conflict-ridden history of white minority rule, I focus on a narrow range of memory-markers made and remade during and after the end of apartheid and the transition to parliamentary democracy. My intention is not to treat South Africa's history and cultural complexity too cavalierly or too lightly, but to acknowledge that it is impossible to do justice to these important considerations in a single study.

In South Africa, collective memory is inevitably the product of the intersection of settler colonialism with modernity. What this peculiar mixture has engendered in the "new South Africa" is a yearning for progress under circumstances where virtually every aspect of everyday life remains inextricably tied to the past. This awareness of the specificity of South African history enables us to see how collective memory emerges out of the ruins of colonialism and the dreams of modernity. Hopes for the future cannot escape the enduring traces of the past.

The methodological approach that I take here is to disaggregate, or to loosen up, the ties that bind universalizing, grand narratives to a single story of nation-building. Collective memory is situational, linked to multiple stories of sacrifice and heroism, victimhood and resentment, triumph and tragedy, and dispersed across sites that inhabit landscapes littered with ruins. The field of collective memory gives meaning to the historical past.

Introduction

Memory and Amnesia after Apartheid

The end of apartheid and the transition to parliamentary democracy brought to the surface a host of deeply entrenched tensions that were long suppressed under white minority rule. Yet as the "new nation" has struggled to establish a firm footing, the lingering ghosts of the past have continued to haunt the present. As retired South African constitutional court justice Albie Sachs once suggested, "We all know where South Africa is, but we do not yet know what it is."[1] The dilemma—at once ethical and practical—confronting the creation of the "new South Africa" has revolved around how much of the past to preserve and remember and how much to erase and forget.[2] According to John Gillis, national identity depends upon the creation of a "sense of sameness" stretched over time and distributed over space, that is to say, a "structure of feeling" (to borrow a phrase from Raymond Williams) that is sustained by the intertwined processes of remembering and forgetting.[3]

The imbricated layering of the hybrid histories of early colonization, settler colonialism, racial segregation, and apartheid—along with both organized and unorganized resistance to these forms of oppression—combined over time to produce a complex and sometimes confusing legacy of multiple identities all linked to different memories of the past and all vying for a stake in the shaping of the "new South Africa."[4] As a consequence of this peculiar history of racial oppression, the past—and the collective recollection of it—

occupies a complex, contradictory, and deeply ambivalent place in the new post-apartheid social order.[5] Fluid, unstable, and ambiguous identities in the "new South Africa" invariably produce tremendous social, political, and psychological tensions, which in turn give rise to sometimes unexpected anxieties and fears.[6]

The unsettled circumstances that accompanied the birth of the "new South Africa" gave rise to complex and often bitter conflicts over how to define, remember, and commemorate the fragmented past. As Marita Sturken has argued, the practice of collective remembrance is always a field of politico-cultural contestation, negotiation, and compromise in which different stories compete for their own place in history.[7] Despite the rhetorical flourishes about "new beginnings" and "starting afresh," the birth of the "new South Africa" did not take place outside its own historicity.[8] The matter of the "afterlife" of white minority rule—that is, the ways in which white minority rule "remains an ineradicable trace" in the everyday life of post-apartheid South Africa—has remained an irredeemable part of the present.[9] This lack of consensus over what to remember and what to let go engendered a kind of memory crisis, putting in motion disputes over what is deemed worthy of remembering, and ultimately what collective remembrance means, particularly with respect to what needs, interests, and fantasies it satisfies, and what is to be forgotten.[10] Disputes over the past reflect deeper and far-reaching struggles for control over the future.[11]

Yet memory, whether individual or collective, is a notoriously slippery term that lacks the analytic rigor so often attributed to it. The unanticipated consequence of the recent fascination with collective remembrance—what some scholars have referred to as the "memory boom"—has been to elevate the conceptual status of collective memory.[12] Used carelessly, collective memory, it appears, has sometimes assumed the exalted role of a metatheoretical trope and has laid claim to the valorized position—once exclusively reserved for empirically verifiable truth—as a privileged site of authenticity.[13] Where scholars once talked about folk history, popular history, oral history, or public history (and even myth and commemorative rituals more generally) as separate fields of inquiry, they increasingly turned to collective memory as a metahistorical category that subsumes all of these under a single rubric of "memory studies."[14]

In warning against the "terminological profusion" and "semantic overload" of collective memory, a number of scholars have argued that the overextended and sometimes indiscriminate use of the term can result not only in conceptual confusion but also in unwarranted entanglements with such related ideas as cultural identity, subjective experience, and popular consciousness.[15] The inherent danger of "memory" is its seductiveness as an all-encompassing term without precise meaning.[16] As Kerwin Lee Klein has argued, the extravagant employment of memory has enabled it to figure as "the therapeutic alternative to historical discourse."[17] The difficulty of attaching a generally agreed-upon definition to "memory" lends an unfortunate flexibility and malleability as to how it is used both in everyday speech and in scholarly writing. For this reason, one must take considerable care not to overextend its use or to compel it to bear more analytic weight than it is capable of handling.[18]

Collective memory works to pull the past into the present. Because it is so malleable and fungible, it presents the past in ways that are rarely a simple matter of factual recall.[19] To speak of the recovery, the collection, the excavation, or the layering of collective memory requires that one take care not to treat shared remembrance as an object-in-itself, or a "thing," that exists outside of those who do the remembering. Yet as Alon Confino has put it, collective memory is ultimately connected with "the intermingled beliefs, practices, and symbolic representations that make people's perception of the past."[20] Framed in this fashion, it can be argued that memories are written in stone, carved into granite, and preserved in photographs. Memories can be recovered in the form of autobiographies, collected in museums, displayed in monuments and memorials, and layered at particular sites. It is in this sense, metaphorically at least, that collective memory takes on a life of its own—as a shared understanding that belongs to social groups and collectivities of all kinds.

This focus on cultural or the symbolic dimension of politics, although a broad and amorphous category, can assist us in reaching a more inclusive and sophisticated appreciation of the ways in which such vehicles of memory as monuments and memorials, museum exhibitions, autobiographical writing, documentary film, popular cinema, and the visual arts are instrumental in forging a sense of shared national identity. Rather than interpreting the meaning of these mnemonic devices as mere expressions or reflections of a deeper substratum of material realities, I take these cultural productions as objects of inquiry in their own right. The cultural realm—the "symbolic universe" of shared meanings—is a crucial sphere for the communication of ideas, hopes and fears, anxieties, memories, and myths that accompanied the birth of the "new South Africa."[21]

National trauma that gives rise to political transition is almost invariably the catalyst for the construction of collective memory. White minority rule left a bitter legacy of crimes and victimhood that sprang to life with the end of apartheid and the transition to parliamentary democracy. Shared experiences, whether lived directly or lived vicariously, engendered collective memories of past wrongs that were captured in stories, protest songs, poetry, and the visual arts. A common but misplaced assumption is that national memory takes shape, at least ostensibly, as a harmonious fusion of shared values. Clearly, in the "new South Africa," where political divisions and social polarization have not disappeared, this assumption is a fallacy, a hollow promise.[22] As a general rule, collective memory is not a fusion of shared values but a multitude of perspectives, debates, and images of the past.[23] These fissures have produced a multiplicity of different modes of remembrance, including personal memories, national memories, local memories, ethnic memories, official and unofficial memories, civic memories, vernacular memories, and so on, ad infinitum. The confusion produced by too many memories, and too many people remembering, produces a crisis of memory, expressed as a kind of cacophony of discrepant (and competing) voices laying claim to some "authentic" reading of the past.[24]

The Making and Meaning of Collective Memory

Collective memory is produced and embodied in multiple forms, including monuments and memorials, commemorative events, ceremonies and rituals, anniversaries and public holidays, folk festivals and pageants, museums and exhibitions, public art and performance, architecture, popular culture, archives, visual displays of all kinds, legal discourses, historiographies, autobiographical writing, fiction, documentary film, recreational tourism, cultural-heritage sites, commodities, and social activism. What these vehicles of collective memory have in common is an abiding interest in excavating vanished places and lost times, and "reliving" them in symbolic, figural, and ritualized ways.[25] Whether in the official, institutional, or popular imagination, acts of remembrance signal an interest, desire, or need to preserve a connection with the past. Collective memory is always entangled in complex political stakes and meanings. By holding a mirror to the South African psyche, these vehicles of collective memory provide a useful way of observing contemporary anxieties, ambiguities, and uncertainties about the future.[26]

Regimes of memory fill in the physical and psychic space that the passage of time inevitably creates. Every regime of past memory is equally a vision of a possible future. Those who remember the past with nostalgic longing typically seek to preserve as much of it as they possibly can. Conversely, those who recoil at the bitter memories of past injustices typically look to the future for redemption, solace, and distance, and they yearn for a promising new age that will be simpler and purer than what came before. Regimes of memory operate as screens upon which people project their anxieties about repetition, change, representation, authenticity, and identity.[27] Focusing attention on these regimes of memory can offer insights into how the citizens of the "new South Africa" live in harmony with, or in stark opposition to, their past. The past and the present collide at those sites where those entrusted with the responsibility of preserving a semblance of what came before construct public domains for collective memory, such as monuments, museums, exhibits, memorials, and other commemorative sites.[28]

Commemorative practices have always been deeply invested in the shaping of political and national identities, and the recasting of new memory-markers provides us with significant clues as to the social stability of the "new South Africa" and about the ways that the custodians of memory—both from the top down and from the bottom up—project its future.[29] A close reading of the memorial landscapes that have proliferated after the end of apartheid can reveal insights into the power of collective memory to shape national identity. Looking at the cultural politics of "nation-building" through the lens of an assortment of mnemonic devices—such as monuments and memorials, museums, and autobiographical writing—enables us to grasp how the lingering, ghostly presence of the past, always contested and never stable, haunts the present. While the "new South Africa" is located in the historical conjuncture that has been called " post-apartheid," it must be recognized that the legacies and impositions of white minority rule are far from over, and that they have remained embedded and intertwined with, and imprinted upon, the here-and-now.[30]

Put at the service of recalling historical trauma or celebrating triumph of "good" over "evil," the practice of commemoration possesses a singular power to generate through the built form of architecture, statuary, monuments and memorials, literature, art, and other means of aesthetic expression what might be called "landscapes of remembrance." White minority rule left an enduring legacy of shared memories of forced displacement, state terror, and racial segregation that are now officially remembered in the "new South Africa" in physical sites and material objects, as well as visual images and written words. If all memory-markers are semiotically underdetermined, then it is not difficult to understand why the signs of remembrance are particularly open to different and sometimes conflicting interpretations. Collective memory is generated in the context of conflicts over who defines it, what is deemed worthy of remembering, and ultimately what it means, particularly with respect to what needs, interests, and fantasies it satisfies.[31] While the relationship of the present to the past is a purely temporal and continuous one, the connections between history and memory, cultural heritage and national identity, rhetoric and power, and remembering and forgetting, are inextricably intertwined in complex ways.[32] Looked at from the vantage point of the present, the historical past is always implicated in the here-and-now: these "presentist" concerns shadow every memory recovered, lurk behind the desire to "relive" past experience, and consciously or unconsciously shape every interpretation of what happened and why.[33]

Understanding the practice of collective memory entails unpacking the means by which social groups reconstruct, assimilate, and make sense of their past. Recent scholarship has suggested that neither forgetting nor remembering is a homogeneous practice. Whether incidental or deliberate, the conjoined processes of forgetting and remembering work in tandem. Instead of treating them as mutually exclusive categories, remembering and forgetting are constitutive processes that create the conditions for the practice of collective memory.[34]

The Politics of Forgetting in the Service of Social Amnesia

The end of apartheid and the transition to parliamentary democracy was greeted with a veritable flood of journalistic accounts and scholarly analyses that hailed the birth of the "new South Africa" as nothing short of a "miracle."[35] For the most part, these commentaries reinforced a celebratory narrative that recounted the story of how a few men of goodwill (particularly F. W. de Klerk and Nelson Mandela) almost single-handedly overcame all sorts of obstacles to orchestrate a largely peaceful transfer of power that marked a decisive break with the odious past. With the passage of time, this early fixation on "Madiba magic" (Mandela's Xhosa clan name) and the promise of new beginnings have lost much of their original appeal. The warm embrace of free-market capitalism—along with the elevation of the attendant values of individualism and acquisitiveness—marked a decisive turn away from the principles enshrined in the 1955 Freedom Charter.[36]

"If that brief historical moment after the end of apartheid seemed saturated with long repressed memories of tragedy and suffering," as James Statman has argued, "then subsequent years have been subjected to the pressures of willful forgetting."[37] Just like the many Germans who could not recall ever having supported the Nazis or seen evidence of the oppression of Jews, white South Africa seems to be developing a serious case of amnesia to complement its symptoms of privileged indifference and denial. Close to two decades after the end of white minority rule and the successful transition to parliamentary democracy, the initial obsession with unmasking the injustices and injuries of the racially oppressive apartheid system has begun to fade. In the headlong rush to get out from under the apartheid past, a rising chorus of voices urgently called for a quick resolution of grievances held over from the past. In the absence of a full-fledged political commitment to expose the long-term effects of the structural violence of apartheid and to seek ways to offer compensation, an "insubstantial culture of distraction" has filled the void.[38] Concerns with making money and the lure of conspicuous consumption have contributed to a cultural of amnesia.[39] The uneasy tension between remembering and forgetting has produced sharp divisions where the battle lines are firmly entrenched between the custodians of memory, who contend that only a firm grasp and appreciation of the historical past can provide a solid foundation for building the future, and those who argue that only by letting go of the past is it possible to start afresh.[40]

The novelty implied in invoking the terminology of the "new South Africa" suggests a decisive and recognizable break with the historical past. Yet, as Saskia Sassen has argued in another context, the "new" in history is rarely *ex nihilum*. The apparent "newness" is deeply implicated in the past, saddled with the kinds of path dependence that are not easily broken.[41] In short, the end of apartheid and the transition to parliamentary democracy was indeed a much more complicated, messier process, and tied to older lineages than the birth of the "new South Africa" suggests.

The end of apartheid and the transition to parliamentary democracy came about through what has been called "transmutation," that is, a brokered transfer of political power from an authoritarian regime to a new multiparty democratic order through negotiated compromise that produced a partial modification in the prevailing "rules of the game" rather than a wholesale restructuring of the existing state administration.[42] Because this process of transmutation involved only a partial dismantling of the old regime and its political institutions, there was no clean break with the past. The lack of clarity about what was old and what was new produced a crisis of memory, where the simultaneous impetus to construct, distort, exploit, and suppress collective remembrance resulted in an awkward terrain of compromise and contradiction.[43]

Under such unsettled circumstances, collective memory is always a two-edged sword: creating pressure for more radical transformation extending outside the boundaries of the negotiated compromise, on the one hand, and enlisting support for the preservation of elements of the old order, on the other. Shared remembrances of grave violations of human rights typically give rise to resistance to any compromises that threaten the rule of law. At the same time, unearthing the past may so alarm holdovers from the old regime and their allies in the new order that they threaten to disrupt the political compromise that produced the "new South Africa." In the effort to forge a democratic future under the terms and conditions of a negotiated settlement, collective memory is always accompanied by selective amnesia, in the sense of a largely pragmatic drift toward pseudo-forgetting. Selective amnesia serves as an instrument of smoothing over, and sanitizing, the rough edges of the negotiated settlement and the resulting political compromise.[44]

As the uncompromising rhetoric of socialism and revolutionary transformation subsided, it was replaced by the softer language of reconciliation, multiculturalism, and the "rainbow nation." As Eve Bertelson and others have suggested, this abrupt *volte-facie* required that the newly enfranchised citizenry undertake a rather wholesale "un-remembering" of the ideals and values that animated the anti-apartheid struggle.[45] By adopting the orthodoxies of free-market capitalism, the ANC leadership moved close to effectively redefining "liberation" as less a wholesale, radical transformation of the prevailing social order than a struggle for more inclusive participation in a preexisting system of spoils. Accommodation with the status quo has required a dramatic shift in thinking. For those whose entrenched power and privilege has gone unchallenged and for those who have experienced upward mobility in the "new South Africa," the past and what lessons it might contain all too often appear to have been set aside and forgotten.[46]

The end of apartheid and the transition to parliamentary democracy produced a volatile situation where collective memories of the structural violence of white minority rule were under constant threat of erasure, where bitter legacies of the past were so easily set aside in the name of national reconciliation, and where meanings attached to particular places and events became unstable and fluid.[47] While proponents of the "rainbow nation" have sought to forge a new shared national identity through deliberate exposure of the "truths" of the past, there are skeptics who argue that historical fissures and divisions are so great that the past should be left alone, unexamined and untouched. Rather than generating a harmonious fusion of values as the proponents of the "rainbow nation" had hoped, the resurrection of collective remembrances of the past has produced a range of debates, a multitude of different perspectives, and conflicting images that are not easily bracketed under the rubric of reconciliation and forgiveness.[48]

1 The Power of Collective Memory

Collective memory is not at all like a living organism that develops and matures on its own accord in linear time, as present disappears into past. Instead, it is something that is socially constructed and socially situated—not only incubated in the shared desire to preserve that which is worth remembering but also fashioned in such a way as to connect it to an "eternal present." Collective remembrance is absolutely essential for connecting the past with the future. Without memory, there is no grounding in the present or ability to imagine the future. It endows past events and persons with historical significance. It enables us to see selectively, and to alter and save what is deemed important to preserve from the past, but it also "inspires emulation in the likeness of the present."[1]

In the much-acclaimed novel *Midnight's Children,* Salman Rushdie uses his fictional characters to reflect upon what he calls "memory's truth." Memory, he says, has its own special kind of truth. "It selects, eliminates, alters, exaggerates, minimizes, glorifies, and vilifies also; but in the end it creates its own reality, its heterogeneous but usually coherent version of events; and no sane human being ever trusts someone else's version more than his own."[2] The idea that memory creates its own truth points to a kind of skepticism often associated with acts of remembrance. "Monuments, festivals, mottoes, oratory," as William Graham Sumner remarked more than a century ago, "never help history; they protect errors and sanctify prejudice."[3] More recently, in suggesting that "the past cannot be literally construed; it can only be selectively exploited," Barry Schwartz reiterates this suspicion about the power of memory to remain true to dispassionate objectivity and factual accuracy.[4]

Filtered through the lens of shared remembrance, collective memory renders scenes, events, persons, and actions that were ambiguous or inconsistent in historical accounts straightforward and clear. Whereas actual experience is a welter of conflicting images, confusing thoughts, and subjective remembrances, collective memory has the power to simplify the past, constructing coherent stories of heroism and sacrifice, or trauma and loss, which are "brought into line with contemporary circumstances."[5] For these reasons, collective memory is never settled or fixed but is always open to revision and modification.[6] It not only has the power to reshape past events; it can create wholly new ones.[7] In recounting the past, collective memory relies upon stories that typically "add background details absent from the originals, fabrications that become fixed recollections" endowed with a social life of their own.[8]

Collective memory is everywhere.[9] It moves easily back and forth through official, unofficial, public, popular, and vernacular guises. Collective memory appears in the routes of marches or parades, the location and semiotics of murals and graffiti, and the staging of elections and political campaigns.[10] Even more broadly, the choice of architectural stylistics, building sites, place-names, and streetscapes become repositories of shared remembrance.[11] Although typically unacknowledged, the visual memories of the past are embedded in the physical landscape of walls, gates, and barriers. Memories are also embodied in particular places, visual images, ritual reenactments of the past, personal stories, and casual conversations. Taken together, these "memory texts," as Annette Kuhn has argued, serve to connect private experiences and public life, and to link personal and social memories.[12]

Laying Claim to the Past: Acts of Remembrance and Sites of Memory

Collective memory, as Omer Bartov has suggested, is "elusive and ambiguous."[13] It is only tangentially related to empirically verifiable truths, but it is a vital ingredient in the symbolic discourse of politics that mobilizes popular opinion and animates a spirit of national identity.[14] By conflating remembrance, place, and history, sites of memory render the past comprehensible because they testify to an essential continuity across time. Even the most durable acts of collective remembrance are located in the "contact zone" between the past and the "eternal present." Faced with continual destabilization of their original intentions, sites of memory constantly re-create the past in ways that typically reflect "presentist" concerns.[15] Looked at closely, it is possible to grasp how the "temporal messages" that emanate from all kinds of memory-markers disrupt and unsettle the linear logic of sequential time, that is, time unfolding from a past "then" to a present "now." By simultaneously harkening back in historical time and pointing forward to an imagined future, memory-markers enable us to comprehend how past, present, and future are imbricated in every historical conjuncture. It is sometimes the case that the symbolic meanings attached to a particular event can become as significant as the event itself. As David Lowenthal has argued, "Memory not only conserves the past but adjusts recall to current needs. We make the past intelligible in light of present circumstances."[16]

The practice of commemoration is as much a politico-cultural process shaped by the anxieties of the present as it is a historical narrative influenced by an accurate reconstruction of the past. The translation of memory across space and time is a central feature of both the rituals of everyday life and to the exceptional moments of remembrances associated with tragic events and untimely deaths.[17] Social memory, as recollection, remembering, and re-presentation, is crucial in the mapping of historical moments and the articulation of identity. As Jonathan Boyarin has suggested, "Memory is neither something pre-existent and dormant in the past nor a projection from the present, but a potential for creative collaboration between present consciousness and the experience or expression of the past."[18]

Because it is socially constructed, communicated, and institutionalized, collective memory is never static or monolithic. It is always incomplete, contested, and subject to elisions, omissions, and gaps.[19] Remembrance is a contingent process where the "past is endlessly constructed in and through the present."[20] Rather than focusing primarily on the preservation of the past, collective memory reconstructs it in the context of the present. This insistence on the continuing presence of past in the present determines what "history" we remember and how we remember it. Seen in this way, collective memory is never dissociated from considerations of power.[21] In the same way that myths are flexible discursive forms open to embellishment and elision and to polysemic interpretations, symbolic sites often condense the messiness of history into easily decipherable shorthand.[22]

History, Memory, Place

Since the mid-nineteenth century, what Frances Yates called the "art of memory" has been separated from history.[23] While history and memory share a common fixation with the past, they are indeed quite distinct. Widely accepted conventions guiding contemporary historiographical research and writing have distinguished between memory as subjective, instinctual, and (consciously or unconsciously) selective, and history as objective and truth-seeking, submitting its findings to empirical verification and tests of validity.[24] Critical and systematic attention to the idea of social memory has its modern origins in the works of Maurice Halbwachs, particularly his monument treatise, *On Collective Memory*.[25] For Halbwachs, collective memory was intimately linked shared experience. Memory bound social groups together, reanimating their commonality by reference to shared identity. Conversely, he regarded history as an instrumental and thoroughly rationalized version of the past. He argued that it was through membership in a social group—particularly through kinship, religious, and class affiliations—that individuals were able to acquire, localize, and recall their memories. A central organizing principle for his work was the idea that all memory is socially constructed around some sense of place.[26]

In his exhaustive exploration of the making and re-repesenting of national identity in France, the French historian and social critic Pierre Nora focused attention on the instability of collective memory.[27] His project was prompted by a sense of urgency triggered by the belief that collective memory—as the bedrock of national identity—was under threat.[28] For Nora, *lieux de mémoire*—embodied in monuments, memorials, and other places—are places where collective memory is crystallized, and where it finds a place of refuge.[29] These realms of memory come into existence as compensation for the eradication of memory by history, as commemorative sites devoted to incarnating remembrance and entirely reliant on the specificity of past traces that, in turn, engender a kind of superstitious veneration.[30]

Nora's pioneering work has inspired an outpouring of recent scholarship concerned with the widening gap between collective memory and history in contemporary social life. What Nora accomplished was to destabilize the idea that there is only one shared collective memory that exists as a remnant of the real past.[31] Instead, he suggested that social memories are fluid and flexible, subject to competing and multiple meanings. As Raphael Samuel argued, memory is not "merely a passive receptacle or storage system, an image bank of the past," but is "historically conditioned, changing colour and shape according to the emergencies of the moment, that so far from being handed down in the timeless form of 'tradition' it is progressively altered from generation to generation."[32]

Commemorative Practices and Nation-Building

Constructing a national identity involves, literally speaking, mapping "history onto territory."[33] In the service of nation-building, these symbolic landscapes become "sacred sites" that are the repositories of shared memories, animating myths, and common traditions and the central locus for both collective and individual performances of ritual and pilgrimage.[34] The power of these symbolic landscapes lies in their elevated status as "points of physical and ideological orientation." Taken together, they constitute materialized "circuits of memory" and repositories of meaning.[35] Public monuments have long served as the focal point for collective participation in the politics of remembrance of towns, cities, and nation-states. The specific location that these monuments occupy is not just an incidental or unimportant backdrop, but actually inscribes the statues with symbolic meaning.[36] Sites of collective memory assume symbolic importance as places "to authenticate and legitimate selective stories about the past and thereby construct a [shared] identity in the present." At times of uncertainty and unease, memory-markers provide fixed reference points and a sense of stability.[37]

Conversely, the mass removal or systemic destruction of public memory-markers that celebrated discredited political figures and the political values and ideals they served represents the concerted effort of the victorious political forces to promote a kind of organized forgetting of what came before.[38] With the collapse of the Soviet Union, for example, a new generation of post-socialist political leaders moved quickly to dismantle or demolish memorials dedicated to socialist leaders, rename streets and buildings, and relocate Soviet-era statuary from their prominent place in the urban civic landscape (public parks and squares) to largely invisible "heritage sites" tucked away in inaccessible places.[39] These "disappearing acts" conformed to a general pattern in history whereby political victors almost invariably assert their newly acquired power over the vanquished by removing, eliminating, and erasing repositories of collective memory that legitimated the deposed regime.[40]

By providing a sense of shared attachment to particular histories and territories, collective memory is an essential component in the process of nation-building.[41] In the social construction of the cohesion and identity of social groups, nation-building relies upon a variety of mnemonic devices to translate the "ties that bind" into a collective awareness of belonging, or an "imagined community," in the sense defined by Benedict Anderson.[42] Yet as Michael Ignatief has argued, the collective awareness of belonging, in some cases, gets its inspiration from the politics of fantasy and myth.[43] The imaginative use of symbols, rituals, and stories is the foundation upon which collective identity, tradition, and heritage are built.[44]

Insofar as it resists the totalizing regimes of official histories, collective memory becomes a political act, enabling us to grasp onto alternative understandings of the past. Memory exists in the form of narrative, obsessively revising our relationships to places that have changed or vanished, and rewriting stories that conform to what we want to believe.[45] Seen from this angle of vision, monuments, memorials, and other commemorative practices are always open to different interpretations, where their changing meanings are refracted through shifting beliefs, values, and rituals. Ironically, what endows sites of memory with historical longevity is their almost infinite capacity for metamorphosis, a seemingly endless recycling of their symbolic importance.[46] The very act of memorialization—that is, the practice of capturing memory so that we do not forget—can, by its focused exclusivity, push aside and even deny the claims of others for their own collective remembrance and identities.[47]

Looking at efforts at memorialization suggests that the practice of collective memory is a highly problematic and contested terrain. "If the Holocaust and its memory still stand as a test case for humanist and universalist claims of Western Civilization," Karen Till has suggested, "one might argue that these place-making processes in Berlin are central symbolic and material sites of the crisis of modernity, uniquely embodying the contradictions and tensions of social memory and national identity."[48] Despite its special significance both to Jewish people and to the international human rights community as a painful symbol of the Nazi Holocaust, the symbolic landscapes of memorialization at Auschwitz have not gone uncontested. As Andrew Charlesworth has shown, the efforts of postwar Polish Communist authorities and later the Polish Catholic hierarchy to lay claim to the memory of Auschwitz as a symbolic site of sacrifice and martyrdom effectively promoted a "layering over," or "de-Judaising," of the specificity of Jewish suffering at the Nazi death camp.[49]

Monuments, Memorials, and Other Commemorative Sites

Sites of memory consist of the organization of material objects in space. The assemblage of iconographic forms in particular places materializes memory.[50] Physical landscapes are repositories of collective memory, forming a kind of vast archive that bears witness to the past. Sites of memory are not only places in space; they are also dramas in time. Such mnemomic devices as gravesites, battlegrounds, and actual places where tragic events occurred contain material traces of past activities that can be selectively used to justify collective remembrance in the present and future. History and myth often blend together to forge a shared sense of the common past.[51] Monuments, memorials, museums, and exhibitions communicate in an unusually direct and silent way the symbolic importance of shared identity and collective belonging.[52] These enable collective memory to inscribe itself into history, to be registered and codified into popular consciousness.[53] Once embedded in memorial sites, the recollection of triumphant or traumatic events seems less susceptible to the "vagaries of memory." By resisting the pressures to forget, sites of memory become vehicles for popular identity.[54]

Sites of memory come into existence as compensation for inevitable loss as the eternal present inevitably recedes into the past. Monuments and memorials, museums, cultural-heritage sites, and public commemorations are the embodiments of social memory that commemorate heroic figures, recall traumatic events, and draw attention to civic ideals. Their construction and maintenance signals the commitment of the custodians of memory to maintain a connection between the past and present.[55]

Whether in the form of silences or outright deception, fictions are embedded in the creation of monuments and memorials. Every commemorative site represents a kind of performative re-creation—of an event, a person, or a deed—that seeks to bind future generations to a moral lesson, if not to an actual truth. In the case of the remembrance of heroic events, the process is straightforward. As Douglas Allen argues, "resurrect the memory and convert it to architectural form that appropriately dignifies it." In such cases, the fiction that accompanies the act of commemoration is typically a kind of requisite hyperbolic aggrandizement or willful embellishment useful for securing the obligatory moral commitment. But when efforts are undertaken to commemorate events associated with senseless tragedy, the route toward creating an authentic remembrance is often more convoluted. Under circumstances where the pain and suffering associated with particular events seem to defy rational explanation or justifiable purpose, acts of commemoration often deflect attention from too close a reading of what actually happened in order to suppress memory.[56] The substitution of "whole-cloth fiction for the recall of actual events" creates a kind of "thwarted memory" that acts to erase or bury uncomfortable truths. Those commemorative sites of "where the original event has been so camouflaged that it presents an entirely new, fictional memory" construct what amounts to an injunction not to critically engage with the past.[57]

Monuments, memorials, and other iconographic statuary freeze time in physical space. In this way, they preserve stylized images of the past that are fixed in place. These stylized images keep alive uplifting myths of origins, and they offer assurance that the passage of time is both linear and continuous. In this way, monuments, memorials, and other commemorative statuary help to establish collective fictions: those self-conscious narratives recounting tragic loss, or romantic triumph, that are the building blocks for collective identities.[58]

More than simply a material form, a physical shape, or a visual image, a monument or memorial is also a quality: the quality that some specific places or physical objects have to make us recall, evoke, and imagine something beyond and outside ourselves. As a place of memory-work and shared remembrance, monuments and memorials are produced to be historically referential. Yet as embodiments of art in the public realm, their value and significance is not just derived from noteworthiness as artwork, but from their ability to direct attention to collective memory.[59] Their significance lies in the "dialogic character of memorial space," as James E. Young has suggested, the fluid space between the stories recounted, or the events remembered, and the act of commemoration—the memory-work—they help to frame.[60]

The rhetoric of monumental space, that is, its most powerful form of address, is narrative.[61] Put simply, collective memory is primarily transmitted through stories that seem to move seamlessly between celebrating triumphs and achievements and recalling sacrifice and tragedy. Whatever their particular form, telling stories is central to identity formation and identity affirmation. In constructing narratives, we can "discern the meaning of any single event only in temporal and spatial relation to other events."[62]

As Edward Casey has suggested, public memory is radically bivalent in its temporality, for it is both attached to a past (typically, to an originating or traumatic event of some sort) and simultaneously seeks through persuasive rhetoric to secure a future of further remembering of that same event. By simultaneously harkening back in historical time and pointing forward to an imagined future, such memory-markers as monuments and memorials produce "temporal messages" that disrupt and unsettle the linear logic of sequential time, that is, time unfolding from a past "then" to a present "now." Recognizing the Janus-faced qualities of these "temporal messages" enables us to grasp how past, present, and future are imbricated in every site of collective memory.[63]

More than innocent aesthetic embellishments of public space, monuments and memorials have political and cultural meanings attached to them.[64] Spaces of public display and ritual embody power and memory.[65] Sites of memory also embody ethical, moral, and philosophical concerns. The ways that history, memory, and trauma are appropriated, valued, and represented are also contested. The work of those who construct monuments and memorials lies in unveiling—uncovering as well as anchoring—histories and memories.[66] Monuments and memorials are physical markers for the display of collective remembrance, but they can just as easily signal the crisis of memory. As the traumatic events or heroic figures that they memorialize lose relevance, they "join the life of the street, brought into the extensive time of the everyday," their original meaning ignored or forgotten.[67] Memorial spaces that deal with trauma and tragedy function as sites of mourning.[68] Yet when they become embarrassing reminders of a discredited past, calls for their removal invariably arise. Removed or destroyed, monuments and memorials become invisible markers of oblivion—the "absent absence" of the historical past.[69]

By their very nature, commemorative sites raise all sorts of questions about history and heritage, national identity, and the role of public art in a modern democracy, especially regarding suitability, architectural style, and location. Monumental statuary commemorating past injustices always provokes a cautionary uneasiness, a wary discomfort about the lingering past, and unresolved anxieties about living in the here-and-now with the ghosts of the past. Old statuary signifying discredited political regimes stand at the center of contested histories and memories.[70] Calls for the removal or demolition of monumental statuary typically arise out of a collective desire not only to erase, at least metaphorically, the events and persons commemorated at the site, but also to recast the history that these events and persons had hitherto signified.[71]

As a general rule, monuments and memorials signify the past in the present. Despite the commemorative rhetoric that accompanies their construction, memorials and monuments typically have a relatively short life span after which their overt meaning and relevance diminishes, and they become anonymous landmarks or background ornamentation. With the passage of time and without careful attention, they tend to fall into a state of suspended animation, neither fully alive as active signs of collective memory nor completely dead as sites of indifference.[72] Separated from substantive histories and sentiments that inserted them into public consciousness, commemorative sites become easily stranded in a present that has no commemorative use for them.[73]

Monuments and memorials are crucial flashpoints around which group identities and national narratives get articulated, gain power, and claim authority. They transform a version of the past into a "living symbol," a central pillar in the assertion of cultural heritage. The remains of the past, now irretrievably lost, become symbolically reconstructed in material form as stone or bronze. The acts of remembrance that take place around the physical durability of the built object become a process of group solidarity, of shared resolution to always remember or never forget. The logic of monumentality is to unearth group origins and to imagine group destiny. Monuments and memorials are essential elements in the practice of cultural heritage. The power of remembrance cast in the built form of monuments and memorials is the capacity to assert group identity.[74]

Specific places act as fluid mosaics of shared memory, bringing together at particular locations a flood of overlapping and sometimes conflicting remembrances of the past. Places are haunted by shifting and unstable structures of meaning. Shared remembrances, when subjected to distortion and undue stretching, can easily become unanticipated instruments of forgetting. In this very real sense, collective memories have a fragile, unstable status in the contemporary age of globalization.[75] The didactic logic of monuments, their demagogical rigidity, and their "authoritarian propensity" to reduce viewers to passive spectators can undermine the power of collective memory. To the extent that the custodians of memory encourage monuments and memorials to do the work of remembrance, they may actually promote forgetfulness. In taking on the work of memory, monuments may actually relieve viewers of their own personal burdens of remembrance.[76]

In erecting formal reminders or replicas of events or persons who ought to be remembered, one risks slipping into forgetfulness. By making symbols or remnants stand for the whole, one can easily succumb to an illusion. "Once we assign monumental form to memory," James Young has argued, "we have to some degree divested ourselves of the obligation to remember." As monuments imperceptibly blend over time into the landscape, they seem to become part of the past rather than a meaningful reminder of it.[77]

Displaying Memory: Museums and Exhibitions

Such built spaces as museums, archives, and exhibitions act as repositories or storehouses for material traces of the historical past. The physical presence of these "memory-banks" provides tangible signs of historical continuity and stability in times of dramatic upheaval. Museums have a special status as official or semiofficial carriers of collective memory, repositories of cultural heritage, and mediators of historical consciousness. Like memory itself, museums mediate the past, present, and future. But unlike the memory that is animated by lived experience, museums typically give material form and shape to authorized versions of the past, which in time become institutionalized as official public memory. Yet ironically, this process of institutionalizing public memory involves both remembering and forgetting, along with inclusion and exclusion. In making decisions about what to collect and how to display it, museum curators determine criteria of significance, define sociocultural relationships and hierarchies, and establish linkages and connections between artifacts and ideas. Viewed in this light, museums influence the historical consciousness of those audiences that view the displayed exhibits. Because of the allure of authenticity and objectivity, museums are privileged locations that "validate certain forms of cultural expression and affirm particular interpretations of the past."[78] Without the counterweight of alternative interpretations and understandings, they can easily serve to legitimate or "naturalize" official versions of public memory.[79]

Because of their multiple functions and histories, museums assume particularly significant roles as depositories of collective memory. In seeking to attach meanings to symbols, scholars have described museums as "memory palaces," secular temples, shrines, storehouses of dead artifacts, rooms of inquiry, and ceremonial time capsules.[80] What distinguishes museums from other kinds of memory-markers is their "inscapes," that is, their interior designs or indoor landscapes. As mnemonic devices, museum exhibitions are theatrical spaces, or performative sites, that stage selective versions of the historical past. Because museum displays are primarily constructed around objects and artifacts, the interpretive narratives that accompany them largely stress material culture. Museum curators extract material objects from their physical settings and historical context, arranging and displaying them in new ways. The experts who create these kinds of exhibition space give a particular meaning to the past by bringing places, objects, and texts into distinct relationships to one another in ways that seek to provide particular understandings of what happened and why. Objects originally made to be used become artifacts to be displayed and seen. The ability of museums "to function as machines for turning time into space enables them to be used as an apparatus of social memory."[81] By displaying artifacts that convey a sense of what is "normal, appropriate, and possible," museums communicate a sense of permanence and stability.[82]

Museums are ritualized sites of collective memory.[83] Because they rely primarily upon physical artifacts to reconstitute the past as it might have been, museums have the unusual capability of turning culture into a collection of material objects. They play a role not just in "displaying" the social world, but in structuring a particular way of seeing and comprehending the social world as "if it were an exhibit."[84]

Museums have become contested sites where national histories and personal memories grounded in lived experience are sometimes at odds.[85] In formal academic histories, scholarly accounts of the past are conventionally structured around the concatenation of singular events into a narrative whole. In contrast, the collective memory preserved in museum exhibitions typically operates through the spatial arrangement of objects and displays around a common theme. Displays and exhibitions pull events out of a seamless narrative order and rearrange them as a series of juxtaposed "free-frame" images. This disruption of historical continuity creates space for distortion and misrepresentation to fill in the gaps.[86]

In the contemporary age of global tourism, museums are called upon to perform multiple functions ranging from storehouses for collections of "found objects," exhibition and display venues, repositories of cultural artifacts, income-generating business enterprises, educational institutions, research organizations, communal spaces, places of memorialization, and tourist-entertainment sites.[87] Subjected to the pressures of maintaining financial stability, museums have shifted their focus from their mono-functional places specializing in the collection and conservation of cultural artifacts to multidimensional tourist destinations that emphasize an "entertaining experience."[88] The traditional core activities of museums—the collection, preservation, archiving, restoration, and display of collections of artifacts and the pursuit of scholarly research—have been replaced by a stress on multiuse entertainment sites and "cultural supermarkets" that combine spectacle with consumption.[89] No longer serving a primarily educational function, museums have become something akin to cultural amusement parks for housing temporary, traveling exhibitions and for sponsoring themed blockbuster events.[90]

Urban Space and Collective Memory: Scattered Memories in the Fragmented City

Cities are theaters of collective memory. Because urban landscapes are repositories for the material traces of the past, the built environment represents a kind of preserved archive of collective memory.[91] Memory-markers, or the physical signs of collective remembrance, are everywhere in the city: they are inscribed in statuary and commemorative plaques, woven into popular literature and visual cultures, hidden in language and dialect, and etched into the names of places and objects. Signs of memory are also powerfully encoded in popular cultural practices—like theatrical performances, music, and the visual arts, and the facilities that have sponsored these activities.[92] Vehicles of memory range from the monumental to the vernacular, that is, from such officially sanctioned sites of memory as monuments and memorials, museums, and art exhibitions to spontaneous, impromptu expressions of remembrance embedded in such activities as official commemorations, pageants, and political rallies.[93] Everyday life in the city is saturated with an almost endless variety of mnemonic devices for shaping collective memory: festivals, public celebrations, and other regular events.[94] Such localized and place-specific mnemonic devices as parades and staged reenactments of historical events are mechanisms for telling stories, recalling what happened in the past as a way of reliving it in the present.[95] Signs of memory also appear in the most unlikely places: in graffiti, political slogans, and place-names.[96] As Raphael Samuel has put it, the names of streets, neighborhoods, and buildings are "almanacs, registering those personalities and events, mythic or real, which have imprinted themselves on public consciousness."[97] Place-names are "communal registers," to borrow a phrase from Spiro Kostof, that create mental maps and memory-markers in the public realm of cities.[98]

Collective memory in cities is rooted in the experience of being and moving in urban space. The very process of remembering and recalling grows out of spatial metaphors of connection and topography.[99] Collective memories are embedded in the built form of cities and inscribed in individual encounters with specific places and particular objects. Particular places come to express and embody popular memories of the city "through a complex interplay of production, consumption, re-construction, interpretation, and diverse tactics of remembrance."[100]

Places of memory resemble public stages upon which the drama of history is continuously performed. Yet these places are never simply a background for action or inert containers for the past. They are active agents that constantly shape and reshape collective memories of the past. By dispensing with the archaeological metaphor that presumes the existence of a stable historical meaning beneath the present, such scholars as Karen Till, Andreas Huyssen, and others are able to draw out the tension in marking absence and loss in places of memory. This emphasis on depth, erasure, and contestation opens up questions about the multiple readings of meaning at sites of memory.[101] Places of memory are not so much bounded physical sites as open and porous networks of social relations. This condition reinforces the idea that place-identities are always multiple. In short, the meaning of place is always a matter of contestation and, as a consequence, invariably changes over time.[102]

The reorganization of space—place-making—is an instrument for the shaping of collective memory.[103] Through their encounters with specific places and particular objects, individuals and social groups invoke their shared remembrances. In this sense, landscape and memory are co-dependent. Collective memories are literally impossible without physical landscapes to store and preserve them, and to serve as touchstones for the active work of recollection. Places are bearers of history, meaning, and memory. They give rise to stories that evoke, variously, nostalgia, melancholy, and loss. By assigning meanings to their physical surroundings, individuals and social groups endow specific places with social significance they might not otherwise possess. Places are not mere settings or inert backgrounds for staging shared activities and social events; they are active agents in shaping popular consciousness. Attachment to place links social groups and local communities to the past.[104]

The shaping of urban space is an instrument for the production of collective memory.[105] Cities hold onto memories through their built structures, Aldo Rossi argued, so the historic preservation of old buildings is analogous to the preservation of memories in the human mind.[106] Collective memories lay buried, hidden below the surface, in the physical artifacts and traces of the past. The past is carried forward to the present through the physical sites that remain. City streets, squares, monuments, and statuary are topographical markers that often contain not only the grand discourses on history but also local stories that reflect the microhistories of local communities.[107]

To the extent they are invested with historical significance, objects scattered around the city operate as signs of memory. Cities are physical landscapes that embody the past through residual traces of sequential cycles of building and rebuilding. As assemblages of objects, cities facilitate the formation of collective memory by triggering involuntary recollections of what once was. City builders ranging from architects and other design professionals, urban planners, historical preservationists, and real estate developers contribute significantly to the shaping, maintenance, and reproduction of urban memory. Yet urban memory is much more pervasive than professional practices and entrepreneurial exercises.[108]

Impermanent Cities, Disrupted Memories

Collective memory is inscribed in the material fabric of urban landscapes. As Umberto Eco has persuasively argued, "Memories are built as a city is built."[109] It is the place itself that initiates and activates the formation of collective memory through its tangible and visual signification. Such topographical markers as streets, squares, parks, and buildings become primary agencies in the communicative interaction that enables urban residents to remember the historical events recounted there. Spatial memory-markers are vehicles that articulate through their material presence the echoes of the past inscribed in them. Seen in this light, collective memory is the translation of this silent, wordless language of urban topography into the commemorating discourses that enter the public realm of the spatial landscape.[110]

This translation is a kind of hermeneutic deciphering of the textualized signification of spatialized locations that Walter Benjamin theorized in his magisterial *Arcades Project.* In this masterful work, Benjamin sought to explore various tactics of remembrance, ways in which subjective memories might serve to break the grip of historical continuity over the present. For him, the Paris arcades constituted the main memory-traces of the collective unconscious of nineteenth-century capitalism.[111] Even the destruction or demolition of such sites of memory as the Paris arcades leave behind an "absent absence" that, as the reverse of its former presence, continues to articulate meanings.[112]

The public spaces of the city are not simply the aggregation of autonomous subjects that come together in social congregating space but function as the medium through which collective memory is preserved, transformed, and communicated. Multiple memory-markers are inscribed in the materiality of urban topography, and these compete for validity and legitimacy.[113] In an age of ferociously competing ideologies, the widespread corrosive effects of the entertainment industries, and obsessive fixations on "virtual reality" scenarios and digital simulations of history, collective memories of the past are threatened with distortion and even extinction.[114]

Yet the pace at which city-building processes remake and reshape the cityscape undermines and disrupts the foundations upon which collective memories are produced and sustained. Cities are impermanent places where technological innovation and the evolving built environment ensure that urban landscapes are always in a process of becoming something new and something different.[115] As John Urry has argued, cities are "economically, politically and culturally produced through multiple networked mobilities of capital, persons, objects, signs and information."[116] Rather than taking shape as self-contained, fixed locations, cities are better understood as "dense networks of socio-spatial practices that are simultaneously human, material, natural, discursive, cultural, and organic."[117] While the material existence of urban space relies upon the continuous circulation of money, materials, ideas and information, people, and technologies, the networked relations that constitute cities are precarious, impermanent, and only stable for limited durations.[118]

Cities are dynamic sites of flows, movements and mingling of people, information, and things.[119] The historical recomposition of networks, coupled with the constant building and rebuilding of places, contributes to what Doreen Massey has called the "mixity" of cities.[120] Architectural remains of old buildings are eloquent testimonies to the disappearance of connections, obsolete networks, and the failed dreams of permanence and stability. Without constant vigilance "to exclude matter out of place and also to keep matter in place," buildings and the sites they occupy fall into ruin and disrepair.[121] The impermanence of place is intimately connected with the disruption of urban collective memory. The spatial and temporal porosity and volatility of city-building processes compete with attempts to retrieve displaced or suppressed memories, to hold onto vanishing traditions, and to sustain nostalgic desires for what once was.[122]

2 White Lies

Mythmaking and Social Memory in the Service of White Minority Rule

What becomes of the social memories of settler colonialism and white minority rule when the myth-laden, sociocultural world of their making lies in ruins?[1] The end of apartheid and the transition to parliamentary democracy triggered what amounted to a crisis of collective memory that left citizens of the "new South Africa" without the stable reference points necessary for building a shared sense of national identity. Pierre Nora captured a sense of this dilemma in his famous aphorism: "We speak so much of memory because there is so little of it left."[2] What should be remembered and how? Where do old-fashioned monuments and memorials that extolled the virtues of white minority rule fit into the new national narrative of political stability, economic progress, and racial reconciliation? These are the kinds of questions that immediately provoked widespread debate and controversy. While discredited memories have lost their privileged place in official stories of the past, new ways of remembering have not yet crystalized into a shared national consciousness.

At the beginning of the 1990s, an estimated 97 percent of all cultural-heritage sites recognized by the National Monuments Council (NMC) in South Africa reflected the cultural values and significant experiences of the white citizenry. The remaining 3 percent covered the cultural heritage of all other population groups combined, much of which was included under San/Khoi [Bushman] rock-art sites. The unmistakable message was that so-called nonwhite people never produced any material culture worthy of mention, and that in fact they were "people without history,"[3] classified as objects of nature, reduced more or less to physical types and specimens, and relegated to museums of natural history along with wild animals and picturesque landscapes.[4] These narrowly framed commemorative practices affirmed official racist discourses about black inferiority and lack of civilization, thus providing legitimacy for discriminatory legislation and policies.[5] Another perplexing circumstance of post-1994 South Africa is the surprising survival of names synonymous with the darkest days of apartheid: on street signs, school arches, game-park notice boards, police-station plaques, buildings, and public spaces. Names like Hendrik Verwoerd, Louis Botha, Barry Hertzog, D. F. Malan, C. R. Swart, and J. G. Strijdom appear in the oddest places, conjuring up frightful ghosts of the racist past.[6]

Those vehicles of memory—monuments and memorials, written texts, museums, place-names, and other commemorative practices—that served to justify and legitimate white minority rule suddenly became anachronistic and irrelevant. Perhaps not surprisingly, the collapse of apartheid cast the "new South Africa" adrift, disrupting and unsettling the sense of historical continuity that had sustained the myth of "white South Africa" over the course of its long history.[7] Collective memory in the "new South Africa" remains so torn and so convoluted because remembering and forgetting come face to face with a perverse paradox: the official desire to construct a new national identity on the bedrock memory of the horrendous crimes that have gone largely unpunished under circumstances where the perpetrators remain in many instances adamantly unrepentant. The shape and content of a new unifying national identity is a field of contesting discourses and ideologies. Contentious conflicts over collective memories are a form of politics fought on the terrain of bitter struggles over what kinds of remembrance to embrace and preserve, how to commemorate the past, and in whose name, and for what purpose.[8]

Myth and Memory: The Making of White South Africa

The "new South Africa" that came into being with the collapse of white minority rule and the transition to parliamentary democracy is only the most recent effort to build a nation and to forge a collective sense of national identity at the southern tip of the African continent. As a general rule, the collective identification with geographical territory involves weaving together, in a set of shared narratives, memories of particular places and past events. Yet rather than being the true records of past events and experiences, these shared memories are a selective, socially constructed set of fragments from which collective identities are crafted and recrafted.[9] Collective memories are mediated by cultural representations that stress historical roots, geographical boundaries, and a sense of belonging to an "imagined community."[10] The very idea of nationhood and national identity is impossible without the mediating force of collective memory. Nationhood is founded on a "narrative of descent" that isolates and reifies a variety of identity-forming principles (race and ethnicity, religious affiliation, cultural practices, continuity of embedded habitation) that link the nation to a shared past in a common territory.[11]

The discursive construction of national identity is always contingent to appeals to shared memories. Collective identity rests on the construction of narratives of descent (or originating myths) that create a sense of shared membership in the larger, abstract imagined community of nationhood. In white South Africa, these narratives of descent refer almost exclusively to European settlers who arrived at different times and typically shared few identity-forming principles (such as language, religious affiliation, or ethnicity) other than they inhabited the same geographical territory.[12]

As was the case with other white settler colonies, the European immigrant communities that staked a claim to territory at the southern tip of Africa by right of occupation were preoccupied with creating a sense of themselves and their place in the world. Nationhood and national identity are integrally linked with shared memories of places and past events. White identity was shaped and mediated by everyday practices of boundary-marking and memory-making that came together to legitimate and naturalize the connection between race and power.[13]

From the time of the original European settlement in the seventeenth century to the present, the story of South Africa is, and yet has always been, more or less one of continuous construction and reconstruction of memoryscapes. All sociocultural groups, from the original San/Khoi inhabitants to the early Dutch settlers, from the Boers to the English settlers, from the Bantu-speaking Africans to the European immigrants, and from mixed-race (so-called) Coloured people to those who trace their heritage to indentured servants who came from India, have distinctive sociocultural experiences that have produced historically specific memoryscapes that remain alive, in one form or another, in popular consciousness.[14]

In some sense, white South Africa has reinvented its sociocultural memories at least three times prior to 1994. The efforts of the Boer communities to become and remain autonomous from European (but particularly British) domination involved an almost continuous struggle of cultural invention and political innovation. The war between Britain and the Boer Republics, which broke out two months before the end of the nineteenth century and lasted until early 1902, brought to a head long-standing conflicts that had divided white communities along the lines of language, cultural identity, and national/imperial ambitions. No other event heightens the connections between history and geography—and hence, identity formation—like the violent disruption of war. The South African War of 1899–1902 was undoubtedly the single most important event shaping white identity in the subcontinent during the next half-century. Among many things, the conflict left a legacy of place-specific memories that would, directly and indirectly, be used to anchor and shape collective identities for decades to come.[15] The experience and shared memories of concentration camps where thousands of Boer women and children died, the British "scorched earth" military strategy that resulted in widespread destruction of property, the trauma of displacement from the land, and the undermining of an entire way of life, among other things, produced a shared resentment that was kept alive in stories, gravesites, poetry, literature, and song (even to this day). The memories of these events formed the bedrock for the revival of Afrikaner nationalism, which culminated in the 1948 electoral victory of the National Party.[16]

Fashioned from a collection of victorious British colonies and defeated Boer Republics, the "new South Africa" that came into being with the 1910 Act of Union produced what William Beinart called a "state without a nation."[17] This new Union of South Africa constituted a single political entity, yet one with uncertain borders, no consensus on what constituted citizenship, and deeply divided by language—"the most fundamental badge of cultural identity."[18] Concerted efforts to bring about the reconciliation and partnership between the two "white races" that constituted the "new South Africa" were only partially successful.[19] In the immediate aftermath of union, two strands of political ideology emerged. Although latent in the subcontinent before 1899, the South African War of 1899–1902 provided the touchstone for what eventually blossomed into a carefully orchestrated ethnic mobilization around Afrikaner nationalism. Over the next several decades, these two ideological positions struggled for hegemony and control in South Africa, became entrenched in white party politics, and hardened into increasingly divergent constructions of national identity. One construction of national identity envisioned the future South Africa as an integral part of the British Empire. This ideology made use of a homogenizing rhetoric of loyalty and patriotism to erode ethnic, historic, and regional differences and to foster a sense of a unified imagined community. This largely Anglophone ideology claimed to rise above language differences and what were regarded as narrowly sectarian differences to build a nation that "drew upon (rather than was defined and limited by)" the imperial connection with Great Britain to imagine a liberal and progressive future. In contrast, the alternative political ideology conceived of a white South African identity more narrowly and exclusively defined around an indigenous white culture.[20] This ideological current was strongly linked to a distinctly literary-linguistic conception of South African national identity that sought to establish Afrikaans as a modern white man's language and to use it as a vehicle for mobilizing popular support for Afrikaner national identity. It used programs of social regeneration and cultural resurgence to assert an ethnic Afrikaner identity separate from pro-British loyalism. Awakened by a sense of economic disadvantage and political marginalization, this embryonic Afrikaner ethnic nationalist movement was able to dig deep into the reservoir of resentment, triggering shared memories of a "century of wrongs." The combination of words and images kept alive shared memories of past grievances, transforming what had been a more or less dispersed, disempowered, and semieducated group into a single *volk*. Every story, every picture, and every monument became a place where shared memories of the past could be constructed, reconstructed, and stored for future generations. This emphasis on language as the key signifier of cultural identity became a powerful mobilizing force that appealed to economically disadvantaged "poor whites," who feared for their own socioeconomic security if and when Bantu-speaking African people were able to find a legitimate place in South Africa.[21]

Despite their seemingly irreconcilable differences, these twin political ideologies shared a common commitment to racial exclusivism. Beginning in the mid-1920s, a white settler identity began to take root, fueled by the shared belief that South Africa should remain a "white man's country." The strengthening of a sense of white national identity took shape through the active promotion of racial segregation and the continual political disenfrancisement of so-called nonwhite peoples.[22]

The Dreamscapes of White Settler Colonialism: Imaginary Pasts, Fictive Histories

The social memory of "white South Africa" is a product of the settler-colonial past. In the main, the first European settlers who immigrated to the southern tip of Africa understood themselves as making history on a subcontinent without history. Yet ironically they were obsessed with their own historicity, that is, their own "being-in-history." The stories that they told about themselves—the ubiquitous tales of discovering, exploring, pioneering, and settling in a new land—formed the bedrock upon which an entire historiographical carapace of beginnings and endings, periods and times, continuities and discontinuities, and connections and disjunctures was fashioned. Viewed through this narrow prism, history and memory appeared to operate in tandem, in large measure because official accounts of the national experience—expressed by the schools, churches, mass media, commemorations, and popular culture—largely shaped public remembrance. The meaning of names and places, dates and times, events and turning points, derived from their location within a familiar narrative of European settlement and conquest, encounters with indigenous peoples, tribal wars and dispossession, mineral discoveries, segregation, and apartheid. These stories of national character, founding institutions, and nation-building inculcated a sense of collective belonging to an "imagined community"—or an understanding of nationhood that was constructed around an evolving (and permeable) idea of "whiteness."[23]

One corollary of the politics of forgetting is the construction of an imaginary past, or what Eric Hobsbawm called the invention of tradition.[24] Instead of operating as a substitute or replacement for an elided or erased past, the fabrication of a fictive past fills in the imaginary space for what might have been, but never really was. In Ridley Scott's 1982 science-fiction film *Blade*

Runner, so-called replicants (cyborgs with four-year life spans) are provided with photographs depicting families constructed out of whole cloth, childhoods and homes they never had, and events they never celebrated. These photographs provide fictive remembrances of their own subjectivities to compensate for the absence of their humanness. The replicants who mistook the counterfeit photographs as evidentiary proof of their human existence acted "as if" they were real subjects with actual identities.[25] "It is not important whether or not the interpretation is correct," as W. I. Thomas once put it in a well-known aphorism, "If [people] define situations as real, they are real in their consequences."[26]

As a distorted kind of sociocultural memory, mythmaking in the service of white minority rule originated in the early days of European settlement beginning in the seventeenth century. In large measure, these myths were bound up with such key events as the Great Trek (1834–65), the birth of the independent Boer Republics (the Transvaal Republic and the Orange Free State), the wars of conquest against indigenous African peoples, and the First Boer War (1880–81) and the Second Boer War (1899–1902), remembered in Afrikaaner nationalist folklore as *Vryheidsoorlog,* or "freedom wars," these two wars pitted the ragtag guerrilla forces of Boer farmers against the military might of the British Empire. The Second Boer War, which ended with a British victory and the annexation of the two defeated Republics into the British Empire, featured the introduction of new tactics in the conduct of what amounted to "total war," including the "scorched earth" policy of burning Boer farms, the destruction of crops and livestock, and the establishment of concentration camps, where an estimated twenty-eight thousand Boer women and children died of disease and malnutrition. While they eventually reached political accommodation, the defeated Afrikaners never forgave the British for their humiliation. The radicalization of Afrikaner nationalist sentiment was born out of the memory of destroyed farms, ruined earth, and uprooted people. In a real sense, the memory of a particular architecture of humiliation becomes the prototype for the construction of another one.[27]

The animating myths that formed the foundational pillars for the idealized construction of "white South Africa" can trace its historical roots to European conquest and dispossession, that is, to the failed dreamscape of settler colonialism shared by Boer and Briton. But they acquired a more fixed, stable, and permanent form when they became embedded in the official state ideology of white supremacy. The surprising electoral victory of the Nationalist Party in 1948 provided Afrikaner nationalists with the political opportunity to unveil their grand master plan for racially inscribed "separate development." The official heritage culture of the apartheid state administration was directed at ensuring the purity of Afrikanerdom both by maintaining a clear distinction between the Afrikaner people and British settlers and a spatial separation with the "African races." In refusing to admit indigenous peoples, black Africans, the mixed-race descendants of slaves, and other "nonwhites" into its charmed circle of origins, the custodians of official memory reinforced the myth of "white South Africa." According to the circular logic enshrined in the racially exclusivist principles of apartheid, "nonwhite people" had no right to claim a legitimate role in the founding of the nation, and hence had no place in its destiny, because their historical roots and hence their destinies lay elsewhere, tied to Bantustans, or fake homelands, noncontiguous pieces of barren landscape carved out of the inhospitable veld. Imaginatively constructed to fit the logic of "separate development," "Bantu cultural heritage" consisted of *faux* tribal histories rooted in a debased regime of traditional folkways and primordial customs that had only a tangential connection with the modern world of "white South Africa."[28] The custodians of official memory endowed these "invented traditions" of rather recent historic origins with a fictitious continuity and a *faux* historic past of varied accuracy.[29]

In order to establish the desired continuity with a suitable historic past, the architects of the Bantustan policy sought to invent hermetically sealed "tribal" traditions and separate "surrogate histories" capable of recalling the semblance of a glorious past, of instilling a sense of loyalty to a hereditary chieftaincy, and of gesturing toward a promising future embodied in full sovereignty status, rights of citizenship, and political independence. The creation of this legal fiction of ten separate, self-governing "tribal" homelands—each with their own distinct tribal integrity, sociocultural coherence, national identity, and imagined political independence—depended upon deliberate acts of blatant falsification. Beginning in the 1950s, the Nationalist Party used the pseudoscientific discourse of highly suspect archaeological findings and shoddy anthropological scholarship to bolster their claims to the existence of ten separate African tribal entities. The invention of these distinct tribal traditions—at times, new ones were readily grafted onto older ones, and at other times they were fabricated virtually out of whole cloth—enabled the white minority regime to establish and legitimate relations of authority and status hierarchies, and, in time, to cobble together fictive nation-states where none existed before. They wished to consecrate this illogical mixture of fact and fantasy by appeals to historical genealogies, Holy Scripture, and the pseudoscientific findings of archaeology, anthropology, and linguistics.[30]

Repeated often enough, these mythical constructions of white superiority in opposition to "native" inferiority, ownership of land by right of conquest, and the legitimacy of racial segregation took on the status of "revealed truth," that is, normalized beliefs that had no actual basis in reality but nevertheless operated in the terrain of commonsense understanding. Afrikaner nationalists did not simply replace one set of myths and beliefs with another, but engaged in a process of recycling, reconfiguring, and reworking established myths to conform to the changing circumstances of rapid industrialization and urbanization.[31] Lodged in stories and shared beliefs, collective memory looks backward into the historical past in order to project forward in time.[32]

The theorist W. J. T. Mitchell has suggested that landscapes are an integral feature of the European imperial project, merging the narration of the "natural" expansion (and geographical extension) of the "civilized world" to the transformation and naturalization of the colonized territories.[33] White settler identity was intimately connected with the landscape imagery of uninhabited space. Left behind as memory-traces, these afterimages of empty territory became naturalized as a kind of birthright.[34] The motto inscribed on the statue of Cecil John Rhodes in Cape Town's Gardens (with his outstretched hand pointing northward)—"Your hinterland lies yonder"—captures the essential connection between imperial conquest, possession, and nationhood. As David Bunn has argued, "The future of Empire, the [motto] says, rests on a return to unmediated mastery. It is a vision of heroic boldness and manorial authority, closely associated with feudal nostalgia for a time before class, and made possible by the violent context of the colonies."[35]

As Jeremy Foster has pointed out, this "discursive construction of the imaginary geography of nationhood is seldom conscious or directed toward a specific goal, and it often evolves through a series of detours, false starts, and dead ends, all of which leave traces in the physical landscape."[36] But above all else, this imaginary geography of nationhood rests on the conjoined belief in (racial) superiority and natural rights. In their self-fashioned stories of conquest and triumph, the Voortrekkers and their descendants brought civilization and progress to a virgin interior only sparsely inhabited by indigenous peoples.[37] Similarly, English-speaking settlers typically imagined the landscape as a territorial extension of Europe rather than a part of the African continent. They also marked the physical landscape with their own peculiar brand of architecture, aesthetics, and symbolic imagery.[38] But whatever their differences, Afrikaans- and English-speaking white settlers, intruders, and new arrivals shared in the process of naturalizing their national identity in the ongoing drama of frontier conquest, narrated through the encounter with landscape and environment. The lingering "afterlife" of white settler colonialism—that is, the ways in which white supremacy has inosculated itself into the social fabric as an intractable trace in the social relations and visual cultures of the present-day—has remained a potent force acting against the forging of a single national identity in the "new South Africa."[39]

The historicity of landscapes means that present-day sites are inevitably inundated with the multiple politics of the past.[40] As Simon Schama has suggested, "Veins of myth and memory . . . lie beneath the surface of our conventional sight-level."[41] The spatial layout of townships, the great distances between the historic "white" and "black" residential districts, the architectural design of homes for the white wealthy and the black poor, and so on, are grim reminders, silent testimonies, and living memories of the topography of apartheid social engineering.[42]

History and Memory

One significant source of unease that accompanied the birth of the "new South Africa" is the stark realization that history and memory no longer move together in unison. In the past, history and social memory appeared to operate in tandem because official accounts of the national experience—expressed by the schools, churches, mass media, and popular culture—largely shaped what was remembered and what was forgotten. The meaning of names and places, dates and times, derived from their location within a familiar narrative of European settlement and conquest, tribal wars and dispossession, mineral discoveries, segregation, and apartheid.[43]

White minority rule depended upon separate and unequal domains of heritage production. The custodians of official memory under apartheid rule both extended and codified the marginalization of the nonwhite population of South Africa. Almost without exception, museums, monuments, and memorials in apartheid South Africa found their raison d'être as physical embodiments of the dominant ideology of white supremacy. As sites dedicated to legitimating "separate development," they carefully constructed one-sided and singular versions of history aimed at an exclusively white audience. This mode of constructing history, as Jo Noero has suggested, operated on two principles: erasure and clearance.[44] Erasure entailed the deliberate omission of any traces of the past that might undermine or disrupt the official narrative, thereby "effectively confining history to a hermetically sealed box." Clearance involved the systematic eradication of traces of the past in order to ensure the construction of a historical perspective that functioned entirely on its own terms, untainted by destabilizing influences or unsettled by alternative versions of the past. This mode of selective remembering and deliberate forgetting "ensured that the dominant ideology became the only version of the past," ignoring and suppressing alternative stories as irrelevant.[45]

Under white minority rule, the state-sponsored practice of commemoration functioned as a narrow, sectarian, and self-aggrandizing locus of national memory. It should not be surprising that the victors of history almost always have built memorials to remember their triumphs. The cultural landscape was littered with granite and bronze statuary, monuments, and memorials that encouraged the remembrance of the heroic sacrifice, hardships, and achievements of the white minority. As a general rule, state-sponsored collective memory of a national past aims to affirm the righteousness of a nation's origins by drawing attention to key figures and eventful turning points.[46] During the apartheid years, the white minority regime used public holidays, museums and exhibitions, commemorations, visual displays of all sorts, monumental art, burial sites, and the mass media to construct and entrench their racialized understanding of the past and impose their bifurcated vision of the future on white citizens and "nonwhite" subjects. These commemorative acts were expressions of a kind of "victor's mentality."[47]

Looking at the Jan van Riebeeck Tercentenary Festival of 1952 illustrates how the custodians of memory at the time used pageantry in order to reinforce the mythical past. This festival was carefully orchestrated to celebrate the anniversary of the arrival of Jan van Riebeeck at the Cape, transforming this minor functionary of seventeenth-century Dutch imperialism into the founder of South Africa. The purpose of this festival was "to display the growing power of the apartheid state and to assert its confidence."[48] As in the South African Pageant of Union in 1910 (an event that marked the birth of modern South Africa), the organizers of the Van Riebeeck Festival favored "visual spectacle" rather than literary drama in their creation of a procession that moved through the streets of Cape Town. This celebrated "People's Pageant" incorporated two separate processions: the "Historical Pageant" and the "Pageant of the Present." The "Historical Pageant" began with a float labeled "Africa Dark and Unknown," which served to justify European conquest and settlement in South Africa. It ended with a float called "Africa Awakes," which stressed the enormous benefits of settlement.[49] The "Pageant of the Present" promoted the singular contribution of white settlers and entrepreneurs in developing South Africa's natural resources and in industrializing and modernizing production by parading industrial and agricultural workers with the fruits of their labor.[50]

Modes of expression like festivals, pageants, and commemorations inscribed in the values, attitudes, and worldviews associated with "whiteness" and its absence into popular consciousness. The sites for institutionalized social memory ranged across the sociocultural landscape, from "whites-only" schools (with their official textbooks, national anthems, place-names, and the like) to public sites of commemoration.[51] Under white minority rule, vehicles of collective memory functioned less to remember events with genuine historical accuracy and more to bury them altogether beneath layers of national myths and romantic sentiments.[52] As reified cultural practices, these commemorative acts obscured historical understanding much more than they fostered any appreciation of the past.[53]

For close to three hundred years, the symbols and rituals of white minority rule infiltrated the iconography and symbology of a succession of state administrations. From school curricula to coins, from flags to the selection of national holidays, and from the national anthem to the dominance of the

Afrikaans language, the emblems, signs, and rituals of white minority rule largely shaped daily life. Public spaces, landscapes, monuments and memorials, and architecture were transformed into sites for the celebration of white minority rule. From the monuments that adorn public parks to the place-names for streets and buildings, the emblems and markers of white minority rule still remain a visible part of everyday life, disturbing reminders of a racialized past. These are not ephemeral features of cultural life but are powerful forces that influence public opinion, that call people to action, and that shape cultural identities.[54]

The urban landscapes of post-apartheid cities have remained cluttered with the physical reminders of the old white minority regime. What historical preservation that occurred has stressed the European roots of architecture, visible symbols of the settler dream of establishing a permanent beachhead on the African continent. Material remnants like statuary, memorials, street and building names, along with commemorative gravesites for Boer commandos who lost their lives during the Anglo-Boer War (1899–1902), can be found everywhere.[55] The spatial impact of racial segregation has left physical remnants that have remained at the very center of urban South Africa.[56] Under white minority rule, museums functioned primarily as depots for storing objects that lent legitimacy to the claims of European superiority over African backwardness. The municipality of Cape Town, for example, has continued to operate according to a "language of monumentalization," which sought to essentialize colonial domination by evoking an endless repetition of monuments and other memory-markers—what Martin Hall has called a "continual call on memory."[57] The private rituals of apartheid are still enacted by ordinary people through the continued realities of everyday life that confine people to their predetermined subject-positions.[58]

Naming and Recalling

Exploring the process of naming and recalling enables us to examine the complex relationship between language and identity, history and memory, and the past and the present. The act of naming and recalling establishes points of reference, or standards of comparison. Whenever we are confronted with some phenomena that we do not understand, we search about for a concept or label—a name—by which we might come to know it. Time and again, we are forced to construct and convey our understanding of things through the use of terms previously reserved for other things, on the basis of some perceived or conjectured similarity, or homology, between them. This cross-naming, or knowing-by-comparison—provides the means by which we manage to locate and classify our experience of things, thus giving these objects a place and a context.[59]

The authoritative act of naming is a social practice embedded in social and political struggles between social groups for power and legitimacy.[60] Naming practices are inherently unstable and historically contingent.[61] The naming and renaming of places, streets, and key events inscribe the dominant discourses of political legitimization into the social fabric, thereby naturalizing the existing political order. The act of naming is a twofold procedure directly linked to the process of remembering and forgetting: an existing place-name is first eliminated along with its meaning, and is replaced by a new one carrying its own sociopolitical significance.[62] The coexistence of place-names from different historical periods can be read as the layered effects of successive waves of political conflict and upheaval.[63]

Understood properly, place-names are not passive signifiers but are actively engaged in place-making practices.[64] As the early Voortrekkers moved tentatively into the unknown interior from their temporary bivouac at the Cape of Good Hope, they put names to the places where they wished to establish permanent settlements. *Afrikaans*-language place-names often end with suffixes like *-kruil, -pan,* and *-fontein.* These "watery names that confirm the dryness of their ways," as Jeremy Cronin has written, betray an ironic wishful thinking, as if these *trekkers* hoped that the very name itself would magically transform these barren places into a hospitable Garden of Eden.[65]

Because of its animating power to bring into existence something new, naming is an essential component of identity formation. In the early twentieth century, Afrikaner nationalists used the inspiration of the poetry of "Totious" [Ds. J. D. du Toit], Jan F. E. Celliers, and Eugene Marais to nourish and promote the Afrikaans-language movement as part of a wider cultural revival. Written texts of all kinds made it quite clear that "the Boers wanted to develop an exclusive culture, in which they saw themselves as a God-fearing people, guided by divine purpose to tame a wilderness, the African 'savage.'"[66] Likewise, they enlisted the support of secret cultural organizations like the

Broederbond to keep alive the bitter memories of military defeat and social humiliation at the hands of British imperialism. They built museums and other commemorative sites to celebrate their achievements.[67] They used the classrooms of Christian National Schools, the platforms of political leaders, and the pulpits of the N. G. Klerk (Dutch Reformed Church), to promote the idea of common heritage and to foster attachment to place and spirit. They exploited the cultural appeal of festivals, commemorative events, and storytelling to instill loyalty, sociocultural unity, and common purpose around the principle of "strength in isolation."[68]

Acts of naming and recalling are inextricably linked with discourses of political legitimation.[69] One of the principal "founding myths" that historically undergirded Afrikaner national identity revolved around the idea that the early Dutch-speaking settlers who followed in the footsteps of Jan van Riebeeck encountered a sparsely inhabited land devoid of indigenous inhabitants and ready for the taking. In the discursive constructions that accompanied their rise to political power, Afrikaner nationalists downplayed, ignored, or flatly denied a wealth of existing archaeological evidence authenticating the long-standing presence of indigenous peoples in order to justify their territorial claims by right of occupation.[70]

The 1948 electoral victory of the National Party enabled Afrikaner nationalists to impose virtually carte blanche on their racialized vision of what they hoped would be a radiant future for what they considered "white South Africa."[71] Once firmly in power, the Afrikaner nationalists inaugurated an orchestrated campaign of remembering and forgetting. "When a big power wants to deprive a small country of its national consciousness it uses the method of *organized forgetting*," Milan Kundera has argued. "A nation which loses awareness of its past gradually loses its self."[72] To be sure, the most brutal form of forgetting involves what Paul Connerton has called "repressive erasure," where totalitarian regimes deliberately set out to replace, displace, or otherwise obliterate alternative interpretation of the historical past that differed with their own cherished versions.[73]

The white minority regime sought to create places of memory congruent with their political and cultural goals of racial segregation. A succession of political leaders sponsored a variety of disparate, and at times contradictory, projects to reorient a number of prominent historical places to reinforce the goals of white minority rule.[74] The emphasis on particular commemorative events to the exclusion of others imposed their own version of the past on "white South Africa." When they unveiled their grand plan of racialized social engineering, they named it apartheid—a difficult-to-translate Afrikaans term that roughly means "separateness" or "apart-ness." But the apparent blandness of the name itself fails to capture the true meaning of what apartheid policies has meant in practice, or to give any indication of the deep imprint these practices have left on the mind-sets, consciousness, and discourses of the "new South Africa." A great deal of the language of apartheid lives on, continuing to reinforce an "us-versus-them" mindscape, a viscerally reactive way of cognitively mapping the social world that "naturalizes" the existing order of things as given, immobile, and immutable.[75]

Used judiciously, philological analysis can help us to parse the language and unpack the meaning of apartheid from the official discourses that its clever wordsmiths fabricated, sometimes out of whole cloth.[76] The deliberate racialization of ordinary language and common speech, the frequent use of euphemisms that invariably obscured social realities, and the repetitive stereotyping of opponents enabled National Party ideologues to subvert the language in order to alter, modify, and transform the ways in which (white) citizens of South Africa thought about politics and history, about race and national identity, and about their lives and their futures.[77]

This urge to classify, to regulate everything along strict racial lines from residence and marriage, to work and leisure, is what linked the public sphere under apartheid with cultural and pedagogical practices of the white minority regime. It is not by accident that seemingly benign acts of naming and labeling were merely the symbolic expressions of a deeper desire to codify, to order, to regulate, and, ultimately, to control and pacify.[78] Afrikaner nationalists were obsessed with questions of national origins—or the idea of "being first," which is intimately connected with the settlement of putatively unoccupied lands—and the notion of racial purity, or the idea that "full-blooded" constitutes the ultimate source of identity. In adopting a "cult of the past," they created a grand master-narrative that was "overt in its acts of celebratory remembrance, [and] covert in its editing out and erasure" of inconvenient facts that muddled or contradicted their own story.[79] Afrikaner nationalists experienced little difficulty in absorbing the founding myths of the "white tribe" of Africa, struggling on two fronts against British imperialism on the one side and African chiefdoms on the other, into their enduring dream of a "whites-only" *volkstaat* carved out of the same geographical space inhabited by indigenous African peoples. When they looked back on a turbulent sequence of retreat and defeat, they found inspiration in the spiritual heritage of Calvinist orthodoxy, the common thread of language, and their shared animosity to British over-rule. Afrikaner nationalists fashioned themselves as "chosen people" whose spirit was replenished by divine inspiration and who were morally obligated to carry out a sacred mission in a profane world. They sought to locate lines of continuity that linked their origins with opposition to oppressive British over-rule.[80]

Afrikaner nationalists largely succeeded because they had a coherent story to tell about their singular place in Africa that could bind the past and future into a single narrative, and they taught that story with firm conviction to generation after generation of future citizens. The troubled relations between English-speaking white South Africans and Afrikaner nationalists were indelibly marked with the sentiments of suffering, uncertainty, defeat, shame, and doubt. Unlike white English-speakers whose cultural identity was connected with their European heritage, Afrikaner nationalists took great care and trouble to commemorate their role/place in Africa, to celebrate their cultural heritage, and to bind future generations to their narrow vision. They were able to forge a national identity rooted in African realities in part by a steady accumulation of monuments, memorials, solemn inaugurations, and folk festivals, not to speak of deliberate efforts to silence critics, to punish heretics, and to marginalize opponents.[81]

As a powerful mnemonic device that inscribes social memory into places and objects, the act of naming creates an existential presence where none had existed before. In Afrikaner nationalist folklore, the Day of the Covenant—formerly Dignaan's Day—assumes totemic significance as a cultural symbol of solidaristic group identity. This annual commemorative event marked the solemn blood oath that the outnumbered Boer commandos vowed on the eve of their military defeat of an assembled force of ten thousand Zulu warriors at Blood River on December 16, 1838, where they pledged to always keep the day as a covenant should their prayerful pleas for divine intervention prevail. Parliamentarians in the "new South Africa" were acutely aware of the symbolic, gestural significance of the calendrical date when they declared December 16 as Heritage Day. Like the medieval Catholic Church, which attached itself to existing pagan celebrations as a way of incorporating these primordial folk traditions into their own sacred rituals, memory-makers in the "new South Africa" have taken very seriously the symbolic significance attached to place-names, commemorative events, and public holidays.[82]

The flip side of the politics of remembrance is the politics of forgetting. In creating their own sanitized memory of the past and their formative, heroic role in it, Afrikaner nationalists deliberately sought to silence the voices, erase the memories, and reconstruct the histories of others whose hopes and dreams clashed with their own. In 1956–57, under the terms of the Natives Resettlement Act, city planners in Johannesburg carried out the forcible removal of African residents from a densely settled urban neighborhood called Sophiatown located on the western edge of the central business district. Apartheid officials hailed this ignominious act, conducted with the precision of a well-planned military operation, as "a triumph of social engineering," handing the vacant land over to real-estate developers who built modest houses atop the rubble for Afrikaner working-class families.[83] In demolishing Sophiatown and renaming the new whites-only suburb Triomf [Triumph], Afrikaner nationalists hoped to erase the earlier, past memories of the existence of a vibrant African urban community and to bring historical closure to what they regarded as the evil of "race-mixing."[84] The custodians of apartheid conducted scores of similar slum-clearance schemes. But what made the destruction of places like Sophiatown and District Six in Cape Town different was that their memory survived, kept alive in memoirs, popular imagery, and visual remembrance.[85]

Racist Stains That Will Not Fade Away

Myths narrate versions of the past by accentuating selected aspects of it while marginalizing or ignoring others. Mythologized versions of memory become powerful social forces that acquire their strength through appeals to loyalty, sentiment, and cultural identity. As a general rule, monuments and memorials are a conventional way for constructing and disseminating the animating myths of national identity.[86]

Official memories are typically mobilized through the practice of place-making. They are rooted in "a geography of belonging, an identity forged in a specific landscape, inseparable from it."[87] From Cape Town in the south to Beit Bridge in the north, the commemorative landscape of South Africa is dotted with the icons of an exclusive social order founded on conquest and exclusion. Take the numerous monuments that memorialize the concentration camps that the British military forces constructed during the Second Boer War (1899–1902). They typically gloss over or ignore the thousands of black South Africans imprisoned alongside Afrikaner women and children.[88] More than in most countries, much of South Africa's history has remained out of sight—hidden behind monuments that celebrate a narrowly conceived "official view" of the past, stored in the recesses of popular memory, and buried under ideology and wishful thinking. None of this selective remembering was an accident. It served evolving political and ideological purposes. The apartheid system, and the forms of colonial rule that preceded it, only had space for one view of the events and people who formed the country because those memory-makers who were entrusted with commemorating the past were determined to keep the country for their white heirs alone.[89] The monuments, museums, and designated places of remembrance conveyed a view of the past—cast in stone or bronze, inscribed on plaques or parchment, displayed in photographs and landscape paintings—that was "one-sided, jaundiced, [and] predicated on justifying a system which excluded most of the country's people."[90] Museums built during the apartheid era were "bastions of ideology," extolling the virtues of white European civilization while framing indigenous peoples as something akin to the flora and fauna of the "found landscape."[91]

Beyond concrete monuments and disgraced statues, countless visual images and physical artifacts have remained in place as recognizable symbolic residues of a bygone era. Collective memory of the past lives on in the most mundane of ways, certainly in unfriendly gestures, snide remarks, coded phraseology, racist jokes, and intolerant attitudes of those who embraced white minority rule and cherished its ideals of racial separation. Nostalgia for the past makes its appearance in the flag-waving pageantry of sporting events and other public festivals. These memory-markers that express nostalgia for the apartheid past continue to haunt social interaction across racial lines.[92]

The physical landscape itself bears witness to collective memories of the past. The spatial layout of townships, the tiny houses on small plots, the treeless terrain, and the main thoroughfares wide enough to accommodate military vehicles testify to segregationist planning practices under apartheid. These spatial markers resemble what Pierre Nora called "true memories," which have taken refuge in gestures and habits, in skills passed down by unspoken traditions, in the body's inherent self-knowledge, in unstudied reflections and ingrained memories."[93] Collective memories of the past are embodied in buildings, streetscapes, spatial grids, and architectural styles of apartheid-era housing stock. Shared memory is a kind of social understanding. The shared remembrances of social life under apartheid constitute a form of local, popular, and vernacular knowledge that exists outside the parameters of official memory.[94]

3 Facing Backward, Looking Forward

The Politics of Remembering and Forgetting

The end of apartheid and the transition to parliamentary democracy produced a paradoxical situation. With the collapse of white minority rule and the dismantling of apartheid, citizens of the "new South Africa" have been called upon to look two ways in time: back to the racially divided past to confront painful memories born of discrimination and oppression, and forward to the future—with its attendant risks, uncertainties, and contingent possibilities. Looking backward, they hold onto the past by remembering and commemorating. Looking forward, they envision a radiant future unencumbered and unburdened by the sordid apartheid past. The central conundrum that arises from this Janus-faced, schizophrenic vision has to do with resolving the tension between the politics of remembering and the politics of forgetting.[1] On the one hand, the collapse of apartheid has triggered an enthusiasm for the recovery of those aspects of the national past that white minority rule had tried to erase, suppress, and elide from collective memory. On the other hand, finding a common ground of shared values upon which to forge a unifying national identity requires moving beyond—escaping—the past that had divided the country along racial and ethnic, "tribal" and linguistic, lines.[2]

This delicate balancing act between remembering and forgetting lies at the heart of nation-building. The ebb and flow of remembering and forgetting are not innocent activities but strategic undertakings that streamline the historical past in ways that cohere in the present and project a positive image into the future. In situations that call for starting over, new national identities are constructed and held together as much by forgetting as by remembering. Such "new beginnings" invariably require the erasure of uncomfortable secrets of the past and engagement in what Benedict Anderson has called "collective amnesia."[3] While forgiveness is a necessary therapeutic ingredient for bringing closure to the painful memories of the past, glossing over past injustices in the name of reconciliation effectively enables perpetrators of gross human rights violations to go unpunished and the enduring structural inequalities nurtured under white minority rule to go unattended.[4] As Timothy Garton Ash has so eloquently put it, "[O]ften it is the victims who are cursed by memory, while perpetrators are blessed by forgetting."[5]

The task of settling accounts with the past converges with the need to build a different future. Reconciling these past- and future-orientations requires that collective memory be put at the service of "nation-building," that is, the construction of a shared identity of belonging to the same "imagined community," as Benedict Anderson suggested.[6] Letting go of the past—starting afresh—means laying aside long-standing grievances and the painful memories that accompany them. Ironically, the impulse toward forging a new national identity requires what Milan Kundera has called "organized forgetting."[7] As a forward-looking undertaking, "nation-building" demands a kind of obliviscent attitude toward those corrosive, disruptive, tangled memories rooted in a disturbing, sorrowful past. The construction of a new national identity requires the kind of social closure that loosens the ties between the present and the past. For fear of opening old wounds never completely healed and losses never fully mourned, "nation-building" necessarily downplays the sordid past, blunting disturbing memories, transforming and eviscerating them, penetrating and ossifying them.[8] This lack of consensus over the delicate balance between remembering and forgetting unleashed conflicting interpretations over how to represent the past in the present, thereby producing an unsettled situation that the cultural critic Andreas Huyssen has called "mnemomic convulsions."[9]

Collective Memory and Nation-Building

The birth of the "new South Africa" put into motion an extensive search for a new, unifying national narrative that would be able to forge a collective identity, to articulate shared aspirations, and to bind together a disparate citizenry.[10] This process of constructing an "imagined community" for the culturally diverse citizenry of the "new South Africa" has involved nothing less than a wholesale redefinition of the meaning of cultural heritage and reinterpretation of the place of history in the context of debates over what should be stressed and what should be downplayed as part of the new national identity. This nation-building exercise came into being in response to the colonial and apartheid preoccupation with articulating and legitimating white minority rule. As an artifact of the transition to parliamentary democracy, this unifying narrative stressed truth in opposition to secrecy, forgiveness over retribution, democratic dialogue in opposition to authoritarian rule, and a culture of human rights in opposition to organized state terror. Efforts to construct this new nation-building narrative proceeded in tandem with attempts to distance the "new South Africa" from what came before.[11] It is this sense that remembering and forgetting are intertwined elements that partake in the same nation-building project. While these twin processes can work together, they sometimes stand in stark contrast with each other.[12]

Memories are part of the domain of the present. As Alison Landsberg has persuasively argued, they are "less about validating or authenticating the past than they are about organizing the present and constructing strategies with which one might imagine a livable future." In this sense, remembering is not a means or method for closure, that is, it is not a "strategy for closing or finishing the past. On the contrary, remembrance acts as a creative force, a vehicle that "propels us not backward but forwards."[13]

Always and everywhere under circumstances where a new forward-looking politics of inclusion has replaced an atavistic politics of exclusion, collective memory plays a central role in the nation-building project. The power of collective memory is its capacity to selectively eliminate unwanted and uncomfortable aspects from the past, highlighting favorable moments and rendering history "tidy and suitable."[14] Remembering offers a way out of the shadow of white minority rule where a single narrative imposed a kind of "organized oblivion" over public culture.[15] The subjective, creative, and constructed nature of collective memory has enabled the "new South Africa" to use its problematic and contested past to reconstruct its new national identity in symbolic ways, and, in doing so, to manage simmering social conflict and create a unified sense of national purpose.[16]

The centerpiece of this effort has been strong top-down support and encouragement for the creation of new vehicles of collective memory, particularly monuments and memorials, museums, public art, exhibitions, and artistic performances, aimed at promoting and nurturing the new national ideals of unity in diversity, reconciliation, and forgiveness.[17] These new vehicles of memory give pride of place to those people who were previously ignored, marginalized, or silenced under white minority rule, offering spaces for reconciliation and healing within a social order that continues to struggle with the legacies of trauma and suffering. The construction of a new national identity comes face to face with the paradox of multiple allegiances of the citizenry. "Nation-building" requires a kind of civic sensibility that is able to reconcile conflicting interests, beliefs, and future visions and to weave these into a shared sense of loyalty, commitment, and trust. Commemorative practices act to retrieve displaced or suppressed memories, to hold onto vanishing traditions, and to sustain nostalgic desires for what once was. Official acts of remembrance seek to connect an understanding of past realities with future hopes.[18]

In seeking to forge a new and integrated national identity grounded in cultural diversity, policymakers, public officials, and key political leaders have grappled with the legacy of spatial partition, racial oppression, and narrow nationalism. The cultural machinery of apartheid rule systematically devised and disseminated repressive measures designed to divide groups in accordance with fictive racial classifications. The centuries-long experience with white minority rule actively promoted a particularly narrow kind of historical understanding and institutional memory that stressed the accomplishments of European civilization and the achievements of "Great White Men," while simultaneously downplaying, ignoring, and erasing the historicity of indigenous African peoples and cultures. In seeking to redress the biased landscape of collective memory that prevailed under white minority rule, the commemorative practices that have gained a foothold in the "new South Africa" perform double duty: they function as devices both for recalling the past and for representing an imagined future.[19]

While great strides have been made in rectifying the imbalance, it can be argued that the post-apartheid social order has only partially begun to address, in a systematic fashion, the psychological trauma, cultural mind-set, and distorted consciousness that the racialized bigotry and everyday stereotypes of apartheid inflicted upon ordinary people.[20] Both the officially sanctioned and unofficially sponsored efforts directed toward transforming and democratizing the commemorative landscapes of the "new South Africa" have typically stressed the goals of reconciliation and inclusiveness and called for the celebration of cultural diversity in the "rainbow nation."[21]

Yet the "rainbow nation" is a roseate catch phrase that is used endlessly, but never in an analytical sense. On the surface, it is an uplifting and inspirational slogan, asking citizens to lay aside past grievances, and to look forward to a new dawn where racism fades into the past. But behind this innocent-sounding, and well-meaning, request is the suggestion that a racially harmonious social order is at least logically possible under the present conditions of massive socioeconomic inequality, and unequal access to socioeconomic resources are closely associated with racial differences. Rainbow multiculturalism suggests an attitude of conciliatory and benevolent consensuality. With the demise of the apartheid social order, it can easily fall into a new posthumous complacency. The "rainbow nation" is thus more a hopeful design for the national future, which tends to overlook the invidious ways that the past still inhabits the present.[22]

Building the "new nation" has required not only the recovery of the buried past as a way of acknowledging the gross human rights violations committed in the name of white minority rule, but also pushing aside the past as a necessary step in starting anew. In the discourse of healing and reconciliation exemplified by the Truth and Reconciliation Commission (TRC), the exposure of buried pasts and the recovery of traumatic memories created the foundation for "letting go" of the past as a way of moving forward into the future.[23] Yet putting memory in the service of a consensual public history and a shared national identity invariably involves reshaping, streamlining, and channeling of individual remembrance of trauma and suffering to fit the requirements of a forward-looking "nation-building." As the cornerstone of the project of "nation-building," the commemorative practices that have shaped national identity in the "new South Africa" have mediated and framed personal experiences of trauma and suffering in ways that subsume individual stories into a homogeneous and disembodied narrative of collective memory.

Where does remembrance of the past find its place? How do the relationships between stories of places and the places of stories shape our appreciation of public history and commemorative practice in South Africa at a time of uncertainty about the future? How do the reciprocal pressures of remembering and forgetting come together in the construction of a shared national identity? How does the relationship between stories of places and the places of stories shape public history and commemorative practice in post-apartheid South Africa? How do memorial and commemorative practices transform the subjects of history into objects of historical representation? Addressing these questions lies at the heart of understanding the nation-building project and the construction of a shared national identity in South Africa after apartheid.[24]

The Challenge of Collective Memory in Nation-Building

In the face of an uncertain future, a vibrant culture of collective remembrance has gained a significant foothold in popular consciousness in the "new South Africa." As long-repressed memories of the evils of apartheid came to the surface, ordinary South Africans and local communities took matters into their own hands, organizing pilgrimages to sites of memory, constructing spontaneous memorials in places of unspeakable tragedy, and staging impromptu acts of commemoration designed to bear witness to personal and collective trauma and loss, to honor victims and survivors of the oppressive apartheid system, and to reveal truths about the past that had long remained shielded behind the official cloak of secrecy.[25]

Memories—both individual and collective—of the apartheid past have continued to haunt the present.[26] The outpouring of various kinds of popular remembrance—what Jill Liddington and Graham Smith in another context have called a "memory boom"—has assumed a wide variety of forms, ranging from the monumental and official to the popular and vernacular.[27] As a way of keeping the collective memory of the past alive, all sorts of new sites of memory, such as the District Six Museum (Cape Town), the Apartheid Museum (Johannesburg), the Hector Pieterson Memorial and Museum (Soweto), Constitution Hill (Johannesburg), the Red Location Museum of Struggle (Port Elizabeth), the Sharpeville Exhibition Centre and Monument (Sharpeville), and Freedom Park (Pretoria), have greatly expanded the symbolic landscape of the "new South Africa." The recognition of new national holidays that commemorate significant milestones in the struggle for freedom include the Human Rights Day (formerly known as Heroes Day or Sharpeville Day, March 21), Freedom Day (April 27), Workers Day (May 1), National Youth Day (previously Soweto Day, June 16), Women's Day (August 9), Heritage Day (September 24), and the Day of Reconciliation (December 16).[28] These commemorative acts "help the nation appreciate the importance of history, heritage and memory in the crafting of the present and future of the country" as Yonah Seleti, heritage manager for Freedom Park Trust, has argued. They seek "to counteract amnesia as the basis for nation-building."[29]

Efforts to forge a coherent national identity in the "new South Africa" have relied heavily on collective memory and cultural heritage as indispensable tools within the wider framework of the search for transitional justice, healing, and reconciliation. This obsession with memory has spilled over into the world of public art and other forms of aesthetic expression. Artists, writers, and performers from a variety of backgrounds and cultural experiences have refused to abandon the past, using their voices, their words, and their creative talents to "never forget" what came before the birth of the "new South Africa."[30] The public articulation of shared remembrance, specifically with regard to suffering and trauma, has come to occupy a privileged position within those nation-building efforts to deal with and make sense of the past.[31]

Commemorative practices play an ethical function: that a confrontation with tragedy prevents us from "going on with the usual business of life," forcing us to look backward and reflect on the past before moving forward.[32] The significance that remembering and recalling holds for communities and individuals affected by trauma and loss cannot be overestimated. But what does coming to terms with the past actually mean? Does truth always lead to reconciliation? Commemoration practices can never compensate for collective trauma or human tragedy. At best, they can engage dialogically with the events they reference and help frame a process toward understanding and healing.[33] As Andreas Huyssen has convincingly argued, collective memory, after all, can never be a substitute for social justice, and social justice itself is inevitably entangled in the unreliability of remembering.[34]

Seeking a Usable Past for a "New Nation"

Central to the question of the imbrication of memory and forgetting are the ways in which the strategic reworking of built environments transforms landscape identities and affects the ways that social groups relate to place. On the one side, "creative destruction" erases existing built environments, thereby rendering certain activities, people, and place memories invisible. On the other side, "destructive creation" represents more than just the redevelopment of material landscapes but also the creation of "new symbolic meanings—and ultimately memories—for places."[35]

As the apartheid regime began to falter and its ideology of "separate development" was no longer capable of justifying the brutality required to keep it afloat, the cracks in its once solid armature exposed the excess and waste of white minority rule. By the early 1990s, it was clear to all except the most hardened and myopic supporters of white minority rule that the monumental architecture of white minority rule and the national narratives that justified and legitimated "separate development" were in ruins. The end was imminent. Monuments standing on the ruins of the failed dreams of apartheid, or the ruination of monuments, were the visible signs of the collapse of a singular, carefully circumscribed, national narrative that conveyed in all domains of daily life white (Eurocentric) superiority and African inferiority.[36]

The collapse of the apartheid state apparatus left behind a vast stockpile of unusable history and discredited heritage. Yet unlike discarded rubble, which is nothing more than useless material without significance (or "matter out of place," to cite a well-worn metaphor coined by Mary Douglas), ruins are saturated with meaning. They project an image, however partial and truncated, of the historical past. As evocative objects that continue to bear the traces of what once was, ruins offer a window into the past.[37] The question becomes: What to do with the visible reminders of discredited political regimes that have exited the political stage, never to return? Discarding the physical symbols of an oppressive regime gestures toward creating a clean slate, and thereby opens up space for new beginnings. But shared memories of state-sponsored violence and injustice linger, forming a ghostly presence that refuses to fade away. The end of apartheid and the transition to parliamentary democracy did not open up a pure space uncontaminated by what preceded it. As a spectral presence that refuses to accept oblivion, the enduring afterlife of white minority rule lurks just beneath the surface and appears, seemingly out of nowhere, to haunt the present. The ways in which racial segregation remains an indelible trace embedded in the social relations, spatial form of the built environment, and visual cultures of the present are never far removed from questions of group and national identity. The echoes of the past that reverberate in the present should remind us that the "post" in post-apartheid refers to continuities as much as to discontinuities. The symbolic and material markers of white minority rule did not entirely disappear with the birth of the "new South Africa": they have continued to exist as the spectral afterlife of the past, the enduring presence of the past in the present.[38]

In its official version, cultural heritage in the "new South Africa" has been reconceptualized around the twin themes of acknowledgment and redress. Besides the renaming of towns, cities, streets, and other public sites, the reworking of cultural heritage has involved the construction of various legacy projects designed to highlight and showcase the achievements of key individuals and social groups long ignored under white minority rule.[39] The end of apartheid signaled a profound and enduring rupture in the language, the politics, and the symbolic imagery of remembrance that prevailed under white minority rule.[40] From the start, political leaders, cultural workers, and academics in the "new South Africa" began seriously to explore ways of redressing the balance of official memory.[41] High-ranking state officials were acutely aware that "nation-building" required a new contextual framework, symbols, and heroic figures from which to draw sustenance and inspiration. In the official view, an inclusionary interpretation of the historical past can contribute to healing divisions, recognizing the genuine diversity that has always existed, and restoring dignity and self-confidence to those whose heritage has been denied or ignored.[42]

The process of replacing old memories with new memories has careened between the extremes of radical erasure and deliberate delegitimation, on the one side, to benign neglect and gradual abandonment, on the other.[43] The adoption by the first post-1994 Cabinet of nine key "legacy projects" opened the way for a broader interpretation of South African history, commemorating the origins and contributions of all the people of the country. The new custodians of collective memory pinned their hopes for an ultimate sense of historical balance on a "legacy mega-project" called Freedom Park outside Pretoria. Planners envisaged a centrally located agglomeration of memorials, museums, computer-age interactive sites, galleries, and learning facilities. While its creators have argued that its greatest strength is its ability to combine a diverse range of experiences linking the past and the present, its critics have suggested that the greatest danger is that it resembles a poorly conceived "heritage Disneyland on the hill somewhere outside of town."[44]

As a general rule, place-names hold a great deal of symbolic value in the process of memorialization.[45] Places are like storehouses of memories, ranging from personal recollections to official histories of momentous events.[46] As Jennifer Jordan has argued, names inscribed on plaques, street signs, and buildings constitute a form of collective memory refracted through political and bureaucratic processes.[47] Place-names attached to specific landscapes are like "tapestries" consisting of different threads and patterns of meaning that have been left behind by the victors in earlier political struggles.[48] In the immediate aftermath of the transition to parliamentary democracy, acts of installing memory within the commemorative landscape proceeded slowly. Three years after the historic 1994 "liberation" elections, the hallways of Parliament were still adorned with the portraits of the whites-only cabinet ministers serving under such apartheid stalwarts of J. G. Strijdom, H. F. Verwoerd, John Vorster, and P. W. Botha. Politically and racially offensive place- and street names that have their roots in the racist past—like Kafferboom Crescent in Birchleigh (Kemptom Park), to give an egregious example—can be found throughout South Africa. Place- and street names honoring iconic figures of the bygone era and glorifying the names of many Boer republic officials remained largely unchanged.[49]

Place-names left over from discredited regimes typically act as disturbing reminders of the terrible way it once was. Postcommunist regimes in European cities like Moscow, Bucharest, and Berlin moved quickly to remove street names, statuary, and other material symbols that provided political legitimation for the state administrations they replaced.[50] In contrast to this practice of "toponymic cleansing,"[51] the post-apartheid state administration pursued a considerably more cautious strategy, ever-mindful of the coexistence of competing political ideologies and nostalgic sentiments in the "new South Africa."[52]

Yet with the passage of time, acts of institutional inscription that alter, balance, or erase the painful reminders of the racist past have begun to occur with predictable regularity. A wide range of "liberation heroes" has been gradually memorialized in monumental statuary, place-names, public buildings, monuments and parks, street signs, anniversaries, celebrations, gravestones, and official commemorations. In Johannesburg, city officials successfully renamed Showground Road to Enoch Sontonga Avenue to honor the composer of the national anthem *Nkosi Sikelel' iAfrika*. Water Affairs Minister Kader Asmall renamed the Kafferskuil River by calling it the Goukou River.[53]

While the act of naming for commemorative purposes may appear somewhat mundane and harmless, it is often subjected to a great deal of debate and controversy.[54] All sorts of memory-markers can easily become representational battlegrounds where a variety of stakeholders, including artists, victims, members of political parties and community organizations, political officials, representatives of cultural-heritage boards, and so forth can take very different positions. Controversies over aesthetics, architectural stylistics, iconography and symbolism, appropriateness, and financial cost can easily reflect deep-seated ideological conflicts over the interpretation of the past.[55]

The Liberation Struggle as Foundation Myth of the "New South Africa"

With the end of apartheid and the transition to parliamentary democracy, South African citizens have been asked to confront their painful past, both as a way of exposing the terrible truths associated with white minority rule and as a way of laying the groundwork for moving forward toward a radiant future.[56] Like other deeply divided countries that have broken free from an oppressive institutional and political order, South Africa is not alone in having to grapple with questions dealing with painful memories of the past. Few people will deny that there is a need to remember the past, but there is only partial consensus on what aspects of the past should be commemorated or how these should be represented.[57] Yet because they tell some stories while glossing over others and speak to some audiences while ignoring others, commemorative sites are never immune from conflict and controversy. They can easily become embroiled in questions regarding who is allowed to speak and which audiences are addressed.[58]

As a general rule, the passage from one political order to another involves the forging of a new national identity through a process of selective remembrance and the invention of usable pasts.[59] For a culturally diverse citizenry, the creation of this new national identity involves managing social conflict and overcoming mutual distrust, suspicion, and even outright hostility. As Paul Connerton has argued, the birth of a new nation is always accompanied by efforts to begin with a fresh start, where new beginnings are inevitably rooted in arbitrary and selective recollections of the past.[60] Perhaps the most significant aspect of this process is the construction of a compelling foundation myth, a story that identifies the roots and defines the beginning of the new order in order to demarcate a radical break from the past.[61] To paraphrase Roland Barthes, myths do not deny things; on the contrary, their function is to simplify things, to talk about them simply, to purify them, and make them innocent. In short, myths give things a natural and eternal justification and a "blissful clarity" that "abolishes the complexity of human acts," giving them "the simplicity of essences."[62] Foundation myths operate on much the same terrain as what Eric Hobsbawm termed "invented tradition."[63] Generally speaking, these foundation myths are carefully designed stories about what came before that are not necessarily untrue but are fashioned out of a "suitable historical past" to fit present circumstances.[64] As a kind of invented tradition put at the service of constructing an "imagined community," they generally come into play when those entrusted with "nation-building" seek to cement bonds of social solidarity by establishing continuity with a historic past of varying accuracy.

It is this "blissful clarity" embedded in foundation myths—as opposed to the complexities, ambiguities, and contradictions that characterize all efforts to reach an accurate historical understanding of the past—that makes the messages conveyed by monuments, memorials, and other commemorative practices so appealing to popular audiences.[65] Foundation myths provide the framework into which individual stories, particular events, and specific places can be attached and from which they derive their broader meaning. They also provide a platform around which to construct heroic figures, which become larger-than-life characters that perform their assigned roles in uplifting national stories.[66]

In seeking to counter the regnant British story of domination and Empire, Afrikaner nationalists created their own foundation myth rooted in the story of the mid-nineteenth-century "Great Trek," when thousands of Boer farmers and their families, suffering under the yoke of British domination, set off to the interior in search of "the promised land." In the construction of such foundation myths, it matters little that many of the actual facts of the Great Trek are uncertain, shrouded in mystery, or contested. Scholarly research suggests that the Voortrekkers were a much more diverse and heterogeneous group of people, speaking different languages, and having different sociocultural roots than Afrikaner nationalist historiography has admitted.[67] The period leading up to the watershed Centenary celebrations of 1938 provided the historical context within which a systematic process of selective remembering intended to define and consolidate a narrowly focused metanarrative of Afrikaner nationalism took place. A closely affiliated collection of researchers, writers, and propagandists played a significant role in creating a story of the Voortrekkers as "God's chosen people," who, in intending to escape the yoke of British domination, went in search of "the promised land." This practice of selective remembering and historical fabrication subsequently shaped the dominant view of the Great Trek as a spontaneous, but well-organized, event with clear goals that were more or less unanimously agreed upon. The Great Trek became the key symbol of Afrikaner nationalism, and the annual ritual observance of the "Day of the Vow" (December 16), with its staged performance, rites of passage, and choreographed pageantry, acted to reinforce the foundation myth. Monuments, especially the Voortrekker Monument near Pretoria, played the central role in visualizing, institutionalizing, and perpetuating the collective memory of shared heritage that linked generations of Afrikaner nationalists across space and time. The celebration of the Great Trek—through monuments, rituals, and celebrations—functioned as the driving force behind the construction of a unified, coherent Afrikaner group identity. Repeated often enough in written texts, visual memory-markers, and rituals, the foundation myth of Afrikaner nationalism assumed an exalted status akin to indisputable historical fact.[68]

With the end of apartheid and the transition to parliamentary democracy, the challenge facing the "new South Africa" has revolved around forging an inclusive, transcendent vision and shared national identity that would facilitate the process of putting aside and overcoming the painful divisions of the past. In contrast to the narrow, exclusivist practice of white minority rule, the idea of a "rainbow nation"—terminology introduced by Archbishop Desmond Tutu in the 1980s—became a central building block in constructing an "imagined community." The inauguration of commemorative events, such as Human Rights Day (March 21) replacing Sharpeville Day, Youth Day (June 16) supplanting Soweto Day, and Day of Reconciliation (December 16) replacing the Day of the Vow, not only sought to suppress what these days of remembrance symbolized in the past but to instill universalizing values that reflected the future vision of the "new South Africa."[69]

Public officials have largely embraced a functionalist approach toward commemoration by promoting the notion that commemorative practices should contribute to social and racial reconciliation, to an inclusive culture of human rights, and to the building of a new national identity. In seeking to redress the inherited symbolic landscapes of memory so strongly weighted in favor of the celebration of white minority rule, they have adopted the idea that public art cannot be separated from cultural heritage, that is, public art not as object of aesthetic contemplation, or (more mundanely) as a focal point of urban landscapes, but public art as cultural artifact with a specific purpose.[70] As a result, they have promoted the development of commemorative practices that stress previously neglected historical narratives and cultural values and that honor key figures in the liberation struggle and their noteworthy contributions to human freedom and dignity.[71]

White minority rule was never a homogeneous experience: its impact varied considerably, since it was contingent upon, and negotiated through, local circumstances and the specificities of place. In the repressive, authoritarian context of apartheid South Africa, collective memory was shaped around a combination of gaps, silences, and outright lies. Ordinarily, collective memory provides a way to excavate those silences. How apartheid has been remembered—or not—has in large part reflected the social and political dynamics set in motion after its collapse.[72] The power of foundation myths is to establish legitimacy and provide a platform for the formation of national identity. In fashioning a new foundation myth, the story of the liberation struggle—not only against apartheid but also against all forms of colonial oppression and discrimination—has become the cornerstone of the collective memory and national identity of the "new South Africa."[73]

New monuments and memorials have proliferated across the spatial landscape. These range from the officially sanctioned to the unofficially ordained, from the public to the intensely private, and from the stately and grandiose to the local and vernacular. Monuments, memorials, and other sites of commemoration are places where memories—both collective and individual—converge, condense, and crystallize. In the typical case, they commemorate significant events in the history of popular resistance against oppression and pay tribute to those who died at the hands of the apartheid state machinery, either as innocent bystanders or as political activists in the liberation struggle.[74]

Almost without exception, the message conveyed in the construction of new monuments, memorials, museums, and other commemorative heritage sites revolves around this central theme of the "liberation struggle" and the sacrifice and heroism associated with it. Examples include the Apartheid Museum located on the premises of the Gold Reef City gaming resort southwest of the Johannesburg central city, the Red Location Museum in Port Elizabeth, Freedom Park at Salvokop outside Pretoria, the Walter Sisulu Square of Dedication in Kliptown (Soweto), District Six Museum in Cape Town, and the Women's Memorial at the Union Buildings in Pretoria.[75]

By blending the conjoined themes of suffering and redemption, such cultural-heritage sites as Robben Island and Constitution Hill in Johannesburg represent the sacrifice of those who struggled for freedom, while at the same time they symbolize the eventual triumph over adversity. The new custodians of memory have found ways to recognize the contribution of mythologized "struggle heroes" like Nelson Mandela, Steve Biko, Mahatma Gandhi, Albert Luthuli, Solomon Mahlangu, John Dube, and countless others in monumental statuary (typically in the conventional form of bronze busts or statutes on pedestals), place-names, public buildings, parks, street names, anniversaries, celebrations, gravestones, and official commemorations. In addition, a whole range of "massacre memorials" has been constructed throughout the country, including the Sharpeville Monument near Vereeniging, the Bulhoek Massacre Monument near Queenstown, the Bisho Massacre Memorial near East London, the Trojan Horse Memorial in Athlone (Cape Town), the Ncome/Blood River Museum and Monument in Natal, the Langa Massacre Monument in Uitenhage, and the Duncan Village Massacre in the Buffalo City Municipality (Eastern Cape).[76] In emotionally charged images, symbols, and texts, these commemorative sites typically recount similar, but locally specific, versions of the same story: groups of innocent people, gathered to engage in peaceful protest, are indiscriminately shot and killed by ruthless security forces. With its deliberate stress on children as the nearly universal symbol of innocence and vulnerability, the Hector Pieterson Memorial epitomizes this genre of public commemoration.[77] These kinds of "martyr monuments" speak to the tangled web of mixed emotional responses that range from anger and outrage to melancholy and alienation. They attest to the limits of understanding and the lingering resentment that the perpetrators were never brought to justice.[78]

Finally, a number of less well known small group memorials have been dedicated to the memory of those who sacrificed their lives—usually young, always male, political activists whose untimely deaths are associated with a singular tragic event and brutal murder by the security forces. For the most part, the dramatic stories of these deadly incidents and the complex narratives of their lives are condensed into one succinct, catchphrase label: the "Trojan Horse" incident, the Gugulethu Seven, the Cradock Four, and the Pepco Three, to name only a few.[79]

Even a cursory glance at some of the most well known Afrikaner nationalist monuments—the Voortrekker Monuments at Pretoria and at Winburg, the Blood River Monument near Dundee, the National Women's Monument in Bloemfontein—clearly illustrates the predominant themes of Afrikaner national identity and the Great Trek as foundation myth. These commemorative sites are marked first and foremost by the conjoined ideas of hardship, suffering, and sacrifice—along with unrelenting struggle and unselfish heroic commitment to the common good. Perhaps not surprisingly, these themes and topics also appear in the foundation myth and official depictions of the origins of the "new South Africa." The idea of "foundation myth" is integrally linked to the notion of discontinuities, radical breaks, and "new beginnings" in history. This approach to history, as Michael Lambeck and Paul Antze have argued, is imported unnoticed into memory and practices of commemoration.[80] As a way of constructing group identity in the present, the commemorative practices of the "new South Africa" have mimicked and imitated the values that shaped the memorializing impulse during the colonial and apartheid periods. A rich array of monuments, memorials, and commemorative statuary has become the main mechanisms for visualizing, nurturing, and disseminating the new national identity.[81]

Because they generally make use of conventional features that have not varied over space or time, monuments and memorials are essentially a conservative artistic genre. For this reason, "it is difficult to determine whether it is the inherent quality of a particular shape or element that has the power to trigger virtual universal feelings," Sabine Marschall has argued, "or whether it is the extensive usage of certain elements in recurring specific contexts that has established a cross-cultural tradition of emotional responses."[82] While there are some important differences, memorials to the victims of the liberation struggle in South Africa can be compared with the genre of national war memorials. What they have in common are depictions of idealism, sacrifice for a noble cause, and seeking to maintain or bring about a just political order. As a general rule, memorials encourage remembrance of the war dead by giving it the literal language of narrative. In seeking to encourage the public viewership to "live through" the experience, they often resort to didactic techniques designed to force an emotional response. With the passage of time, such memorials can appear as empty and lifeless. The overuse of the pathos formula can ironically produce distance rather than connection.[83] In contrast, the minimalist formula promotes a kind of existential ethos, encouraging the public viewership "to imagine the experience, rather than to visually consume a prearranged pictorial representation of it."[84] Holocaust memorials typically rely upon this minimalist language of abstraction and formalism to convey tragedy and suffering. To the extent that monuments and memorials in the "new South Africa" mimic this formula, they seek to attach themselves to conventions that have proven successful in other settings.[85]

With the end of apartheid and the transition to parliamentary democracy, South Africa has experienced a building boom in the construction of new museums, monuments, memorials, and other commemorative sites. In trying to deal with contested and traumatic histories, these purpose-built places are, by definition, engaged in a critique and reevaluation of the past by addressing inaccuracies and omissions in the historical record. In breaking from the narrow confines of white minority rule, commemorative sites open up space for a more inclusive interpretation of the past.[86]

Dialogical Memory: The Power of Public Testimony

By its very nature, all memory—collective and individual, popular and official—is always selective and malleable, evolving in response to acts of recovery and processes of suppression or forgetting. Under the repressive conditions of apartheid rule, collective memory was shaped around disturbing silences, secrecy, official lies, and deliberate deception. Ordinarily, memory, and especially oral testimonies, provide a way to excavate those silences and to expose manipulations of the truth. Under apartheid rule, it was the individual experience of violence that held sway over memory, pushing aside other remembrances and reducing the importance of other recollections. This shared experience of violence is central to understanding how so many individual memories, "I-witness" accounts, historical documents, visual images, and personal commentaries converged to create collective memories that came to occupy a place in the public sphere.[87]

As Antjie Krog has argued, "[South Africans] are struggling to find identity for themselves, individually and collectively, within the shadows still cast by their country's brutal history."[88] What accompanied the end of apartheid and the transition to parliamentary democracy was an intense fixation on the systematic brutality and violence of white minority rule. At the time, the prevailing memory discourse focused primarily on the personal and experiential, that is, on testimony, memoir, and subjectivity. The resurrection of traumatic memory served a therapeutic purpose—healing a nation ripped apart by formal racial segregation. The intensity of witness and survivor testimonies reinforced the demand for redress of collective grievances. The focus on trauma is certainly legitimate and understandable under circumstances where groups of people were collectively stigmatized as "nonwhite" and hence "noncitizens." Coming to terms with a history of violence suffered and violence perpetuated is always complicated by the nagging questions of degrees of suffering and extent of complicity. The privileging of traumatic memory formed a thick discursive network that paralleled political discussion and debate over how to address the structural inequities inherited from the immediate apartheid past.[89] As a general rule, the function of public memory discourses is to break free of a melancholic fixation on unspeakable trauma, suffering, and loss with "no exit" options. Memory-markers like truth commissions, exhibitions, personal memoirs, oral testimonies, and public memorials commemorating those who suffered at the hands of oppressors are tools for breaking the grip of melancholic despair.[90]

The collective remembrance of trauma puts a great deal of pressure on conventional forms of representation and commemoration, giving rise to new forms of expression such as public testimonies along with other kinds of performative rituals and symbolic gestures. The centerpiece of the new nation-building project was the Truth and Reconciliation Commission (TRC).[91] In the early years of the "new South Africa," TRC provided a high-profile platform for public debate about healing, forgiveness, and restorative justice. By stressing the power of public testimony as a means of promoting healing, the TRC focused its attention on individual culpability and the admission of guilt as a means of achieving forgiveness and reconciliation. The TRC created a platform for victims to speak without fear of retribution, and to let their voices be heard, thereby enabling those experiences of harm and suffering silence by the apartheid regime to become a part of public disclosure. The offer of amnesty in exchange for truthful admission of guilt enabled the TRC to wrap itself around the moral principle of forgiveness in the service of reconciliation and nation-building rather than retribution and punishment.[92]

Public testimony, particularly the staged reenactment of acts of violence and physical abuse, often resembled a cathartic act of conversion, marking the passage from an old life to a new life. The performative dimension of the public hearings enabled perpetrators to "speak the truth" and ask for forgiveness. The theatricality inherent in the stage-managed public hearings drove a wedge between the search for empirically verifiable "forensic truth" as opposed to the "narrative truth" that allowed witnesses to privilege the particularities of their own individual, subjective experience.[93] As Jacques Derrida has argued, testimony is a mode of telling that "always goes hand in hand with at least the possibility of fiction, perjury, and lie."[94]

For some, the TRC represented the foundation of the new nation—the crowning achievement of the political transition and a new *official* history marked by forgiveness and racial reconciliation.[95] Yet for others, it signaled a fatal compromise.[96] The TRC's institutional discourse of truth-telling and forgiveness reduced horrific episodes into opportunities for reconciliation.[97]

Public testimonies revealed the truth about events but emptied them of historical content. Yet as much as the TRC opened up space to speak, it also reinforced certain forms of silence.[98] The stress on gross violations of human rights at an individual level sidestepped the deeper structural problems associated with collective responsibility for past injustices and the associated questions of reparations and restitution.[99] By "utilizing the narratives of the perpetrators and victims of gross human rights violations to forge a collective memory and an official historical archive," the TRC constructed a narrowly focused version of apartheid exploitation and oppression, limited to two adversaries: those acting to preserve and maintain it, and those acting to dismantle it. As a consequence, the "subtleties and complexities of the historical and structural violence of the apartheid system "were drained away" and effectively relocated in "racially polarized and individual acts of physical violence."[100]

In spite of its commendable role in exposing the crimes and injustices of the apartheid era, the TRC was not immune from the pressures to forgive in order to forget.[101] Put in precise terms, the TRC promoted what Paul Connerton has termed "prescriptive forgetting," or the official injunction to forgive and forget in order "to restore a minimum level of cohesion to civil society and to re-establish the legitimacy of the state [under circumstances] where authority, and the very bases of civil behavior, had been obliterated by authoritarian government."[102] By holding close to its mandate to promote a speedy reconciliation and by privileging forgiveness as the highest form of ethical behavior, the TRC fell prey to what the poet Ingrid de Kok identified as a rhetoric of amnesia.[103] In the rush to forgive, there are always calls to forget.[104] In describing the work of the TRC, even the commissioners themselves occasionally resorted to the language of making "a clean break," closing "this chapter of our history," "getting the past out of the way," and so forth. This amnesiac rhetoric seemed to express the fear that an obsessive fixation on the past threatened the drag the country into unwanted paralysis.[105] For the beneficiaries of white minority rule and for those complicit in the maintenance of apartheid, organized forgetting is actually a part of a wider political strategy that has as its ultimate goal the avoidance of having to sacrifice anything. As the memories of the past recede into a kind of oblivion, nagging questions of complicity and responsibility fade into the background.[106]

To a certain extent, what the TRC produced was less truth and reconciliation than its own story, that is, the construction of a single, coherent narrative organized around the moral conviction that the reenactment of traumatic experience yields necessarily to healing. At a philosophical level, the organizers of the TRC largely operated on the proleptic logic of contrition, that is, the presumption that the victims of state-organized violence were both willing and able to listen to the appeals of perpetrators for forgiveness.[107] The organizers of the TRC failed to entertain the possibility that the extent of pain and suffering was so great as to irredeemably compromise or interrupt the possibility of communication, dialogue, and openness on the part of victims. Avowals of contrition can easily fall on deaf ears. As Ulrich Baer put it in another context, "How does a guilty party reclaim the confidence and right even to address the victim—or to speak on his behalf, in his name, by using his name?"[108]

Collective Memory and Social Amnesia

Collective memory is a concept that expresses a sense of the continued presence of the past. Yet remembrance is never a benign process. For everything that is remembered, there is something forgotten. Certain memories survive and are preserved in some way. The rest are winnowed out, repressed or simply discarded by a process of willful selection by which the guardians of the past decide what is worth remembering and what is not.[109]

"Forgetting," either as a cognitive lapse or a deliberate strategy, has always shadowed discussions of memory.[110] The flip side of collective memory is forgetfulness. Collective memory is an unstable, elusive medium incapable of holding onto the past without the assistance of mnemonic devices. Remembering can just as easily engender paralysis, passivity, and inertia as it can recall the past. With the passage of historical time, some degree of effacement, or forgetting, is inescapable. Remembrance falls prey not just to forgetting but to distraction. These powerful forces can lead to the erasure of memory altogether, or a kind of anchorless social amnesia. Without memory, the present becomes a blank slate, unburdened by its connection with the past. As Norman Klein has put it, only deliberate mnenomic discipline can slow the decay.[111]

Collective remembrance is a process that is never static but open to continual reconfiguration in line with evolving circumstances. As a consequence, it becomes difficult to untangle from where collective memory originates: whether from direct experience or else passed along and mediated through popular cultural forms. The concept of "prosthetic memory"—that is, memories synthetically produced that nevertheless acquire the familiarity of seemingly coming from direct experience—reveals how recollections of the past are often a blend of wishful thinking, nostalgia, myth, and encounters with a variety of popular cultural forms.[112] Because it is "always subject to subtle and not-so-subtle reconstruction," collective memory is malleable and flexible.[113] In an age of postmodern amnesia, where obsessive self-memorialization (through home movies, personal memoirs, confessional literature, and Internet self-fashioning) plays a key part of popular culture, public memorials have to compete for attention. At a time of information saturation and consumer distraction, "a sense of historical continuity, or for that matter, discontinuity, both of which depend upon a before and an after, gives way to the simultaneity of all times and spaces readily accessible in the present."[114] This simultaneity and presentness, suggested by the immediacy of images and the "magical power of simulation," tends to wipe out "the alterity of the past and present, the here and there." This blurring of past and present undermines our capacity to perceive real difference, or real otherness, in historical time or geographical distance. Taken to the extreme, "the boundaries between fact and fiction, image and the real, have been blurred to the extent of leaving us only with simulation, and the postmodern subject vanishes [into] the imaginary world" of images and simulation.[115] The accelerated pace of scientific, technological, and cultural innovation in a social world dominated by consumer distraction and profit-making "produces ever larger quantities of soon-to-be obsolete objects, lifestyles, and attitudes." The temporal expression of such planned obsolescence is amnesia.[116] The conjoined effects of such space-time compression and the blurring of the boundaries between fact and fiction unsettle the relationship between history and memory, and between an authentic past and mythical fabrication masquerading as cultural heritage.[117]

4 Collective Memory in Place

The Voortrekker Monument and the Hector Pieterson Memorial

The erection of monuments and memorials—along with the choreographed ceremonies of commemoration centered on them and the orchestration of public participation around them—transforms particular places into ideologically charged sites of collective memory. Monuments and memorials are powerful mnemonic devices through which the custodians of collective memory seek to encode particular histories and geographies into landscapes of power and resistance. They provide rallying points for shared memories and common identities. They are material signifiers of ideas, transmitters of sentiments, and repositories of ideologies that their permanent affixture to public space intends to immortalize. The elaborate language of symbolism and allegory embodied in these sites of memory serve a variety of didactic functions. By locating events and key personalities in the historical imagination, monuments and memorials can inspire to action, insist on vigilance, and recall the past with either sadness and regret or pride and gratitude.[1]

While the terms are sometimes used interchangeably, the symbolic meanings that monuments and memorials seek to convey are quite opposite. Broadly speaking, the victors of history have long erected monuments to proudly remember their triumphs and celebrate their victories. In contrast, the victims have built memorials to recall their martyrdom and call attention to their trauma.[2] "We erect monuments so that we shall always remember," Arthur Danto has argued, "and build memorials so that we shall never forget."[3] Because they commemorate what is deemed worthy of remembering at the expense of what is left undisturbed, monuments "embody myths of beginnings." They celebrate the triumph of the human spirit and stand as testimonials to courage, self-sacrifice, and heroism. The messages they convey are uplifting, typically emphasizing group cohesion, solidaristic bonds, and shared values. In contrast, memorials "mark the reality of ends."[4] They ritualize mourning and solemnize bereavement. They draw attention to sacrifice, suffering, and loss in the service of a shared cluster of values or uplifting ideals. As Charles Griswold puts it, memorials are a "species of pedagogy" that "seek to instruct posterity about the past."[5] In so doing, they principally serve a didactic function: reminding people of what they already know or think they know, or informing people about what they may not know, or what they may have forgotten, or never learned.[6]

The steady accretion of monuments, memorials, and other sites of remembrance provide eloquent testimony to the "memory boom" that has gripped South Africa after apartheid. Generated both from above and below, and reflecting both official and unofficial memory, these sites compete for space with the material reminders of the apartheid past.[7] Focusing particular attention on two sites of memory, the Voortrekker Monument and the Hector Pieterson Memorial, enables us to examine critically both the parallels and divergent trajectories in these different modes of commemoration. The Voortrekker Monument marked the power of Afrikanerdom at the height of the political confidence in the National Party as the vehicle of (white) national identity. Once a messenger of power, it has become a symbol of the failed promise of white minority rule. Once a powerful marker of triumph, it has become a symbol of hubris.[8]

Places of memory are sites where the "symbolic imaginings of the past interweave with the materialities of the present."[9] Physical structures built in the past represent a direct link to the history of the place, forcing observers to look backward in time.[10] While they were intended to convey specific messages from the time they were built, these places of memory stand a good chance of being interpreted as "frozen signs" with stagnant meanings, or they may not be perceived as signs at all, thus becoming unattached signifiers devoid of referents and drained of all meaning.[11] In short, places of memory cannot escape the process of continuous metamorphosis and transformation.

While they are fixed in place, monuments are never petrified and inflexible. The meanings attached to them are inherently unstable and mutable. Monuments become invisible and disappear into oblivion unless they serve as places of rendezvous and renewal.[12]

The emphasis on the iconography, ceremonies, and rituals of the white minority regime can enrich our understanding of the ways in which the National Party communicated its agenda and priorities to ordinary white citizens, and the manner in which the party sought to involve them in the vision of white supremacy, or at least sought their acquiescence and compliance to the political order. Of the countless monuments created to commemorate Afrikaner nationalism, the Voortrekker Monument is *primus inter pares:* it is the most widely known, the most celebrated and vilified, and hence the most controversial of all. In its elaborate use of the broadest range of cultural archetypes—the typological image of Boer trekkers, the larger-than-life granite statutes depicting key Boer heroes, and its celebratory iconography—the Voortrekker Monument has achieved little critical consensus. Hailed by Afrikaner nationalists as an enduring shrine to the animating myth of "white South Africa," it has been scorned and ridiculed by most ordinary South Africans, who regard it as a lumbering anachronistic relic to a bygone era, a despised symbol of racial intolerance and oppression, and a monstrous curiosity out of place in the "new South Africa."[13]

Under apartheid rule, built form became a material embodiment of racialist attitudes, such that racial hierarchies and value systems became an innate part of architectural design. The Voortrekker Monument marked the genesis of Afrikaner nationalism and, as a consequence, formed the scaffolding for the national identity of apartheid South Africa. As both a site of pilgrimage and of visual spectacle, it operated as the material manifestation of Afrikaner nationalists seeking to celebrate their racial superiority and their special place as a spiritual people aligned with God.[14] The memorializing impulse that produced the Voortrekker Monument represented a shared desire to "generate political legitimization through the symbolic possession of [commemorative] spaces."[15]

Constructed to sustain the myth of white South Africa, the Voortrekker Monument derived its power from its ability to invite those who believed in its message to mistake material presence for immutable permanence.[16] Yet all monuments "always run the risk of becoming just another testimony to forgetting."[17] The permanence promised by monuments cast in stone are "always built on quicksand." Some monuments are toppled at times of political upheaval, while others preserve fading memory in "its most ossified form, either as myth or as cliché." Still others remain in place simply as "figures of forgetting, their meaning and original purpose eroded by the passage of time."[18] "There is nothing in this world as invisible as a monument," the Austrian writer Robert Musil once observed. "They are no doubt erected to be seen—indeed, to attract attention. But at the same time they are impregnated with something that repels attention."[19] In this instance, this "something" that repels attention is what the Voortrekker Monument symbolizes: the dreamscape of white supremacy. The invisibility of this monument derives from its irrelevance in the contemporary age.[20] "For in its linear progression, time drags old meaning into new contexts, estranging a monument's memory from both past and present, holding past truths up to ridicule in present monuments," James Young has argued. "Time mocks the rigidity of monuments, the presumptuous claim that in its materiality, a monument can be regarded as eternally true, a fixed star in the constellation of collective memory."[21] Kurt Forster has defined ruins as "structures which have outlasted their usefulness." In this sense, the Voortrekker Monument, although it has not suffered from physical deterioriation brought about by neglect, is a contemporary ruin. Its original purpose is antiquated and outdated—and insulting.[22]

In contrast, the Hector Pieterson Memorial is an exemplary expression of what Maria Tumarkin has called a traumascape, or a distinctive category of place that stands witness to terrible acts of tragedy, and as a result inadvertently becomes synonymous with the past events themselves. Much more than merely the physical setting for tragedy, traumascapes are cathartic locations, transformed psychically by suffering, grief, and loss. They have become essential parts of people's experience of mourning, remembering, and making sense of the traumatic events that took place there.[23]

At the Hector Pieterson Memorial, memory is intertwined with history. It is simultaneously a *lieux de mémoire,* in the sense defined by Pierre Nora, and a public space that recounts a story about the "new nation." In sites such as this one, actual and imaginary communities both share and shape meanings attached to the urban landscape. The Hector Pieterson Memorial exemplifies the making of a social history of popular struggle that is embedded in a particular location, where particular places are invested with signification, "memories conjured, and public histories constructed."[24]

As a traumascape, the Hector Pieterson Memorial reflects the power of place, indelibly marked by suffering, to transform grief into a commemorative site of mourning. The historical significance of the 1976–77 Soweto student uprising is forever joined to the site itself. As an uncanny place that mediates between the living and the dead, the memorial has become a touchstone of remembrance and a gathering place for commemorative events that evoke the sacrifice of those who lost their lives in the struggle against apartheid.[25]

Dead Places: The Voortrekker Monument as Disgraced Ruinscape

For eight decades, the colossal Voortrekker Monument, looming large atop Monument Hill in *Voortrekkerhoogte* outside Pretoria, has served both as a symbolic expression of Afrikaner national identity and a public meeting place for the faithful who wished to express their loyalty to white minority rule. The idea of the monument was the brainchild of leading *Broederbond* members seeking to restore an authentic commitment to *volk en vaderland.* The foundation stone was laid on December 16, 1938, following the four-month-long ritual reenactment of the Great Trek (1835–54), where various groups in traditional ox-wagons and costumed regalia converged on the site. The placement of the foundation stone marked the high point of the Voortrekker centenary celebrations where an estimated quarter million Afrikaners gathered at the site to commemorate the one-hundredth anniversary of the Day of the Covenant in an unblinkered display of chauvinistic celebration. The mass spectacle that was orchestrated around the site of the Voortrekker Monument represented, as Annie Coombes has suggested, a "calculated attempt to invent a coherent Afrikaner identity where none actually existed."[26] By borrowing from the language of theater that the National Socialists in Germany so successfully employed and epitomized by the large-scale Nazi rallies at Nuremburg in the 1930s, the organizers of the event tapped into the fears of anxious Afrikaners who lived in resentment of what they considered British domination.[27]

Inaugurated on December 16, 1949, by Prime Minister D. F. Malan, the imposing granite monument stands as a lasting tribute to their courageous,

FIGURE 1. Imposing view of the Voortrekker Monument. Photograph by the author.

freedom-loving ancestors, who in the early 1830s organized a large-scale Boer exodus from the Cape Colony into the interior with the aim of establishing their own Homeland, free from meddling British domination and its inconvenient corollary of slave emancipation. In one of the most powerful animating myths of Afrikanerdom, the Great Trek symbolized a glorious milestone in the development of a premeditated Afrikaner nationalist sentiment, and this invented tradition portrays the Voortrekkers as "nationally aware Afrikaners" that doubled as self-conscious "nation-builders," thereby establishing the desired historical continuity between the Age of the Boer Republics and the Age of Apartheid.[28]

The Voortrekkers regarded the Great Trek as an act of defiance against British colonialism and, as a result, Afrikaner nationalists regarded this commemorative marker as both anti-British and anti-African.[29] The Voortrekker Monument highlights the story of the Battle of Blood River (1838), where heavily outnumbered Boers, who encircled their ox-wagons in a closed battle formation called a *laager* (or protective shield), defeated their Zulu opponents, who, despite their considerably larger numbers, paid a terrible price in terms of loss of life. Inscribed through symbol and text on the walls of the

Voortrekker Monument, this story forms the foundational myth for official constructions of Afrikaner identity, a kind of sacred totem that spells out Afrikaner claims to lawful ownership of the land.[30] By obsessively mythologizing the Great Trek as the singular founding event of the nation, Afrikaner nationalists not only claimed proprietary ownership of South Africa but also asserted their rightful entitlement to rule. The story of the Great Trek functioned as the "master narrative" that recounted the story of how these pioneering white settlers were able to take possession of the land by right of conquest.[31] The black Africans who were there before them were reduced both to a vanquished enemy and, along with the flora and fauna, to an elemental aspect of the landscape itself. These two contradictory images deprived the "native peoples" of a founding role in the identity of the nation.[32]

The Voortrekker Monument embodies the most conventional and deliberately immutable form of memory space. As Vickie Leibowitz has argued, it is a "solid and purposely symbolic memorial constructed with the intention of presenting an uncontestable version of the past."[33] With its commanding location and ornate design, the monument effectively spectacularizes collective memory.[34] The site combines classic monumentality with stark realism to affirm, even glorify, the moral conviction of the Voortrekkers. The depictions of history are so lifelike that omissions go unnoticed, elisions are sustained, and what is repressed becomes invisible. The sheer density of metarepresentational signs appears to provide an accurate story of what happened in the past and why.[35]

The Voortrekker Monument was designed by the architect Gerard Moerdyk, who as a young boy had been interred in the Standerton concentration camp, along with his mother, two brothers, and two sisters, during the Second Boer War (1899–1902). In carefully deliberating how to mold size and form into an enduring symbol of power, Moerdyk sought to align the structure within a lineage of other internationally well-known locations, including the Taj Mahal, the Hôtel des Invalides, the Mausoleum of Halicarnassus, and the Egyptian pyramids.[36] The triadic relationship between form, site, and global context provided the foundation upon which Afrikaner nationalists fashioned their national identity and sense of "being-in-the-world." Moerdyk drew his inspiration from Bruno Schmitz's Volkerschlacht Memorial in Leipzig. The Leipzig memorial was built in the early twentieth century to commemorate German soldiers who died in the Napoleonic Wars. Its construction began at the time of the Second Boer War, thereby allowing Afrikaner nationalists to identify its memorialization with their own. Through identification with the Leipzig memorial, the Voortrekker Monument "claims a double origin" for the soon-to-come apartheid state: the sacrifice of the Great Trek and the humiliation of the Second Boer War convert hardship into resolve, culminating in the National Party electoral victory in 1948 and the triumph of Afrikaner nationalism.[37]

Such historical sites as monuments and memorials, as Maoz Azaryahu and Kenneth Foote have argued, are "dedicated to the cultural production of their pasts."[38] From its inception, the Voortrekker Monument functioned as a mythic place where authority, discipline, and power were made visible and legitimate. Each element of the monument—its location, structure, materiality, and form—was infused with a deliberate significance to highlight Afrikaner achievements as both conquerors and state-builders.[39] The monumental site consists of a phalanx of mnemonic devices, including monumental public statuary, evocative insignia, and inscriptions. The designers of the site rendered a pantheon of specterlike heroes in an idealized, devotional imagery

FIGURE 2. Ox-wagon *laager* at the Voortrekker Monument. Photograph by the author.

intended to evoke feelings of reverence and awe. The meticulously carved statutes of Piet Retief, Andries Pretorius, Hendrik Potgieter, and the unknown Voortrekker hero that adorn each of the four corners of the granite monument constitute, as Christine Boyer puts it, a memory system "transcribed in stone."[40] These pious, stoic sculptural forms of the exterior evoke the memory of the founding fathers of the originating mythology of Afrikaner righteousness.[41]

As an expression of the will to power, the Voortrekker Monument is saturated with symbolic markers that point both to the past and to the future. The monumentality of its architectural form fulfilled the demands of political legitimation, both through its deliberate associations with the mythologized past and also the subordination of the individual to the "community." The basic form of the memorial is rectangular, such that "the significance placed on the materials and sculptural elements becomes apparent."[42] The sheer size and imposing scale of the building closely resembles a grand church. The main entrance of the building leads into the domed Hall of Heroes. This massive open space, flanked by four huge arched windows that provide natural light, contains the unique carved marble frieze (constructed of Italian Quercetta marble, known for its durability). In settler colonial settings, monuments and other commemorative statuary typically include narrative gestures that recall the "bravery" of the European colonizers in juxtaposition to the "treachery" of indigenous peoples. As an intrinsic part of the design of the monument, the frieze consists of twenty-seven bas-relief panels that recount the key events of the Great Trek, from the departure of the Voortrekkers from the Cape Colony in 1835 to the creation of the Transvaal Republic with the signing with the British of the Sand River Convention in 1852. The bas-reliefs are heir to a specific tradition of figural memorialization that stresses storytelling as moral discourse. Reading from left to right, the panels tell a story that conveys a sense of the heroism, sacrifice, and indomitable spirit of these early pioneers, who, against seemingly insurmountable odds, were able to establish a Homeland for themselves in the African interior. By incorporating references to everyday life and the work habits and religious beliefs of the Voortrekkers, the set of panels depicts the early Afrikaner settlers as brave, virtuous, determined, and inspired by God-fearing righteousness, in contrast to Africans, who perform their appointed role as treacherous savages.[43]

The Voortrekker Monument exemplifies how fictionalized images become the foundational myths that animate nation-building. The custodians of memory who constructed this monument relied upon highly nostalgic representations of the past in order to forge a shared Afrikaner identity in the present. The assemblage of friezes flattens the past into a series of frozen images that identify "good" Voortrekkers with virtuous and noble intentions and "bad" Zulus with savage, uncivilized motives. The scenes of heroic men and innocent women and children juxtaposed with armed savages, although highly clichéd and melodramatic, resonated with Afrikaner communities faced in the 1940s and 1950s with an uncertain socioeconomic future at a time of rapid industrialization. Rooted in a myopic form of nostalgia, at once signaling fears, anxieties, and uncertainties about the future and a yearning for an idealized past where a unified community overcame seemingly insurmountable obstacles in achieving freedom. These fictionalized images and Christian symbolism became the foundational myths upon which Afrikaner leadership of the National Party justified the implementation of "separate development." Nostalgic images act as historical filters, replacing the cold realities of racial domination with the celebratory story of "white South Africa" born out of heroism and sacrifice.[44]

In accordance with different semiotic conventions, monuments articulate some combination of sacred, emotional, and cosmological meanings. In the center of the floor of the Hall of Heroes is a large circular opening through which visitors can view the Cenotaph (signifying the final resting place of Piet Retief and other Voortrekkers who died during the Great Trek), where an eternal flame burns constantly. The building itself is constructed in such a way so that every year at exactly noon on December 16 (the anniversary of the Battle of Blood River and celebrated annually as the Day of the Vow), a ray of sunlight passes through an opening in the domed ceiling and shines on the center of the Cenotaph, striking the inscription "Ons vir Jou, Suid-Afrika" (Afrikaans for "We for you, South Africa"). The Afrikaner faithful believe that this ray of light symbolizes God's blessing. This sober moment captures a stylized form of remembrance that attaches the earthly site to what participants want to believe was (and continues to be) divine intervention.[45]

Specific places gain significance and maintain a strong hold over individuals and groups by acting as repositories of collective memory.[46] Both the enclosing wall, with its depiction of the Battle of Blood River with its sixty-four

FIGURE 3. Cenotaph inside the Voortrekker Monument: "Ons vir Jou, Suid-Afrika" (Afrikaans for "We for you, South Africa"). Photograph by the author.

ox-wagon reliefs, and the circular interior echo the spatial form of the *laager*. The adjoining museum focuses attention on a rich array of themes linked to Afrikaner national identity: the Great Trek mythologized as a divinely inspired exodus from the land of Canaan; the Boer occupation of virgin territory and the transformation of the landscape into a Homeland; and the simple lifestyle, the republican values, and the social organization of Voortrekker communities. This material rendering of social memory in a mythologized place transforms landscape from an externalized place that exists in generalized visual condensations to a psychic terrain of internalized symbolic meaning that reinforces the overarching metanarrative of *volk en vaderland*.[47] These exhibitions and displays exemplify how custodians of memory can make "effective use of visual and verbal channels of information" not only to "obscure ideological tensions" but also erase unwanted and inconvenient interpretations that might offer a different understanding.[48]

Memory Devices and Historical Time

Although their intended purpose can be read from inscriptions and deciphered from their styles, monuments reflect the iconographic conventions of the era in which they were built.[49] As David Bunn has argued, the memorial impulse exemplified in the twentieth-century Afrikaner remembrance tradition relied upon "rigid upright forms which collect and focus power vertically." Unlike the British tradition of meditative wandering, Afrikaner monumental practice expresses itself through marking and inscription, thereby signifying goals to be achieved or obstacles to be overcome.[50]

In the domain of public building, the sparseness of the modernist architectural style that reigned supreme through much of the twentieth century tended to preclude massive ornamentation and referentiality. But in the realm of monuments, the level of creative play with symbols, signs, references, and styles was often so intensified and exaggerated that it undermines its intended meaning. As a place that imported its memorial practice and visual language from Europe in order to venerate a white settler minority in Africa, the Voortrekker Monument exemplifies one of the operations of what Daniel Herwitz has called "modernism at the margins."[51] The monument takes Art Deco forms and "renders them as ornament, hardening their fluid lines, imposing a religious severity and overstated indomitability." The almost self-parodying kitsch resides in the unresolved tension between the decorative Art Deco elements and the underlying memorializing purpose: the building looks like an Art Deco radio tower made to do double duty as a church or bunker.[52] It is under circumstances like these where the custodians of memory have stylized and twisted models pillaged from the cosmopolitan center to a purpose finally at odds with their "intrinsic" force, with no real attempt to work them through or render them appropriate.[53]

Collective memory is sustained through the interplay of shared remembrance and ritualized repetition. The use of ritualized repetition is crucial in blurring the differences between individual interpretations of events and the social construction of a "single, highly idealized, composite image."[54] In writing about remembrance practices, Paul Connerton made the useful distinction between inscriptive or incorporating memory. Inscriptive processes of remembering are discursive and representational, that is, memories are preserved as texts, scripts, codes, and symbols. Because reading signs as texts are subject to multiple interpretations this kind of collective memory is relatively fluid and porous. In contrast, incorporating processes of remembering involve performative acts "which are impressed upon the body so as to form part" of the "social habit of memory."[55] Participating groups transmit and sustain collective memories through ritual performance and carefully choreographed observance. Unlike the interpretive scope for innovation and improvisation in written histories or myths that constitute inscriptive memory, the practice of incorporating memory instructs and obligates participants to observe stylized and repetitive actions that in turn are regulated by calendrical points of reference, verbal commands, and gestural codes of conduct. These regular, standardized ritualistic practices inscribe habit-memory onto the bodies of participants, a process that Connerton has argued provides "a measure of insurance against the process of cumulative questioning entailed in all discursive practices."[56]

"Incorporating memory" is a particularly useful metaphor to make sense of the annual ceremony enacted on December 16, the anniversary of the Battle of Blood River. On this day, Afrikaners from all over the country streamed to the Voortrekker Monument to commemorate what they regarded as the most important event in South African history. Disciplined rituals of this sort are important commemorative markers that convey the sacred history of the founding myth of Afrikaner nationalism and that booster the worthiness of the participants in the annual event. The aim of this annual ceremony—with its gestures, period-piece dress, weaponry, and impassioned speeches by key political figures—was to renew commitment to the ideals of the original Voortrekkers. By suspending mundane time, this ceremonial observance of the Day of the Covenant created an illusion of sacred time. Incorporative mnemonic performances, such as the ritualized circling of ox-wagons, taking an oath of allegiance to the *volk,* and other ritualized performances, seek to affirm the historical continuity of Afrikaner nationalism. Attendance became a rite of passage for younger Afrikaners seeking admission into the *volk.* This ritual reenactment of mythical origins of Afrikanerdom symbolized a ceremonial observance fixed in time and performed in a specific place. As Connerton suggested, "This narrative is more than a story told—it was *cult enacted.*" Those who took part in the commemorative pageantry of the annual event "became, so to speak, contemporaries with the mythic event."[57] The narrative recollection of the Great Trek was a story told "not unequivocally in the past tense but in the tense of a metaphysical present."[58] The ordering of shared memory around particular sites provides a focus for the performance of rituals of communal remembrance that sometimes merges with forgetfulness. The continuous flow of time is collapsed into a fixed set of key symbolic dates and events. Sites like the Voortrekker Monument become the symbolic landmarks of a remembered geography and history. The visual displays scattered around the site facilitated the mapping of myths about the arduous journey of the Voortrekkers into the interior onto a specific time and place.[59] This mapping process becomes part and parcel of the ongoing project of attaching individual identities as an expression of collective identity symbolically coded in public monuments and their attendant ceremonial rituals.[60]

By combining commemorative pageantry with official remembrance, the Voortrekker Monument tells the story of historical events—"but of historical events transfigured by mythicization into unchanging and unchangeable substances."[61] Myths of this sort are not subject to any kind of alteration or modification. As Connerton has argued, "The myth teaches that history is not a play of contingent forces. The fundamental constants are struggle, sacrifice, [and] victory."[62] But by burying the actual event of the Battle of Blood River under layers of national myths and facile interpretations, commemorative sites like the Voortrekker Monument may just as easily stultify or "coarsen" historical understanding as preserve and enliven it.[63]

Contested Meanings of Disgraced Monuments: The End of History

The construction of monuments by ruling parties in authoritarian regimes almost invariably conforms to what Michael Walzer calls "single-minded spaces." Put in aesthetic terms, their built form consists of functional, authoritative, and didactic features. The public invited to participate in these places is an all-encompassing, universal collective, and the public space that is fashioned is regarded as a privileged arena for the celebration of exclusivist politics.[64]

The Voortrekker Monument prefigured what became in the post-1948 apartheid era an intensified drive on the part of the ruling National Party to build monuments, commemorate events, and display iconographic images of heroic figures, prescient visionaries, and courageous martyrs. In a deliberate act of time-space compression, Afrikaner nationalists constructed an architectural landscape of ceremonial power whose monuments and memorials, commemorative events, and public statuary spoke of exemplary deeds, national unity, and past glories. These *aides-mémoire* were important symbolic vehicles for the propagation of uplifting messages of ethnic solidarity that were grounded in claims to an authentic "whites-only" homeland on African soil by right of occupation, beliefs about racial purity and the dangers of miscegenation and "race-mixing," and ideologies of white supremacy and the concomitant inferiority of indigenous Africans.[65]

Memorials and monuments anchor "collective remembering" in "highly condensed, fixed, and tangible sites" and seek to freeze ideas, sentiments, and ideologies in time and space.[66] Ironically, however, efforts to guarantee their immortalization are never able to withstand the corrosive effects of the steady, linear progression of time. While these edifices may be permanent fixtures occupying a place in the spatialized landscape, the passage of time invariably oversees the transformation and dismantling of old contexts and the creation of new ones, thereby effacing the original meaning and rendering intended symbolism of monumental statuary outdated, or incoherent, or even incomprehensible. As James Young has observed, monuments and their significance "are constructed in particular times and place, contingent on the political, historical, and aesthetic realities of the moment."[67] Hence, the "unyielding fixedness" of monuments in space almost invariably engenders their demise over time: "A fixed image created in one time and carried over into a new time suddenly appears archaic, strange, or irrelevant altogether."[68]

The Afrikaner nationalists who were responsible for anchoring collective remembering in fixed, tangible sites appropriated numerous public places to stage their ritualized performances of remembering. Yet the collapse of white minority rule and the birth of the "new South Africa" have rendered the Afrikaner "nation-building" project anachronistic and outmoded. Commemorative practices honoring fallen Afrikaner heroes and celebrating key events in a mythical narrative of Afrikaner national identity have become so much flotsam and jetsam incongruously left over from the past. They convey a useless, empty symbolism, with dwindling relevance as cultural markers for young Afrikaners coming of age in the "new South Africa."[69]

"Historical memory today is not what it used to be," Andreas Huyssen has noted.[70] With the end of apartheid and the transition to parliamentary democracy, the Voortrekker Monument excites very little attention. Among ordinary South African citizens, there is a great deal of disinterest. While it once served as an iconic site of enormous symbolic significance, it has gradually fallen out of living memory as a place of commemorative pageantry and into a kind of suspended animation, if not oblivion.[71] It is an empty symbol marking time in the present. Without any possibility of pointing the way forward, it can only look back in time.

In its fusion of public art and collective memory, the Voortrekker Monument demands a critique that goes beyond questions of its appropriate place in the "new South Africa." By creating a public space for commemoration, it propagated the illusion of shared memory.[72] Besides grimacing at its excessive kitsch and self-congratulatory justification for white minority rule, we might ask about what role it plays in contemporary history.[73] The Voortrekker Monument survives, like many other symbolic manifestations of the theatrics of Afrikaner political power, as an uncanny reminder of ideas whose "glorious moment" has come and gone. The placement of the monument, and the construction of the elaborate formal setting around it, represented the intrusion of a particular set of ideas of race, nation, and culture. Like other fetishized places of pilgrimage, the site where the monument stands is only one of countless landscapes of memory littered with the ruins of romantic fantasies where every year sentimental Afrikaner nationalists indulge themselves in idle wishful-thinking of a "whites-only" homeland. As David Bunn has argued, such "whited sepulchers" as the Voortrekker Monument "cannot represent the whole body of the nation. The problems of unequal citizenship under apartheid reveal such white monuments for what they are: partial, disjointed, dismembered."[74]

The Voortrekker Monument belongs to that category of empty, lifeless object that Alfredo González-Ruibal has referred to as the "archaeology of ruination."[75] Without the rejuvenation that comes with commemorative rituals that make them a vibrant part of collective memory, monuments, such as abandoned buildings and unvisited graveyards, become less meaningful with the passage of time. While the Voortrekker Monument long stood as a material signifier for a biased, narrow view of the past, this monocular perspective was actually a true reflection of the vision of white minority rule and the ideology of racial superiority that sustained it. The sheer hulking presence of the monument "still exerts social and political energy ostensibly doing the work of perpetuating the colonial fantasy of superiority and suppression."[76]

"Disgraced monuments" devoted to celebrating the triumph of Afrikaner nationalism and white supremacy occupy what Anne McClintock has called "anachronistic space," that is, "in-between" places combining irrelevance and curiosity, inherently out of place in the historical time defined by the end of apartheid.[77] The urban landscape of South Africa is literally littered with sites of historical significance celebrating the achievements of white minority rule and its heroic figures.[78]

How does the "new nation" deal with the monumental architectural fabric that bears witness to a former repressive regime?[79] Since the stories attached to these sites no longer have currency in the new, revised national narrative, these monuments either assume new meaning or fall into ruin.[80] Demolition of the monumental symbols of discredited regimes erased from history indicates a desire not only to obliterate the individuals commemorated but also to recast the history that those monuments were intended to signify.[81]

"Disgraced monuments" that conjure up memories of discredited political regimes lose their elevated status as proud markers of heroic achievements.[82] But as Deborah Cherry has suggested, their removal would enable amnesia to replace memory, thereby suppressing or undermining our ability to make sense of the past.[83] However, rather than seeking to erase memory-markers that have lost their power to inspire shared feelings of national belonging, permitting outdated monuments to remain in place provides a foundation for never forgetting what came before.[84]

The new status of the Voortrekker Monument as a tourist destination not only sanitizes its original message but places it outside the arena of "contested history." Cocooned in a "tourist bubble," the site has undergone depoliticization. The "tourist gaze" has opened up the monument for reinvention as heritage. As David Lowenthal has suggested, "Heritage reshapes a past made easy to embrace." In transforming monumental sites into objects fit for tourist consumption, heritage welcomes distortion, exaggeration, and omission. In fact, "heritage's greatest sin—fabrication—is no vice but a virtue."[85] With its original message largely forgotten, the Voortrekker Monument has entered into a phase of "impotency as a cultural political symbol," suddenly "free to follow a new career, relatively unencumbered by the past."[86] "Heritage means we view reality as something already forgotten," Didier Maleuvre has argued.

"The real itself becomes a cultural heritage—the reminiscence of something which is no longer quite possible in reality."[87]

During the heyday of apartheid rule, Strijdom Square in downtown Pretoria became a monumental public place, an entire city block, devoted to Afrikaner cultural heritage, accomplishments, and national identity. The signature image that constituted the centerpiece of this virtually sacred precinct was the twelve-foot-high disembodied bronze head of J. G. Strijdom (1893–1958), the South African prime minister between 1954 and 1958. Strijdom became known for his uncompromising vision of racial segregation, known as *baaskap* (loosely translated as "domination"), a forerunner of what crystallized into the official state policy of apartheid. As an "ominous and foreboding monument," the floating bust, with its protective dome and accompanying statue of charging horses, appeared as a concrete materialization of the "unbending authority" of the power of apartheid, its unquestionable presence, and a symbol of white supremacy.[88]

The unthinkable happened. On the morning of May 31, 2001, the gigantic Strijdom head collapsed into the parking lot below the square, breaking into five pieces, unceremoniously dumped among piles of broken concrete. As perhaps an uncanny reminder that the past is never settled, the collapse of a key symbol of apartheid rule came on the fortieth anniversary (to the day) of what had long been celebrated as "Republic Day"—the anniversary of the day South Africa left the Commonwealth to continue in pursuit of its policies of racial segregation. Originally unveiled on May 31, 1972, the statute was exactly twenty-nine years old when it disappeared into the dustbin of history.[89]

Counter-Memory: Freedom Park

New monuments and memorials are important sites in the articulation of national identity. They provide a focal point around which a new vision of a new national identity can be forged, linked to a common past and pointing to a shared future.[90] Under circumstances where the birth of a "new nation" evolved out of long-standing conflict pitting communities against one another, commemoration is rarely if ever the result of consensus but, on the contrary, almost always enveloped in controversy and debate.[91]

Memorial work in the "new South Africa" has remained a difficult and contentious process. With few exceptions, new monuments and memorials have been subjected to a great deal of scrutiny and debate over which kind of memories to embrace, how best to preserve them, in whose honor, and to what particular ends.[92] How do the custodians of official memory in the "new South Africa" incorporate the misdeeds and crimes of white minority rule without offending, much less alienating, those who were not so long ago the beneficiaries of apartheid? Under what moral compass does the "new South Africa" remember victims of white minority rule and commemorate those who struggle against it without reinforcing the existing cleavages and tensions that endure beneath the surface calm?[93]

Officially unveiled in December 2007, Freedom Park is the most significant and financially well-funded cultural-heritage precincts out of the eleven Presidential Legacy Projects designed to memorialize the struggle for freedom in South Africa. Located on a sprawling fifty-two-hectare site situated at the top of Salvokop Hill outside Pretoria, this ambitious project was the brainchild of then-president Thabo Mbeki, who sought to instill the philosophy of the African Renaissance into the "work" of commemoration.[94] Inspired by the national-monument tradition popular in the late eighteenth and early nineteenth centuries, Freedom Park combines two distinct strands

FIGURE 4. Hill of Contemplation, Freedom Park, Pretoria. Photograph by the author.

of commemoration: on the one hand, the mourning of victims of oppression and a spiritual stress on healing and reconciliation, and, on the other, the representation of the rich tapestry of diverse national heritages and the celebration of the significant contributions and achievements of iconic figures.[95]

The official custodians of memory who created Freedom Park proudly identity it as "a leading national and international icon of humanity and freedom," a "place of pilgrimage and inspiration," and a symbolic expression of the "triumph of the human spirit."[96] The location of Freedom Park on a hilltop adjacent to the Voortrekker Monument outside Pretoria was no accident. This sprawling cultural-heritage precinct is an exemplary expression of a counter-monument designed to provide an alternative not only to the nearby Voortrekker Monument but also to the rather rich palette of commemorative statuary celebrating the achievements of white minority rule that remained scattered around the landscape. The rationale behind its assemblage of visual displays, commemorative practices, and written texts is to address the gaps, distortions, and biases that characterized memory-making under apartheid. As a counter-monument, Freedom Park seeks to challenge conventional understandings embodied in the ideology of "white South Africa," and in so doing, to stimulate collective memory against the grain of existing commemoration. This cultural-heritage precinct functions as a site of resistance to the once-reigning perspective of white minority rule, a focus for disrupting collective memory as well as shaping it.[97]

The power of Freedom Park resides in its success in resisting the temptation to monumentalize, to capitulate to the grand, self-aggrandizing gestures of huge statuary inscribed with bold messages that overwhelm and, metaphorically at least, swallow its audience. In contrast to the Voortrekker Monument, which deliberately conveys a sense of enclosed space, the spatial layout of Freedom Park is open and inviting. Instead of seeking to dominate and close space, the physical landscape of Freedom Park blends its assembled elements into a collagelike whole.[98] The goal of Freedom Park is to create a new national identity across a fragmented history of intolerance and oppression by fostering a culture of mutual respect through acknowledgment, forgiveness, and restoration.[99]

"Nation-building" requires a kind of civic sensibility that is able to reconcile conflicting interests, beliefs, and future visions and to weave these elements into a shared sense of loyalty, commitment, and trust. At Freedom Park, the construction of a new national identity—in the form of public commemorations, pageants, statuary, and other acts of public remembrance—comes face to face with the paradox of multiple (sometimes overlapping, and sometimes divergent) allegiances of the citizenry. The conceptual underpinning of Freedom Park and the process of its implementation symbolize the tensions and contradictions of public memorialization in post-apartheid South Africa.[100] The ultimate aim of this cultural-heritage precinct is to pay tribute to those who sacrificed their lives in the struggle against oppression. But in order to be credible as a national symbol and an inclusive site of identification in the "new South Africa," Freedom Park not only recognized the historical continuity of resistance to colonial rule beginning with the seventeenth-century aboriginal Khoi peoples and slave uprisings but also placed a strong emphasis on diversity, inclusiveness, and nonsectarianism.[101]

The core element of the construction of sacred places rests with their differentiation and separation from the secular and the everyday.[102] The spatial layout, the architectonic schema, and its prominent location are all features designed to imagine Freedom Park as a sacred site imbued with a kind of spiritual meaning absent from the surrounding landscape. In its visual displays

FIGURE 5. Eternal Flame, Freedom Park, Pretoria. Photograph by the author.

and written texts, Freedom Park embodies a carefully scripted, uplifting, and overly romanticized vision of the future.[103] In 2007, two ceremonial pieces were inaugurated: the Isivivane is the symbolic resting place commemorating those who died in the liberation struggle, and the Sikhumbuto celebrates the universal values of humanity and freedom. Like the didactic unifying imagery of the nine provinces recognized at Constitution Hill, the Isivivane has assembled nine boulders from historical locales from each of the provinces to create a symbolic burial ground. This remembrance of a painful past seeks to integrate history, culture, and spirituality in a celebratory embrace of a new beginning. Sikhumbuto takes the spiritual theme a step further, invoking ancestral intercession and assistance in resolving current and future conflicts. Making use of the familiar imagery of war memorials (walls of names, eternal flames, a gallery of heroes, and a sanctuary for contemplation), the precinct not only addresses the struggle against apartheid but also precolonial wars, genocide, wars of resistance, the Anglo-Boer War (1899–1902), and World Wars I and II, as well as the liberation struggle. The declared aim of Freedom Park is to embrace the great themes of South African nationhood, namely, the struggle for liberation, democracy, and nation-building through healing. It seeks to address past gaps, distortions, and biases that characterized commemorative practices during white minority rule. Freedom Park is a cultural-heritage site that seeks to bring together and blend "antagonistic, competing, conflicting, non-compatible histories" under the universalizing umbrella of humanity and freedom.[104] In this sense, Freedom Park is not just a site of memorialization but also an instrument for the invention of a new national identity that stresses a shared national vision over fractured histories and common goals over divisive factionalism.[105]

The traditional function of state-sponsored monuments is the creation of self-aggrandizing sites for celebrating the achievements and glories of the "new nation." As a general rule, commemorative sites emplot "the story of ennobling events, of triumphs over barbarism, and recall the martyrdom of those who gave their lives in the [heroic] struggle for national existence—who, in the martyrological refrain, died so that a country might live."[106] But who belongs to the nation, and how can the collective memories of various communities be reconciled in relation to one another has remained a complex question with no easy answers.

FIGURE 6. The Isivivane Memorial, Freedom Park, Pretoria. Photograph by Niel Chen.

Acts of remembrance include forgetfulness. The choices that undergird the transformation of history into institutionalized memory require that certain forgetting is sanctioned and certain memories are disallowed. But because of what the custodians of official memory chose to commemorate and what to leave out, Freedom Park has attracted the ire of various constituencies. Rather than serving as a cohesive and instructive healing field built around public consensus, it has become a disconnected and fragmented battleground.[107]

The purpose behind Freedom Park was to create what Peter Carrier refers to as a "dialogic site of memory," that is, monumental sites that catalyze a conversation about national belonging and that facilitate "the open exchange of plural understandings of history."[108] But as a general rule, "official" memories that are produced in state-sponsored public spaces cannot avoid offending some communities. It should not be surprising that critics have charged that this ANC-sponsored cultural-heritage project promotes a one-sided viewpoint of history. Some have suggested that omissions, exclusions, and evasions only reinforce fissiparous tendencies that undermine the construction of a single national identity and the formation of an "imagined community."

The Wall of Remembrance, which includes the names of seventy-five thousand South Africans who died in the various struggles for freedom, became a flashpoint for controversy. Some critics objected to the inclusion of the names of remembrance of Cuban fighters who died fighting apartheid-era South African troops in the Border War in Namibia and Angola in the 1970s and 1980s, while names of the South African Defense Force soldiers who died were omitted. Others objected to the choice of the twenty-four key leaders honored in the gallery, who include the (Argentinean-born) Cuban guerrilla Che Guevara and South African communist leader Braam Fischer. Afrikaner nationalists were equally angered that the names of Boer leaders who fought against British occupation were excluded as well.[109]

Taken as a whole, Freedom Park exemplifies the difficulties associated with how to remember a past. With its overt spiritual focus on cleansing and healing, this site has become a species of public memorial art. Yet perhaps by trying to accomplish too much, Freedom Park epitomizes the tendency to turn collective memory into a theater of spectacle.[110]

Commemorative Acts: The Hector Pieterson Memorial and Museum

By all accounts at the time, Hector Pieterson was the first youth to die on June 16, 1976. It was on that day that overzealous police fired on high school students from Orlando High School and Morris Isaacson High School who had staged a peaceful march to protest against Afrikaans as the principal language of instruction. His death is forever memorialized in the shocking black-and-white photographs of Sam Nzima, a free-lance photographer who happened to capture on film Hector Pieterson's dying moments as he was carried away from the scene of the shooting by his cousin, Mbuyisa Makhubu.[111] The photograph quickly became the most widely used image to illustrate the tragic events of the day precisely because its depiction of suffering and death evokes such strong emotions from shocked viewers.[112] This powerful image captures the anguish on Makhubu's face and the hysteria of Pieterson's distraught sister, Antoinette. The photograph symbolizes innocence and victimhood in the way it tells the story of the needless loss of life of a thirteen-year-old child.[113]

There were at least another twenty-one fatalities on June 16, 1976.[114] The protests, street demonstrations, and rioting quickly spread to other parts of

South Africa, and by the time the state security forces restored a modicum of calm and order eighteen months later, an estimated seven hundred black people had been killed. Taken together, these watershed events became known worldwide as the 1976–77 Soweto Children's Revolt.[115]

In the conventional historiography of resistance politics, the student protests that began on June 16 signaled the renewal of an enduring "liberation" tradition that stretched back in time to the earliest days of European occupation and settlement of the African subcontinent. The Soweto Uprising marked the opening battle in an undeclared civil war that flared and sputtered until the collapse of white minority rule eighteen years later. Because Hector Pieterson was at least initially considered the first martyr of the student cause, his death became an enduring symbol of the "freedom struggle" and transformed an ordinary site into an extraordinary landscape of public memory.[116]

From the start, the location at the corner of Moema and Vilakazi Streets (Orlando West) where Hector was shot and killed became an unofficial, makeshift place of pilgrimage for those wishing to mourn his death and to honor the estimated seven hundred people who lost their lives over the course of the sixteen-month-long rebellion.[117] As Dolores Haden has argued, such tributes attach popular memory from below to particular places.[118] It is in this way that personal remembrances of tragedy and loss endow specific locations with social meaning, transforming them into sites of collective memory.[119]

The meaning of Hector Pieterson's death is not self-explanatory. The fortuitous circumstances that led to the chance encounter between Sam Nzima and Hector Pieterson on that fateful morning of June 16 left an indelible mark on the historical record. Although the media often named Hector as the first child to die that fateful day, subsequent research based on oral testimonies has revealed that another boy, Hastings Ndlovu, was actually the first child to be killed. Apparently, the police singled out Ndlovu because he was a "troublemaker," deliberately shooting him, whereas Hector Pieterson was killed by a stray bullet.[120] But in the case of Hastings, there were no photographers on the scene, and his name was not immediately known. If Hector Pieterson's dying moments had not been captured on film—frozen in time forever—and if the small march had not blossomed into full-scale revolt, then his death, like the deaths of countless other victims of apartheid security forces,

FIGURE 7. Hector Pieterson Memorial, Soweto. Photograph by Liz Ogbu.

would have surely faded into historical obscurity, one more grim statistic in a long litany of personal tragedies. But because of the worldwide distribution of the shocking photographs, Hector's death was transformed overnight into a symbolic expression of the callousness of the apartheid security forces, and because the small march blossomed into a full-scale revolt, Hector's life, cut tragically short, assumes historical significance of enormous proportions.[121] It is in this sense that the memorial itself, along with the accompanying collection of time-frozen photographs chronicling the moments immediately following his shooting, are genuinely iconic, visual images that stand symbolically for the larger whole.[122]

Landscapes of Violence: The Remembered Space of Tragedy

As Katharina Schramm has suggested, violence invariably leaves traces, which can become powerful mnemonic devices. Whether it is habitually remembered or deliberately evoked to mark particular occasions, the experience of violence has a way of living on in collective consciousness. Moreover, memories of violence are not only embedded in commemorative practices but also are inscribed onto particular places in the form of monuments, memorials, shrines, and other physical markers.[123]

In an effort to stress the heroism and sacrifice of young people, the custodians of official memory tend to downplay, ignore, or exclude historical complexity. The day of June 16, 1976, becomes significant only after the fact. In the grand narrative of the liberation struggle, "the death of Hector Pieterson" was transformed from just another obscure, senseless killing at the hands of overzealous police into an archetypal moment in a chronologically ordered sequence of events that constitute familiar markers in the "unbroken thread" of resistance to oppression. Understood cumulatively, these events constitute "the past" crystallized in particular interpretive frameworks that have a name, a story, and a lesson. As an emblematic episode in what Chris Healy has called "monumental history," "the death of Hector Peterson" acquires its historical significance not as an actual event, but only when it is understood in its historicity, that is, in the ways in which it has been remembered and commemorated in historiographies, photographic exhibitions and essays, reenactments, theatrical performances, and monumental statuary.[124] Put more broadly, "the death of Hector Peterson" becomes meaningful as an integral element of social memory, as an emblematic reminder of the heroic sacrifice of "the youth"—a social category purposefully selected to distinguish the courage of young people in the cause of freedom in contrast to their submissive, intimidated parents, who failed to take a stand in resisting injustice and tyranny.[125] As a particular approach to the past, "monumental history" selects, recites, and disperses key episodes like "the death of Hector Pieterson" as integral moments of social memory, thereby giving coherence, order, and meaning to the grand narrative of liberation.[126] In this sense, sites of collective memory read history backward, using what might be called "retrospective intelligibility," as Louis Mink put it, to connect discrete events from the past into a kind of teleologically inscribed, unbroken chain marking the continuity of the past with the present.[127]

Acts of cruelty and injustice, atrocities, and other equally traumatic events always engender ways of naming, recalling, and remembering. There is an almost "universal willingness," as Sybil Milton has suggested in regard to Holocaust memorials, "to commemorate suffering experienced rather than suffering caused."[128] Memorials are sites of symbolic exchange where living persons admit a degree of indebtedness to the fallen that can never be fully repaid. The Hector Pieterson Memorial invites us to reflect on the sacrifice of youth, which must never be allowed to happen again. For grieving family members and friends, remembering the death of a loved one is a private, personal matter. But under circumstances where the loss of life is conceived in the aggregate, commemoration of large-scale dead becomes a public, collective event with wider implications. The construction of sites of remembrance, like the Hector Pieterson Memorial, translates individual responses to suffering and loss into a collective commemoration that seeks to give cultural meaning to death on a prodigious scale. The act of naming transforms the memorial into a site of mourning, inscribing it with a particularity that tries to honor and pay tribute to those who died in the struggle for freedom. Attaching a name to a memorial constitutes an integral part of a signifying process that seeks to transcend memory and its limitations by assigning it, in its constructed "collective form," a historical role to play.[129] In this way, private sorrow and individual grievance are transformed into public remembrance.[130]

For years, the place where Hector Pieterson was shot served as an unintentional memorial site that reflected the multiple layers of meaning attached to the history of popular resistance to apartheid. On June 16, 1992, the ANC Youth League presided over a ceremony where Nelson Mandela unveiled a memorial stone to commemorate Hector Pieterson at a location two blocks from the site of the shooting.[131] This official inauguration transformed the site from an unintentional site of mourning into an intentional memorial site, thereby making visible and showcasing a new version of old South African history. What the construction of this intentional monument did was to allow for "the recuperation of a single moment in history, made exemplary for the purpose of the present."[132]

In its appearance and purpose, the Hector Pieterson Memorial stands in marked contrast to the Voortrekker Monument.[133] Whereas the gigantic Voortrekker Monument is intentionally and unapologetically didactic, the memorial site commemorating Hector Pieterson is conspicuous but unobtrusive. The memorial is minimalist in form, and the design is simple and modest. The monument itself consists of a four-foot-high block of granite. On the left side is etched "In Memory of Hector Pieterson and all other young heroes and heroines of our struggle who laid down their lives for Freedom, Peace, and Democracy." Mirrored on the right side is an engraving of a man carrying a dead child. The monument itself is situated inside a fifteen-by-fifteen-foot enclosure marked by what amounts to a simple ornamental wall.[134]

Like all historical sites dedicated to preserving collective memory, the memorial cannot avoid the complications that arise from the selection of which people to pay tribute to and what events to remember.[135] Given the complexity of the events leading to the 1976 Soweto Uprising, it should not be surprising that there remains debate—sometimes heated—over "ownership" of the historical event. Competing claims over what persons and organizations played key roles in the events have continued to be put forward.[136] On June 16, 2001, the formal unveiling of the refurbished (and much larger) memory site combined all the elements of the creation of a social memory: the placement of an aesthetically pleasing monument in stone and bronze to serve as a material prompt to the sacrifice of youth in building the "new nation"; a ceremony in which key figures from both the internal and the "exile" leadership of the ANC, along with overseas dignitaries, anointed the proceedings by their presence; the participation of thousands of performers and spectators who attended the event in a massive, choreographed public ceremony; and the widespread dissemination of information about the event through conventional media channels. The symbolism was self-evident: by grafting their name and reputation onto the memory of Hector Pieterson, the ANC leadership sought to incorporate the Soweto Uprising into their own overarching metanarrative of national liberation, to effectively claim ownership over the freedom struggle against apartheid, and to define the terms of national unity.[137]

In the calculus of tragedy, people's deaths are often rounded up to a higher station than the one they enjoyed in life. Hector Pieterson may well have lived an ordinary life in relative obscurity had he not been mortally wounded on that day. Because he was long regarded as the first to die, his name is elevated above the anonymous others who also lost their lives.[138] His death has come to symbolize the senseless loss of life in the bitter struggle for freedom. The memorial serves a solemn, existential purpose: by creating an enclosed space set aside from the rush of daily life, it creates sacred "hollowed ground" where friends, family, activists, and participants in the anti-apartheid struggle and sympathizers are permitted to mourn. As commemorative devices, memorials provide first and foremost a framework for, and legitimation of, individual and communal grief. Yet as the highly personalized feelings of pain, suffering, and loss fade with time, this ritual significance of commemorative art is often overshadowed, or even obscured, by an enduring political symbolism, a feature that remains long after the moment of bereavement has passed.[139]

The place-relationality of museum spaces presupposes a walking tour, that is, an established route that provides direction and order for viewing and reading the pictorial displays, information boards, and commentaries. Displays and exhibitions are a system of signs, working in the realm between the visual and the verbal and between information and persuasion. They create, in effect, a self-enclosed microworld that assigns more importance to some stories over others. As a particular site of collective memory, the Hector Pieterson Memorial and Museum is encased within a redemptive aesthetic that dispenses with melancholia in favor of a kind of reverence and respect.[140]

As a general rule, monuments and other commemorative sites "make frequent use of images and iconographic formulae which, through extensive repetition and a long process of cultural diffusion, have become instantly recognizable and which appear to trigger similar feelings in people of a wide range of cultural backgrounds."[141] In its metaphorical language, the Hector Pieterson Memorial adapts and modifies the Christian story of salvation, condensing a field of disparate emotions and projecting them onto one person, whose visible suffering symbolizes the trials and tribulations of all those nameless and faceless others. From the minute it was published, Sam Nzima's photograph, the third of six sequential snapshots taken with a 50mm Pentax SRL camera, became an iconic symbol of the liberation struggle, capturing what words could not possibly convey. This haunting image lingers as an indelible reference point of the postliberation imagination.[142]

In line with standard conventions developed in the visual arts, photographs often focus on specific motifs and follow familiar compositional schematic approaches to representation. Whereas moving pictures provide images that disappear almost as quickly as the time it takes to view them, still photography "interrupts, actually stops time, freezes a moment: it is inherently elegiac."[143] As a kind of documentary art form, they create spaces of contemplation.[144] In compositional terms, Nzima's photograph conforms to the well-established Christian iconographic tradition of the Pietà (or sculpture with mourning figures)—a formula that in turn has informed the sculptural conventions of war memorial statuary across the Western world. As a highly stylized form of visual representation, it expresses a combination of innocence and martyrdom, mixed with the implications of resurrection and ultimate triumph.[145] Enlarged to roughly life-size dimensions, the photograph is the centerpiece of the memorial, displayed in such a way as to force viewers to be confronted with the lifeless body of Hector Pieterson and the anguish and fear on the faces of his sister Antoinette and cousin Mbuyisa. The mnemonic power and resilience of this image is remarkable. When a photograph achieves the status of iconic image, it enables its public viewership to anchor the history of events to it by virtue of its clarity.[146] Because it is not a relief sculpture or any other kind of artistic representation, but a documentary photograph, it lends a great deal of authenticity and "truth" to the scene.[147]

The story that this photograph tells is one of tragedy, suffering, and anguish. But the position that the viewer occupies ensures that something cannot be seen. Because the image does not provide sufficient depth, the photograph does not engender a stable sense of place. The setting and context must be filled in by the imagination. The palpable power of photography to capture the real—the sense that "nothing in the image can be refused or transformed," as Roland Barthes put it—undergoes a subtle yet significant transformation.[148] Encoded in the language of sacrifice and bravery, the image of Hector Pieterson becomes an iconic symbol of heroic resistance to apartheid.[149]

The museum itself is a two-story building consisting of a number of interlocked exhibition spaces combining period-piece photographs and textual commentaries. This configuration of the interior space provides a means of focusing attention on martyrological and heroic figures who sacrificed their lives.[150] Arranged as a serial montage of tragedy and loss, the old photographs evoke the uncanny, spectral presence of persons who played crucial roles on June 16, but who now only exist in memory.[151]

The large windows located on the upper level of the building offer an unobstructed vantage point from which to view the geographical location of the key sites that figured prominently on June 16. These include the street corner where Hector Pieterson was fatally wounded, the Orlando police station, and the Orlando Stadium, the destination of the student protest march. Written texts inscribed in the glass windows explain the significance of these sites, thereby transforming them into symbolic markers in their own right. This method of pointing out places of significance and drawing out their symbolic meanings allows visitors to visualize the course of events in time and space—the intended route of the protesting students, the location where the police began shooting into the crowds, and the subsequent breakup of the march. Equally, if not more important, this "visualization" of the events of June 16 enables visitors to grasp more fully "the township context, in which the 1976 Soweto Uprising is firmly anchored, not as an incidental geographical location, but as a highly significant site of sociopolitical control."[152]

The Hector Pieterson Memorial blends two conventional approaches to commemoration. On the one hand, Sam Nzima's photograph provides for the literal repetition of the visual forms of the past, enabling viewers to travel back in time and connect emotionally with the event itself. On the other hand, the architectural forms—the "Garden of Contemplation," the "Wall of Remembrance," the use of water as a soothing device—are highly abstract and ambiguous, facilitating mourning and promoting healing, thereby providing a sense of transcendence.[153]

Collective memory matters because of the ways it inscribes itself materially in the present as narrative, place, memorial, liturgy, or tourism. It matters also "because it tells us perhaps less about the historical events themselves than about the identity and identification of contemporary social groups."[154] Honoring those who lost their lives is not simply a matter of paying respects to the dead: it also forms a potent element in the endorsement of an alternative political culture.[155] The Hector Pieterson Memorial represents a conscious effort to pay tribute to those who suffered and died at the hands of the apartheid state over the course of the 1976–77 Soweto Uprising, and to consecrate some sense of meaningful connection with the past. The valorization of Hector Pieterson alone follows a conventional *memoria technica,* whereby historical attributes, achievements, or events that might have been claimed or associated with a great number of historical actors are congealed over time around a single personage.[156] In this way, commemorative practices provide a certain degree of order to the messiness of history, transforming seemingly ordinary incidents that might otherwise have gone unnoticed into iconic events that metaphorically symbolize an entire era.[157] Along with other memorials in the "new South Africa," the symbolic meaning of the Hector Pieterson Memorial cannot be separated from the *ex post facto* knowledge that the liberation struggle led to the collapse of apartheid and the transition to parliamentary democracy. This implied connection between cause and effect provides a sense of closure (albeit partial). Drawing connections between seemingly disparate acts of defiance that began on June 16, 1976, and attaching meaning to them as part of a long history of resistance to apartheid laid the foundations for the way in which future generations would make sense of the struggle against white minority rule.[158]

Custodians of collective memory use such commemorative sites as the Hector Pieterson Memorial to lay claim to the past and to envision a radiant future. As an exercise in commemoration, this particular place serves as a testimonial to the courage and sacrifice of the youthful protesters who dared to oppose the apartheid monolith. The symbolic power of these commemorative exercises is actually the reverse of what they might seem. Rather than approaching them as repositories of knowledge of the past, it is actually the knowledge we bring retrospectively to them that makes them historically significant, transforming a chance occurrence that happened in the past into a transcendental moment—an iconic signifier—for an entire historical period.[159]

Sites of remembrance construct the spatial and temporal limits to popular understandings of the past. Public commemorations, monuments, and memorials run the risk of oversimplifying what were in actuality considerably more complex historical processes. In erecting formal reminders or replicas of something that ought to be remembered, the custodians of collective memory run the risk of diminishing forgetfulness. By making traces or remnants of the past stand for the whole, they "ease themselves into an illusion" that future generations will share their sentiments in equal measure.[160] By assigning monumental form to memory, they divest themselves to some degree of their obligation to foster remembering. Over time, monuments tend to blend imperceptibly into the landscape, becoming part of the past rather than a reminder of it.[161] Like other "struggle memorials," the Hector Pieterson Memorial simplifies, streamlines, and partially sanitizes the historical past. By directing attention to a single story, it simultaneously leaves many other stories untold. As commemorative practice, the Hector Pieterson Memorial creates a public memory that takes the place of history.[162]

Sometimes the search for the higher truth associated with commemorating the past reveals the subterfuges that sustained people during the time of apartheid rule. Meanings attached to names carry enormous significance. While the popular media at first spelled Hector's surname as "Peterson" and sometimes "Pietersen," the family insisted that the correct spelling is "Pieterson." This minor difference in fact conceals a deeper, inconvenient truth. The Pieterson family was originally named "Pitso" but decided to adopt the Pieterson name in order to pass as *Coloured* (the South African term for people of mixed race). The thinking behind this masquerade was that Coloured people enjoyed somewhat better privileges under apartheid than black people did.[163]

Framed through the lens of the Hector Pieterson Memorial and Museum, the story of the Soweto Uprising has become an integral part of the triumphalist grand narrative of the liberation struggle, which itself functions as the foundation myth of the birth of the "new South Africa."[164] Yet the Truth and Reconciliation Commission hearings revealed the tragic irony in the appropriation of Hector Pieterson as a "struggle hero." In her testimony before the

TRC, his sister, Antoinette, claimed that Hector was not a member of any organization that had mobilized students to join the demonstration. She attributed the presence of Hector and other primary school pupils at the march to curiosity rather than involvement in student protest politics. Both Pieterson and Makhubu were unlikely heroes or martyrs of the liberation struggle. The two were little more than unfortunate bystanders to the events of June 16, inadvertent victims of the heavyhanded response of the police to the student demonstration. Despite this contradiction, the master narrative of the liberation struggle transformed them into symbols of resistance and sacrifice of the youth. Whereas Hector Pieterson is widely remembered, Mbuyisa Makhubu is largely forgotten.[165]

More than any other visual reminder of the uprising, Nzima's photograph is widely acclaimed as the prism through which to focus the collective memories of that time. As a rallying point for shared remembrance, it is this photograph—along with "its innumerable public appearances in multiple forms"—that imbues June 16, 1976, with its historical significance. Yet photographs, like material objects and representations, are not simple, stand-alone "carriers of memory" but rather "technologies of memory" through which memories are collectively shared, actively produced, and inscribed with cultural meaning.[166] Without the accompaniment of critical commentary or explanation, documentary photographs appear as if their historical significance is wholly self-sufficient or self-evident, a kind of objective "visual fact" that speaks for itself.[167] The "beguiling realism" of such raw, unvarnished images such as the Nzima photograph appears to offer a warranty of genuineness, providing its viewership with "the appearance of history itself."[168]

The singular and uniquely powerful image of Hector Pieterson's dying moments provides a window through which the post-Soweto, "born-free" generation of young people come to "know" the Soweto Uprising.[169] Yet unlike many one-dimensional symbols employed as memory-devices, documentary photographs do not appear with ready-made, fixed, stable, and immutable meanings, but instead are fluid, malleable, and subject to change. Social meanings do not reside in sociocultural objects like photographs, but are produced by viewers and their context.[170] In short, photographs are free-floating signifiers that do not possess essential, unequivocal, and timeless meanings. While they may fix an event in a temporal time frame, the meaning of these images "is constantly subject to contextual shifts."[171]

Even a cursory look at the lived history of the image itself, what Elizabeth Edwards has termed its "social biography,"[172] reveals that the photograph has taken on multiple, or polysemic, meanings over time.[173] As a mnemonic device, the Nzima photograph has served as an object of reflection, inspiration, and empowerment for those too young to remember the 1976 Soweto Uprising. Yet at the same time, through its retextualization, this image has also been exploited for commercial use, appearing in clothing designs, posters, and artwork.[174]

Maladies of Memory: Evasion, Distortion, and Effacement

When we want to know about the ways in which custodians of collective memory recollect the past and represent it for public consumption in the present, we focus attention on the connection between the politics of remembrance and the politics of forgetting. The construction of such memory-markers as public monumental art, museums, exhibitions, and memorials operate like a Rorschach ink-blot test, a blank screen upon which official custodians of memory project their anxieties about repetition, change, representation, authenticity, and identity. By examining cultural imaginations of remembering and forgetting, we can learn much about the cultural investments that official memory-makers have in particular versions of the past.[175]

Making memory in the service of nation-building tends to forge a single teleological narrative out of shared everyday recollections. Gaps and discontinuities are glossed over through a coherent and inspiring story of shared identity.[176] In official commemorations celebrating the end of white minority rule, the names and deeds of Pan Africanists like Robert Sobukwe and Black Consciousness leaders like Steve Biko are largely ignored. The neglect, whether benign or deliberate, fuels resentment among those political groups that contributed in their own way to the downfall of white minority rule.[177]

Sometimes remaining faithful to historical accuracy stands in the way of commemoration. In January 1999, high-ranking state officials from South Africa and Mozambique gathered at Mbuzini, a small village along the border separating the two countries, to unveil a monument commemorating

FIGURE 8. Memorial for Samora Machel. Photograph by Nicolas Brulliard.

the tragic death of Samora Machel, then-president of the Popular Republic of Mozambique, who lost his life under mysterious circumstances in an airplane crash at that site on October 19, 1986.[178]

This commemorative act, as the embodiment of social memory, is an important reminder that history and memory do not always move in unison. The plaque fixed on the monument contains, as one political observer put it, "a gross disrespect for history." The name of Nonzamo Winnie Mandela, the former wife of Nelson Mandela, is elided from authorship of the text inscribed on the plaque. This text is a transcription of condolences that she and her then-husband, Nelson Rolihlahla Mandela, addressed to the people of Mozambique after Machel's tragic death. Yet the plaque incorrectly describes the text as a message from Nelson Mandela alone, while he was still detained on Robben Island, to the widow of the slain president, Graça Machel. In the acknowledgment note she wrote at the time, Graça Machel began with the words: "My dear sister Winnie Mandela, my dear brother Nelson Mandela." To add a curious twist to the story, Nelson Mandela and Graça Machel were married in 1998. Motivated perhaps by the presentist concerns to create distance between Winnie Madikizela-Mandela and the ANC and perhaps not to complicate the matters of remarriage, the custodians of official memory—in an act vaguely reminiscent of the Stalinist effacement of Leon Trotsky from official photographs of leaders of the Russian Revolution—erased her from the past.[179]

5 Haunted Heritage

Visual Display at District Six and Robben Island

Urban landscapes are densely textured places where both material and immaterial traces of the past cling stubbornly to the social fabric, refusing to fade into obscurity. The meaning of a place depends in large measure upon the residues of memory that are embedded there. The thickness of these memory-traces indicates the lingering presence of unresolved tensions and unrealized hopes for the future.[1]

"Haunting" is a useful metaphorical device for calling attention to how it is that certain places instill a sense of possession, absence, and loss in the urban landscape.[2] The sense of the spectral presence of those who are not physically there is a ubiquitous feature of the phenomenology of place. As Michel de Certeau put it, "There is no place that is not haunted by many different spirits hidden there in silence, spirits one can 'invoke' or not."[3] To varying degrees, city-sites are inhabited—that is to say, possessed—by ghostly spirits that "we cannot see but whose presence we nevertheless experience."[4] As Karen Till has noted, urban landscapes are saturated with "haunted places" that "simultaneously embody presences and absences, voids and ruins, intentional forgetting and painful remembering."[5]

Making places that commemorate, honor, remember, mourn, question, and forget enables custodians of memory (whether amateur or professional) to mark social spaces as "haunted sites" where they "can return, make contact with their loss, contain unwanted presences, or confront past injustices."[6]

The spectral presence of people and events linger on in particular places well beyond the time they vanished from the site.[7] Returning to these "haunted places" conjures up memories of what once was and what might have been—or perhaps memories of what never was but what one might have wanted to have been. As locations where private memories and public histories intersect, places of memory give shape to powerfully felt absences, to trauma and loss, and to "their desire to remain connected to that which is no longer metaphysically present" but continues to have an important symbolic presence in everyday life.[8]

Memory-markers encrypt the past: they hold onto that which is experienced as a powerfully felt absence. These places of memory indicate collective longing for something extinguished from the past and that no longer exists. To paraphrase Avery Gordon, ghosts are spectral figures through which something lost can be made to reappear before our eyes.[9] Seen in this way, the spectral presence of those who are not physically there helps to constitute the specificity of historical sites.[10] The preservation of sites of trauma constitutes a kind of "topographical writing," or writing of history into landscape. Haunted places evoke strange, uncanny moods. The spectral figures that inhabit these places are more symbolic place-holders than literal apparitions.[11] Haunted sites find ways to "speak the unspeakable"—about shared trauma and bereavement, imprisonment, displacement, separation, and loss.[12]

Like haunted sites, "traumascapes" are a distinctive category of place. These physical settings of tragedy acquire a surfeit of meaning as sites of mourning and remembering. Transformed by the suffering that indelibly marks them as haunted, these places are sites of pilgrimage that "compel memories, crystallize identities and meaning, and exude power and enchantment."[13] When the experience of loss becomes bound to specific physical locations, these places enter into the public domain as sites of shared grief and commemoration. Inscribing stories into landscapes of memory provides a means for preserving historical memory of trauma and loss. In their distinctiveness and resonance, these sites evoke other places and other stories, providing "the enduring, tangible imprints that suffering and loss leave behind." Traumascapes demonstrate that the past is always unfinished business, "never quite over."[14] Yet as unstable sites, they can just as easily radiate melancholy as they can trigger a cathartic experience that provides a release from the burdens of a traumatic past.[15] While they can play a vital role in enabling mourning, traumascapes contribute to shaping meanings and interpretations of the tragic events inscribed in them.[16]

What distinguishes the memory of trauma is the fragmented reception of the past. Sites haunted with a traumatic past have an unsettled, and unsettling, "spectral quality" about them.[17] This spectral quality gives rise to several questions: To the extent that particular sites are able to contain memory, how do places of trauma testify to history? If sites of memory are by nature dynamic and contingent, how can a sense of an authentic past be preserved at a particular site without creating a false unity between historical time and the actual event? Addressing these questions requires that we approach the spatiotemporality of trauma in terms of a logic of hauntings, absences, and voids.[18]

Visualizing Heritage: The District Six Museum

Perhaps more than any other site in the post-apartheid city, a vast expanse of vacant land located at the edge of the Cape Town central city—the physical site of what once was District Six—has been the "locus of public debates on the abstract concepts of history, heritage, commemoration, memory, and nostalgia."[19] As Peggy Delport has forcefully argued, "Above all, the name District Six retains its role in contemporary South Africa as a symbol of the will to remember."[20] Along with Robben Island, District Six achieved an iconic status as a visible symbol of the callous disregard of the white minority regime for basic human rights. This desolate wasteland where District Six once existed as a culturally dynamic and diverse community stands as a grim reminder of the dehumanizing process of forced removals put into motion under apartheid rule and a rallying cry for the redress of grievances in the aftermath of the transition to parliamentary democracy. It is a place synonymous with the worst excesses of racial segregation, a site saturated with traumatic memories, and a metaphor for the largely forgotten, now-invisible program of forced removals under apartheid.[21] The faint physical traces of where buildings once stood and streets once intersected offer only the barest hints of what once was, where absence leaves "lost space" as a bitter reminder of a world turned upside down.[22]

At the time when the demolition began, District Six was an overcrowded, rundown, and relatively impoverished area with inadequate infrastructure and poor services (owing in large measure to municipal neglect). Yet it was also a dynamic place that consisted of a full range of commercial establishments, schools and churches, ethnically diverse neighborhoods, and a lively cosmopolitan culture. Despite their marginal location on the fringes of "white Cape Town," residents shared a real sense of community, cooperation, and belonging that "served as a coping strategy against socio-economic hardship." As a result of the piecemeal process of demolition, residents both witnessed and experienced firsthand the physical destruction of their neighborhoods and the trauma of removal as these unfolded over time. Although the physical site was destroyed, District Six has remained alive in the shared remembrances of those who once lived there.[23]

Even as the surrounding cityscape has remorselessly moved on in time, the ruinscape of the obliterated District Six site has left behind ghostly traces of its previous material forms, the social life of its inhabitants, ways of being, and modes of experience. Ironically, it is this absence created by its demolition that has created the enduring presence of District Six. Absence is made to exist as something performed, textured, and materialized through the work of shared remembrance.[24] The "absent-presence" of the spectral makes itself known through the partial remains and discarded remnants of the once-vibrant community.[25] Found objects—household utensils, broken toys, and old photographs—"speak of past lives and presences that inhabit the contemporary city."[26] More than a specific place linked to collective memory, District Six has posed serious challenges to questions related to restitution, redevelopment, and resettlement in the aftermath of physical destruction, dispossession, and displacement.[27]

The Story of Dispossession

The sheer scale and scope of the apartheid practice of place-making has tended to dwarf the capacity to remember, represent, and reconstruct the unsettling experience of families torn asunder, communities ripped apart, and ways of life obliterated. Estimates vary, but one authoritative report has suggested that apartheid policymakers used a cascade of laws, regulations, and decrees to forcibly uproot about 3.5 million people between 1960 and 1982.[28] Disruption of such proportions defies not only our capacity to reliably measure its overall impact on the lives of those people but also even our ability to imagine it in its totality. Consequently, those who want to keep alive the social memory of forced removals, which were an integral part of the grand master plans of the white minority regime for formal racial segregation, are therefore compelled to reduce the enormity of the experience under apartheid to a more manageable size and more conventional forms. Such mnemonic instruments as photography, documentary film, and "I-witness" memoirs have ensured that the record of racial segregation has not passed into oblivion, but these subjective methods of remembrance are inherently limited.[29]

Remembrance necessarily begins from the details. At the time the NP came to power in 1948, Cape Town was an ethnic mosaic with literally scores of racially mixed neighborhoods, especially in settled working-class districts clustered along the main roads leading away from the city center. Almost immediately, NP bureaucrats set their sights on fundamentally recasting the racial configuration of the Cape Peninsula. An outpouring of racially coded laws, regulations, and directives enabled state officials under the apartheid regime to begin implementing formal residential segregation by forcibly removing "nonwhite" residents in scores of neighborhoods and working-class

FIGURE 9. The Empty Space of District Six, Cape Town. Photograph by Antoinette Engel.

communities close to the Cape Town city center. But it was the wholesale destruction of the racially mixed area known as District Six that triggered the greatest outrage and attracted the most attention.[30]

Originally settled about the time of slave emancipation in 1838, District Six was located at the foot of Table Mountain on gently sloping landscape overlooking the majestic Table Bay in close proximity to the Cape Town central business district. By the turn of the century, it was home to almost a tenth of the population of Cape Town. Because of its central location and its proximity to the economically vibrant docklands, it was already a lively, largely working-class community consisting of former slaves, artisans, merchants, and other immigrants, in addition to significant numbers of Cape Malay people originally brought to South Africa by the Dutch East India Company during its administration of the Cape Colony in the seventeenth century. By the 1960s, District Six had established itself as a vibrant, cosmopolitan melting pot, home to approximately sixty thousand residents, primarily made up of people of mixed race (so-called "coloured" people), but also including black Africans and a smaller numbers of Indians and white Afrikaans speakers. On February 11, 1966, state officials declared District Six a whites-only area under the provisions of the 1950 Group Areas Act. In justifying their decision, state officials claimed that District Six was a crime-ridden and dangerous slum, a den of iniquity where prostitution, gangsterism, and gambling were rampant, fit only for clearance and not for rehabilitation. While these were the official reasons, it was widely believed that municipal authorities sought the land because of its proximity to the city center, Table Mountain, and the harbor.[31]

The destruction of District Six took place in stages. Between 1968, when the eviction order was first put into motion, and 1982, when the process was completed, more than sixty thousand people were forcibly removed and relocated to overcrowded, dreary housing projects on the sandy, windswept Cape Flats some twenty-five kilometers away. Municipal authorities bulldozed buildings that were used for commercial, educational, and religious purposes, demolished boarding houses and private homes, and tore out the paved streets. The only buildings that were left standing were a few places of worship. The denuded landscape that remained became a "monumental emptiness"—an iconic symbol of the draconian measures employed in carrying out forced removals.[32] As if seeking to erase even the memory of District Six, municipal authorities renamed it Zonnebloem and allowed the Cape Technikon (now Cape Peninsula University of Technology) to build on a portion of the site. Yet despite ambitious plans to rebuild the area for exclusive white ownership and occupancy, a combination of international and local outrage was sufficiently powerful to prevent wholesale redevelopment. As if frozen in time, this vacant landscape of razed, bulldozed rubble still continues to bare the faint yet still-visible markings of streets, curbs, and buildings. Amazingly, around 35 percent of the original forty-two-hectare site has remained largely intact, more or less as it was when the municipal authorities completed their task of demolition in the 1980s.[33]

The metamorphosis of District Six into a symbol of apartheid oppression can be attributed to a number of historically specific conditions. Unlike other communities that were demolished and subsequently overlaid with an entirely new built environment, District Six had the advantage of remaining a visible scar on the slopes of Devil's Peak, an open wound not immediately patched over, that became a constant reminder of the callousness of the apartheid regime. From the start, a host of diverse constituencies—local residents, some municipal authorities, elected officials, and liberal intellectuals—joined forces to oppose the demolition of District Six and the forcible removal of its residents.[34] It is the way that this mixture of interested parties held the specific tensions in place "that largely accounts for the unprecedented success" in preventing business redevelopment of the area, unlike similar programs of forced removal at Sophiatown in Johannesburg and Cato Manor in Durban.[35]

The District Six Museum as a Distinctive Site of Memory

The origins of the District Six Museum can be traced to the "Hands Off District Six" campaign, which sought to galvanize resistance in the late 1980s to the plans by British Petroleum to redevelop the area.[36] The museum building first opened on December 10, 1994, in the Old Central Methodist Church at 25A Buitenkant Street, on the very edge of the vacant District Six site.[37] In acting as a genuine archaeological site of memory, the museum uses a combination of personal reminiscences, historical documents, old photographs, artwork, recovered objects, and a sound archive to assemble the collective memory of the lost community.[38] It is a memory bank—a veritable treasure trove—that recounts the story of human resilience in the face of great adversity. As an effective memory-device, it reclaims the social history of the people who lived there. Besides engaging in the conventional museum work of collecting, exhibiting, and educating, the District Six Museum is a genuine community project that arose from the felt need of former residents to retrieve memories of forced removals as a resource of solidarity and social identity.[39] More than simply a repository for objects recovered from a traumatic past, the museum serves as a living testimony to oppression, a memorial to a decimated local community, and a meeting place and community center for Cape Town residents who identify with the history of District Six.[40] As a "living heritage" site, the museum both recovers and manufactures a usable past in service of the present.[41] The collective memory of District Six bridges the gap between a vanished neighborhood and its planned rebirth as part of the anticipated restitution, redevelopment, and resettlement process.[42]

The spatial layout of the museum consists of a large central hall with a second-story balcony that extends around the four sides of the building. Distinct "memory rooms" ring the periphery of the building.[43] These installations include display cases of personal objects (fragments of the social life that once existed) unearthed from vanished sites where houses once stood and photographs of buildings, streetscapes, and the people who lived there. Salvaged from near-oblivion, these remnants from past times and ruined places haunt the present. Portrait prints of civic leaders, artists, and others whose personal lives were inextricably intertwined with the public history of District Six fill the wall space. The piecing together of large numbers of oral histories involved the active engagement of narrators in assembling and interpreting their own materials.[44]

The idea behind the creation of these kinds of exhibitionary displays at the District Six Museum was to establish a sense of intimacy and authenticity. This approach involved the fashioning of a generative space for historical retrieval and interpretation.[45] The inaugural exhibition of the museum was called "Streets: Retracing District Six." It consists of an assemblage of original street signs—Hanover, Tyne, Tennant, De Villiers, and so forth—that hang from the second-floor balcony. These "found objects"—donated to the museum from a member of the demolition team who did not dispose of them in the sea but instead stored them in his cellar for twenty years—are physical

FIGURE 10. Display of street names at the District Six Museum. Photograph by Antoinette Engel.

embodiments of the process of remembering, triggering the memories of former residents who recalled street corners, shops, and buildings.[46]

Through the display of old photographs, personal stories, and salvaged objects, the museum employs an archaeological approach to collective remembrance, but one that does not subordinate these fragments of memory to a single curatorial discourse. This kind of arrangement creates "a surplus of meaning that lies in the appropriation and re-appropriation of carnival, music, recollections and the other attributes of identity."[47]

The District Six Museum projects a plurality of stories that cannot be reduced to a unitary, monolithic narrative that would constitute a single history of dispossession, suffering, and loss. This approach stands in stark contrast to the architects of apartheid, who sought to create an essentialist history by "suppressing the voices that did not conform to its own selective ideology." In challenging the "single authoritarian voice that organizes history according to one homogeneous viewpoint," the museum employs the process of *bricolage,* assembling layered and varied stories that produce a kind of montage. The museum presents history as "situated and interpretive," where the emphasis is on critical engagement and dialogue with visitors, one that calls for a flexible "reading" of the historical past and allows for an open-ended process of commemoration.[48]

The District Six Museum represents a community-inspired (and not state-driven) effort to keep alive the memory of a place—by capturing in visual displays, assembled artifacts, and written testimony what has been physically destroyed, and consequently erased from the living landscape.[49] As a place of memory, the museum represents a social experiment in how to preserve collective memory through a public-history project. District Six reconstructs the everyday experience of apartheid by drawing on popular memories of former residents to contribute to and hence refashion interpretations of a genuine "people's history."[50] Curators have used various visual displays to reconstruct varying images of "how it was" in District Six. The most conspicuous (and emotionally powerful) feature of this "memory strategy" is a large, ten-by-fifteen-foot, two-dimensional, laminated map that covers virtually the entire floor surface of the central hall. This "simple but extraordinarily effective mnemonic device" reproduces the spatial layout of District Six as it once was, naming the streets, locating key landmarks, and identifying particular houses, along with the family names of residents. The museum floor thus becomes an interactive space where, in a poignant display of remembrance, former residents can "put themselves back in the picture," so to speak, by finding their names and written commentaries on the map where their homes once stood. This ritual of inscription of names and commentaries becomes a kind of participatory "memory act" that translates personal reminiscences into public history. This map enables former residents to recall and imagine a lost community and their place within it. As a prompt for remembering, this cartographic device transforms passive "representational space" into a kind of imagistic spacializing that enables former residents to recall the metaphorical reality of a place long gone. In what is a kind of memory-performance, former residents actively engage with the map, "letting entrenched memories to resurface" by fondly retracing old routes and remembering people and places.[51] By assisting in the construction of the exhibit, museum visitors not only nostalgically recall their lives in District Six but also identify the forces responsible for the destruction. In this way, the museum offers an engagement with cultural heritage, public history, and collective memory.[52]

These deliberate acts of naming and recalling add a wrenching poignancy to the exhibit. Yet since there can be no exact replica, there can be no absolute repetition. However carefully crafted, copies only gesture toward a long-lost "identity" they cannot possibly realize and thus silently reinforce the very distinctiveness and disparity that they overtly deny. The visual displays at the District Six Museum act deliberately to recall another time, and, paradoxically, these powerful images can easily foster a melancholic sadness.[53] Acts of commemoration can never compensate for tragedy, trauma, and loss. What commemorative practices can do is to provide resistance to premature closure and to initiate and help frame a process toward understanding.[54]

The museum does not maintain anything that resembles a permanent collection but relies primarily upon the testimonies of former residents and the fragmentary remains of their possessions, often literally unearthed and excavated from the actual sites where their houses once stood. The exhibit that showcases "lost" and "found" objects, the remnants of ordinary life in District Six, enables these artifacts to acquire new meanings over time and changing contexts while simultaneously holding onto traces of their former uses. By displaying articles from the past in new and evolving circumstances, the museum plays on absence and presence, thereby reinforcing the indeterminacy and uncertainty that define the contemporary post-apartheid experience of representation and commemoration.[55] The focus on intimate histories and personal lives gives the museum a poignancy and melancholia that is unusual in museum exhibitions.[56] The museum provides a nonlinear narrative, that is, a thematic collage of singular vignettes that, when pieced together, tell a story of a community destroyed by an oppressive regime. There is no prescribed order but rather a juxtaposition of spaces that provoke reflection and contemplation.[57] This openness to multiple interpretations fosters a self-reflexivity among visitors, who are left to think about what they have seen and what they have learned. The specific techniques of display—not just the artifacts collected and exhibited—convey powerful messages that establish an elaborate visual language of symbolism and allegory.[58]

The politically strategic medium through which the discourse of District Six operates is the textualization of space, that is, the inscription of collective identity onto the vanished site.[59] As Crain Soudien has argued, reading District Six as a text "is structured in a dialogue of absences and presences."[60] Writing represents a means of laying down the overwhelming presence of the past "community-in-memory" on top of the absence at the present-day site. The barrenness and ruin of the present stand in sharp contrast with the pictorial and textual images of the once-vibrant community.[61]

Remembrance, Invented Traditions, and Nostalgia

The District Six Museum is the public face of the tragic story of a particularly egregious episode of forcible removal that took place under the terms of the 1950 Group Areas Act. The pictorial narrative in the museum, coupled with the commemorative language, contributes to the social construction of a mythological past, an "invented tradition." To a certain extent, the unifying myth relies on nostalgic reminiscence about the rich diversity of the communities that inhabited District Six before the apartheid state machinery demolished the built environment. As one commentator notes, District Six "proved" that people from different racial and religious backgrounds could live together in harmony—a moral lesson that contradicted the apartheid dreamscape/fantasy of "separate development" as a natural necessity.[62] In

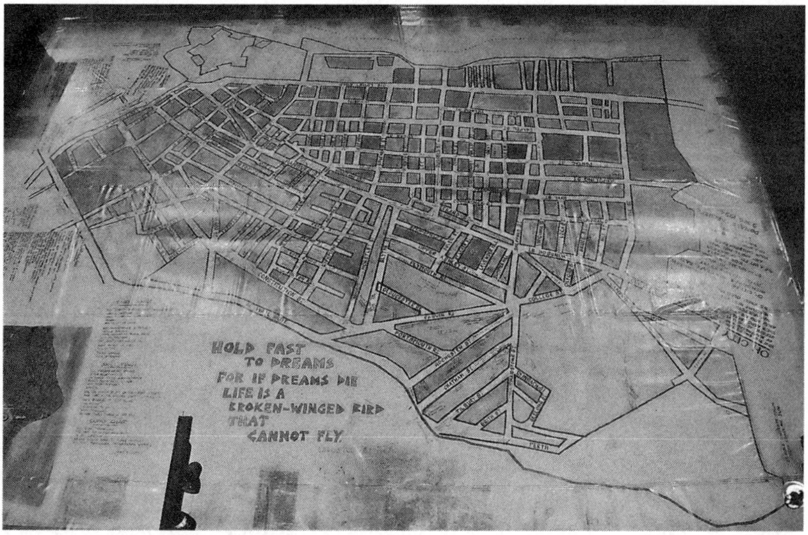

FIGURE 11. Disappearing Acts: Floor map re-creating the streetscape of the original District Six. Photograph by Antoinette Engel.

the words of Sandra Prosalendis, the curator of the museum, "District Six is remembered by many who lived there as a place where they were able to cross religious, class, and social boundaries. As a place where they were able to share their everyday experiences and to live not as 'coloured,' 'whites,' 'Africans,' or 'Indians' but as South Africans, District Six occupies a special place in the history of South Africa."[63]

Seen through this lens, District Six as a cosmopolitan community of diverse peoples from different cultural backgrounds provided nothing less than a prescient vision of the "Rainbow Nation" not yet born, a model of racial harmony not yet imagined or achieved. This remembrance of District Six as a homogenizing melting pot where "community" overshadowed class, religious, or cultural differences stands in stark contrast to the characterization by apartheid bureaucrats that the place was a disreputable slum teeming with gangsters, prostitutes, and the jobless. One of the central goals of the District Six Museum is commemorative, that is, making use of memory-acts as a way of restoring a sense of dignity and authenticity to a place and its people. It builds on a sense of loss of a cohesive community and offers a comforting collective script for fond remembrance.[64] In fostering collective memory of the place, the museum upholds a brand of multiculturalism that can be characterized as a kind of "critical non-racialism."[65]

The exhibitionary space at the museum evokes a memory of "community" that flourished in District Six that is intensely "intractably local."[66] Sites of memory that evoke strong feelings of loss run the risk of falling into a kind of melancholic nostalgia, "longing for a home that no longer exists or has never existed."[67] The inherent danger that comes with ascribing ways of life to a community *post-facto* is that the creeping influence of overly romanticized recollections tends to downplay or ignore negative and unsavory aspects of the past, such as ethnic discord, crime, and violence, in the name of the solidaristic bonds of communitarian unity.[68] Over the decades, the continual exchange of romantic stories about the "good old days" has fostered a narrative community among the families that were forcibly removed. Over time, the telling and retelling of the stories of abrupt eviction gave rise to a "shared set of narrative conventions for remembering a past characterized by traumatic loss." Sharing the experience of trauma produced an implicit and unspoken agreement about what was "appropriate to remember about this past" and the relationships of evicted families to "their destroyed homes and communities." The sharing of individual remembrances can help to explain the "uncanny resemblance" that stories and recounted life histories of evicted families bear in relation to one another. As Henry Trotter has put it, "Their stories were forged in the same cauldron of traumatic loss and were animated by the same moral and emotional purposes."[69]

Through everyday conversation and symbolically choreographed reenactments, this blending of individual stories and life histories produces what can be called a "commemoration narrative."[70] The power of these kinds of mnemonic devices comes from the layering and bundling together of an explicit comparison between two distinct moral universes separated by the traumatic rupture of eviction. This radical divide between an idealized past and the unsettled present is a classical feature of nostalgia. Nostalgic remembrance is a powerful tool that enables the social construction of an Edenic world of a tightly knit community where racial harmony and tolerance prevailed and where unpleasant memories are repressed and reconfigured to suit the present.[71] Remembrance has a way of providing roseate portraits of the past by producing a sanitized, sepia-toned history. As Svetlana Boym has argued, this kind of unrequited nostalgia amounts to a "mourning for the impossibility of mythical return, for the loss of an enchanted world with clear borders and values."[72] As a general rule, there is always a surplus of meaning that lies in the appropriation and reappropriation of shards of memory in visual displays, photographs, found objects, written texts, oral histories, and music.[73] Distorted by the passage of time, memories of a place can sometimes become more real than the place itself. It is not difficult to understand how and why the material remnants of the past at District Six are saturated with associations and longings for a lost, mythical world that once was and can never be again.[74]

The memory of District Six has spawned a significant outpouring of autobiographical reminiscences.[75] Expressions of romantic nostalgia often appear in the personal memoirs and "I-witness" accounts that have proliferated about District Six, where the disreputable features of everyday life are frequently downplayed if not totally cast aside and ignored.[76] In uncritical popular renditions, District Six has long stood for the stereotype of the "Cape Malay." As Bill Nasson has shown, the representational lineage of District Six is that of "exclusively a merry community, with rich, rowdy popular life; a higgledly-piggledly riot of buildings and architectural styles, thronged with characters with an insatiable appetite for conviviality and an insatiable thirst for alcohol."[77] These stereotypical images are sometimes reproduced in the everyday expressions of popular culture.[78]

Yet it should come as no surprise that popular cultural products that market themselves to mass audiences typically bank on nostalgia-in-excess for their own success. Theatrical performances like *District Six—the Musical* (written by David Kramer and Taliep Petersen) provided a "light-hearted look at the people and places that characterized District Six." The message is no more complicated than a simplified version of history which suggests that the residents of District Six were innocent victims of an evil policy. While it proclaimed to capture "the authenticity of the era," this musical performance filled with singing and dancing that played into the reigning stereotypes of "coloured culture" amounted to little more than a fairy-tale.[79]

This staging of the past represents what Arjun Appadarai has called "imagined nostalgia," a sensibility that inverts the temporal logic of fantasy (imagining what could or might happen) and replaces it with a longing for things that never were.[80] In order to guard against an overtly romantic nostalgia, museum curators have deliberately engaged with some of the more controversial aspects associated with District Six. The launch of the *Digging Deeper* exhibition in 2000 provided one way of telling the District Six story with greater complexity and challenging the mythical construction of District Six as the quintessential expression of a distinctive "coloured culture" in Cape Town.[81] Whereas the original exhibitions tended to focus on public spaces and public lives, *Digging Deeper* has sought to investigate the private lives and interior spaces that were largely hidden from view. Rather than falling back on a single and safe narrative, *Digging Deeper* set out deliberately to disrupt and unsettle the popular stereotypes and conventional wisdom that typically accompanied stories about District Six. The exhibitionary space called *Nomvuyo's Room*, a carefully reconstructed domestic interior of a room where a Xhosa woman named Nomvuyo Ngcelwane once lived, challenges the conventional stereotypical image of District Six as an exclusively "coloured" residential area.[82] In other ways, the museum offers a portrait of daily life that complicates the simplified view of District Six as either a crime-ridden slum, on the one hand, or an idyllic, harmonious community without political tensions, group rivalries, and personal antagonisms, on the other. In adopting such an approach, the museum acknowledges that District Six as an actual place was not simply a "space of innocence."[83]

In a notable departure from standard museum practice when dealing with themes of displacement and suffering, the curators have taken great pains to avoid telling the story of District Six through a binary narrative of victim and perpetrator, where the temptation exists to apportion blame and to frame violent acts as the singular responsibility of a few "bad persons." What is perhaps most noticeable in the District Six exhibitions is the absence of images of overt violence. By deliberately downplaying the forcible removal of persons from their homes and the actual demolition of buildings, the museum successfully avoids sensationalizing the story of District Six, which carries the risk of casting visitors as voyeurs, rather than as implicated subjects in a memory project.[84] Rustom Bharacha has characterized the decision to avoid graphic displays of violence as a "curatorial coup," since it permits the exhibitions to focus instead on the familiarity of home and the shared remembrance of community.[85] Yet there is a danger in slipping into a kind of idealistic nostalgia by subsuming the past entirely in a narrative of loss. Without overt acknowledgment of the contradictions involved in calling for the restoration of the site as it once was and encouraging the return of former residents and their children to District Six, the museum risks being "stuck in a time warp," whereby "a particular construction of the past is in the process of being fossilised in its seemingly eternal contemplation of an imminent future." In looking forward, "the challenge for District Six has less to do with assuaging pain and trauma than with negotiating the intricate legalities and bureaucratic mechanisms that determine the logistics and economics of return."[86]

What the vehicles of collective memory that have proliferated in the "new South Africa" have in common is an enduring interest in excavating the past: discovering the truth, setting the story straight, uncovering what had been previously hidden under layers of secrecy. But what questions are asked, what "truths" are considered important, and what approaches are taken vary considerably. For Steven Robins, the District Six Museum evokes what Hannah Arendt termed the "banality of evil"—ordinary individuals engaging in commonplace, mundane practices that reproduced systematic terror.[87] By focusing on the everyday routines of the apartheid bureaucracy, the museum offers a distinct understanding of white minority rule that such memory-makers as the Truth and Reconciliation Commission did not provide. By focusing on the worst crimes committed by individual perpetrators, the TRC overlooked the systemic features of apartheid rule. This narrow approach unwittingly promoted a kind of "organized forgetting" about the everyday structural violence perpetuated by apartheid policies and practices. By shifting the blame for the crimes of the state machinery onto notorious individuals and psychotic killers, the TRC unwittingly promoted the idea that apartheid represented an aberration, an extraordinary moment in South African history. As Robins has argued, the structural violence of the apartheid regime was "largely the result of a 'rational' and modern bureaucracy armed with a sophisticated technology of surveillance and social control."[88]

What distinguishes such sites of memory as the District Six Museum from other commemorative projects is that they are more than silent and symbolic markers of collective trauma. Such "working memorials" invite collective engagement and public involvement; they function as agents for active dialogue. They are premised on the view that memorials dedicated to traumatic memories—not only of the past but continuing to the present—must come into existence and be sustained through a process of engagement with the local communities that share a vital interest in the message and the outcome.[89]

The "District Six Walk" adds a further dimension to the site. The self-guided walking tour is similar to conventional historical city walks and cultural-heritage trails. The aim of "historical city walks" is to "reclaim the hidden or, more specifically masked, histories that lie dormant and unremarked in the civic institutions of an otherwise familiar cityscape."[90] But what makes this walk distinctive is that the physical form of District Six no longer exists. Seemingly against all odds, the District Six Walk reconstructs a vivid sense of place out of a site with few remaining physical remnants. Walking through the ghostly remains of a ruined site animates memory. The site is haunted by presences no longer visible but visceral nonetheless. The scarred landscape becomes repopulated with the ghostly presence of the past.[91]

With limited state financial support, the museum demonstrates how the locally inspired retrieval of collective memory can act as a resource of solidarity and reclamation.[92] The combination of political engagement and community involvement has endowed the museum with a distinctiveness that distinguishes it from other sites of memory in the "new South Africa." The District Six Museum serves three purposes: as an archive for the collection and display of objects, as a memorial that triggers remembrance in its visitors, and as a monument that acts as the physical embodiment of memory. By putting social justice at the forefront of its work, the museum engages with truth, authenticity, and fairness. Restorative projects like the District Six Museum seek to promote social justice by mobilizing memory in the interests of contemporary communities.[93]

District Six embodies the tension between exceptionality and universality. On the one hand, the fashioning of District Six as a "unique and non-exchangeable icon" is linked with present-day political and economic interests related to the redress of past grievances and land restitution.[94] On the other hand, it has assumed a more universal role in the urban imaginary of the "new South Africa" "as a site of memory for recalling apartheid-era injustices and as site of hope for an integrated post-apartheid city, still not realised anywhere in South Africa."[95]

Ruins are palimpsests that evoke feelings of nostalgia for lost places and anger at shattered lives.[96] The call for restoration signifies a longing to "return to the original stasis, to the prelapsarian moment."[97] Whatever shape the rebuilding of District Six takes, it can never be what it once was. Collective memory is no substitute for social justice, and social justice itself is entangled in the unreliability of remembrance.[98] Collective memory consists of "common landmarks," shared frameworks that enable individual recollections to reconcile themselves with one another.[99] The collective memory that the District Six Museum preserves not only mediates between the past and present but also acts as a safeguard against forgetting.[100] It acts as a bulwark against obsolescence and disappearance. The collective memories of District Six evoke an uncanny, haunted place where "what was once imagined as possible, a moment later is possible no longer."[101]

The paradox of cultural heritage at the District Six Museum is that the object of conservation has already been destroyed and no longer exists. In fact, the destruction of its built environment triggered efforts to preserve its memory. As Andreas Huyssen has argued, the international culture industry promotes the manufacture and consumption of mass-marketed "imagined memory" as part of global tourism.[102] The District Six Museum shares this obsession with memory. But what is different is that, unlike many global efforts at remembering, forgetting, producing, and selling trauma, the collective memory cherished at District Six is not depoliticized and packaged for mass consumption. What has politicized collective memory at the museum is its central role in serving as a "hub for displaced community members to negotiate the complex processes of restitution, redevelopment and resettlement."[103]

Because the actual place was demolished and its rubble discarded, it is absence that marks the District Six Museum. Ironically, this absence of physical remains—or the visuality of disappearance—offers freedom to the imagination. Memory seems to function as a vehicle for engagement with broader questions regarding dispossession, loss, and grief. The District Six Museum has established a space for memory where it is possible to imagine how an integrated, nonracial city might work.[104]

Touring the Sites of Collective Memory: Robben Island as the Located Presence of the Past

Located at the entrance to Table Bay, about nine kilometers and a thirty-minute ferry ride from Cape Town, Robben Island is a forlorn, forbidding place. As a topological space, the island is a genuine palimpsest of South African history, from physical traces associated with the aboriginal (Khoi) peoples to colonial buildings and gun emplacements dating from World War II.[105] Yet for the most part, Robben Island came to symbolize the outer margins of expulsion, a liminal space where those who were unwanted were banished. For hundreds of years, beginning with the earliest Dutch settlement at the Cape of Good Hope in the seventeenth century, Robben Island served as a convenient place of exile for political dissidents, a penal settlement, a leper colony, and a dumping ground for the criminally insane.[106] With the upsurge of political unrest in the 1950s, the Department of Prisons commandeered the island for its own use in 1961, transforming the World War II–era military training site into a maximum-security prison for political detainees.[107] During the following three decades, Robben Island acquired a much-deserved reputation as the "hell-hole" of Table Bay—South Africa's own Devil's Island, or Alcatraz.[108] As an impregnable place of banishment for political prisoners, it became a metaphor for the inhumanity, brutality, and capricious violence of apartheid rule.[109] In drawing attention to the historical specificity of this place, Oliver Tambo argued that "the tragedy of Africa, in racial and political terms [has been] concentrated in the southern tip of the continent—in South Africa, Namibia, and, in a special case, Robben Island."[110]

But as popular resistance to apartheid rule gained momentum during the 1980s, Robben Island acquired a different meaning that transcended the constraining image as merely a site of suffering.[111] In the uplifting discourse of the liberation movement, Robben Island was rearticulated into a heroic symbol of defiance, a temporarily inhabited territory, the impermanent residence of a legitimate government-in-waiting. As former prisoner Ahmed Kathrada put it, "[Robben Island] should not . . . be a monument to the hardship and suffering [of former prisoners] . . . [but] a monument reflecting the triumph of the human spirit against the forces of evil, a triumph of freedom and human dignity over repression and humiliation."[112] With the release of Nelson Mandela and other political prisoners and the closing of the prison in 1991, Robben Island has become a symbol of transcendence over oppression and an icon of hope.[113]

Despite the prohibitions of the Prisons Act and various state security laws, Robben Island always featured prominently in South African literary discourse, autobiographical writing, and popular memory.[114] The autobiographical accounts of former political prisoners were primarily responsible for fashioning the meaning of Robben Island as a symbol of political resistance. Their personal experiences enabled them to "speak" with authority through their authorial voice. It was from their ability to analyze and interpret the perversion of power on Robben Island, the ways it affected them within the larger political context, and their sustained resistance to the systematic brutality to which they were subject that the political prisoners were able to develop and sustain an oppositional discourse of solidarity. These autobiographies demonstrate the "power of writing" to establish historical "truth" and to shape popular political folklore. Robben Island memoirs were self-conscious constructions of a collective political self, and, as such, they embodied in their collective self-image a sense of historic destiny, where the worst extremes of ill-treatment, blatant cruelty, and appalling living conditions can be transformed into resistance and eventual triumph.[115]

These conjoined themes of transcendence and triumph were also explored in the documentary *Robben Island, Our University,* a film that chronicled the evolution of the island prison from "hell-hole" to "university."[116] A group of ex-Robben Island prisoners—notably, Neville Alexander, Fikile Bam, and Kwedi Mkalipi—collaborated on the making of this illegally produced documentary, a film that helped to shape public opinion by lifting the official veil of secrecy that had obscured the grim realities of political repression during the apartheid years from ordinary South Africans. By chronicling how political prisoners transformed this place of confinement into an enlightened site of learning, this documentary contributed to dispelling any lingering myths that prisoners were only victims of apartheid and not active participants in shaping their own environment, circumscribed as it may have been.[117] Political activists around the world also packaged the story of Nelson

Mandela's incarceration in order to bring media attention and generate support for the anti-apartheid movement both internationally and locally.[118]

Because of the infamy it gained as an impregnable place of banishment for political prisoners during the apartheid years, Robben Island has become perhaps the most symbolically charged site of collective memory in the "new South Africa."[119] For years, debates about the future of the island—as a nature reserve, holiday resort, and museum—came to represent competing visions through which rival interest groups sought to reformulate the meaning of the place and to transform it into a symbol of something other than merely a maximum-security prison during the apartheid years.[120]

In December 1995, Robben Island was declared a national monument and was placed under the jurisdiction of the Department of Arts, Culture, Science, and Technology. Shortly thereafter, the prison facilities were recognized as an official museum, and in January 1997 regular tours to the island were begun.[121] Designated in December 1999 as a UNESCO World Heritage site, the island prison where, along with many other prisoners, Mandela spent eighteen of his twenty-seven years of incarceration, symbolizes "the triumph of the human spirit over adversity."[122]

FIGURE 12. Robben Island with Cape Town in the distance. Photograph copyright Pierre-Jean Durieu, 2012. Used under license from Shutterstock.com.

FIGURE 13. Entrance to the Robben Island Museum. Photograph copyright Darrenp, 2012. Used under license from Shutterstock.com.

This transformation of Robben Island from a maximum-security prison into a showcase "heritage site" reclaimed the name of the place, reassembling it as a metaphor for hope and redemption. Unlike memorials that commemorate the atrocities of the past, Robben Island has become a symbol for the triumph of human rights over the horrors of apartheid. Within the official memory of the "new South Africa," it stands for the "indestructibility of the spirit of resistance against colonialism, injustice, and oppression."[123]

Robben Island is not simply the material backdrop from which a story is told, but the site itself conveys meaning by serving as both the physical location of trauma and the wellspring of an interpretive narrative.[124] The curators of the museum conceived of it as both a gateway to local tourism and a model of hope and reconciliation for the "new South Africa." In seeking to shape a future rather than simply exhibit a past, they created a living museum that is a special place of engagement. But Robben Island is also a symbolically overdetermined place, saturated with different meanings and rival interpretations. Some former political prisoners question the overly triumphalist official narrative of hope and reconciliation. Others challenge what they regard as the undue stress on Nelson Mandela and other key ANC leaders at the expense of other political organizations. Khoisan lobbying groups look upon Robben Island as a symbol of colonial oppression because it served as a place of banishment for their leaders as early as the 1650s. Environmentalists usually view Robben Island in a wholly different light, as the site of the third largest African Penguin colony in the world, as well as the breeding grounds of rare and endangered birds. Archaeologists have discovered one of the few surviving examples of early eighteenth-century garden walling originally constructed by the Dutch East India Company. The village church is a fine example of early Gothic church architecture. The relative balance between competing interpretations—the stress on the colonial versus apartheid eras, rival political histories, and the focus on natural versus the cultural heritage—complicates any efforts to establish a single official interpretation.[125]

The official message conveyed by the Robben Island Museum is closely aligned with both South Africa's nation-building project of racial reconciliation and the moral aesthetic of global heritage tourism. As Veronique Rioufol has demonstrated, the official story deeply embedded in the Robben Island tourist experience closely matches the uplifting message of reconciliation, focusing on "moving beyond" the oppressive past through a negotiated settlement, which provided something for everyone within the new political culture that respects human rights, freedom, and democracy.[126] In promoting an experiential kind of secular pilgrimage to cultural-heritage sites, the global tourist industry blends travel, aesthetics, and enriching personal experiences. Journeys to sacred places offer inspiration, adventure, and opportunities for personal growth.[127] The production and marketing of niche tourist destinations is big business. The global circulation of images depicting cultural-heritage sites is deeply embedded in the universalizing impulse of Westernized humanist values. Journeys to cultural-heritage sites invoke a "compulsion to proximity" that makes travel to sites a necessary part of the personal experience where subjective meaning is directly linked to "being there."[128]

The centerpiece of the Robben Island Museum is the walking tour of the prison facilities. The story that accompanies this tour follows an uncomplicated, teleological narrative that compresses historical time in one linear sweep divided into two serial episodes. The first stage stresses the fall, that is, the evil the island represented; the second marks the triumphant return to grace and redemption, that is, the uplifting account of human endurance and perseverance.[129]

By following the traditional pedagogic style of the "guided tour," the Robben Island excursion engages visitors with an existential experience of everyday prison life by bringing the ghostly presence of the inmates back to life. Rather than focusing on the unusual or spectacular, this kind of tourism emphasizes ordinary spaces—prison yards, cell blocks, the lime quarry, the dining facilities—that appear extraordinary in symbolic significance. By encouraging visitors to imagine what it was like to be a political prisoner, the Robben Island experience cuts against the grain of the detached and distant attitude typically associated with the romantic sensibilities that underpin the conventional "tourist gaze."[130]

The mythology of Robben Island is so powerful that it overwhelms the narrative of anti-apartheid resistance. The island is an overtextualized place that becomes impossible to make sense of without the prior conditioning of texts and discourses. The site itself and the objects on display acquire a second life, "functioning as representations of themselves and their previous lives."[131] The former prisoners who act as tour guides exemplify this collapse of the real and its representation. What separates the two is just a matter of timing: then and now. The ways that events and memories are encoded with meanings are inseparable from their modes of telling. The highpoint of the official Robben Island tour comes near the end, when the tour guide, an ex-political prisoner, engages in dialogue with the visitors, assembled in one of the sparse dormitory rooms. This dialogical format personalizes the experience of incarceration, allowing visitors to imagine prison life under apartheid rule. The irony of working for wages at the site of their own incarceration is painfully evident. The ex-prisoners, with patience and aplomb, field questions both soul-searching and trivial. It is at this point that the memories of personal suffering and despair blend with an uplifting message of hope.[132]

A historical location is a kind of palimpsest, and the task of those who wish to preserve the memory of what happened there is to allow the different historic "pasts" of each site to find expression on their own terms, rather than fixing upon a single story to the exclusion of others. Tour guides do not focus exclusively on Robben Island as the place of incarceration for political prisoners alone but recount the overlapping histories of the place as an insane asylum, a World War II military training site, a prison for common criminals, and a nature preserve. By making the island prison the primary focus of the memory of political detention and harsh treatment under apartheid, the custodians of collective memory run the risk—as with other memorials—of ossifying and simplifying the meaning of the past.[133] The island prison symbolizes the moral strength and the determined resolve of the anti-apartheid movement, but it also tends inadvertently to draw attention away from memories of other forms of repression. While Robben Island prisoners by some accounts received better treatment than political prisoners confined elsewhere during the apartheid years, their imprisonment has come to epitomize the crimes of apartheid, and their release, the victory over an oppressive regime. For political activists who experienced the darkest hours of apartheid overrule, Robben Island takes shape as a shrine, evoking near-religious veneration. For curious overseas tourists with little knowledge of South African history, the entire experience of the Robben Island tour all too often undergoes a radical reduction, where the site is compressed into the place where Nelson Mandela—as prisoner 488/64—was imprisoned for eighteen of his more than twenty-seven years in jail. The image of Mandela looms larger than life. He is undoubtedly a moral and principled person, whose role as a political activist, leader, and symbol of personal integrity marks him as special. But in the construction of Mandela as a singularly heroic figure, his life story has metamorphosized into a kind of moral fable, a stylized fairy tale that symbolizes the journey from racial oppression to parliamentary democracy. Most visitors become fixated in C-Block, Cell 8, the tiny room that was Mandela's "home" for most of his imprisonment. The preservation of this cell in ways that resemble a shrine contributes to the popular view of Robben Island as a sacred site.[134] If the tourists are mostly Americans, the questions seem to focus on Mandela to the exclusion of everyone else.[135]

Museums introduce a plethora of displacements since curators must select objects for display for their expressive qualities, transforming them into public spectacles—to be viewed in reverent silence—and investing them with a public and very often a historical narrative. Cell 8 (where Mandela was confined for most of his time on the island) and the single-room cottage that was constructed for the purpose of ensuring the solitary confinement of PAC leader Robert Sobukwe fulfill this function at the Robben Island Museum,

FIGURE 14. Mandela's cell at the Robben Island Museum. Photograph by Compact Travels (www.namastesouthafrica.com).

the first symbolizing triumph because of Mandela's heroic ascendancy to the Office of State President, the second, tragedy, because Sobukwe died of cancer while in detention.[136] While the museum is the most well-known cultural-heritage project that commemorates the anti-apartheid struggle, it conveys a largely anodyne message—comforting, soothing, safe—that purposely seeks not to offend anyone. By focusing almost entirely on key figures and their heroic sacrifice to the virtual exclusion of everything else, the museum fails to address the more mundane legacies of apartheid associated with the spatial and social aspects of racial segregation.[137]

Packaged tours to cultural-heritage sites are typically structured around the consumption of standardized narratives and rehearsed itineraries. In seeking to manufacture a memorable "experience" for visitors, these sites often bring together a range of techniques to produce "infotainment": guided tours, information brochures, audiovisual presentations. The aim of these elements is to capture the feel of what it was really like "back in the day." Gift shops provide souvenirs, postcards, and brochures (with their "potted histories" and visual imagery) that testify to the experience of "I-was-there."[138] The inherent danger in appropriating sites of commemoration for crass commercial purposes is the risk of lapsing into the triviality of kitsch.[139]

Yet even such symbolically saturated places of suffering as Robben Island cannot escape the pressures of consumerism that often accompanies cultural-heritage parks.[140] As a sign of the multiple meanings attached to specific places, Liz Westby-Nunn, a member of the South African Tourism Board, suggested as early as 1997 that "Robben Island is bound to become one of our top tourist attractions."[141] The staging area for the ferry ride to Robben Island is located at the Victoria & Alfred Waterfront, the luxury retail and entertainment complex located at Cape Town's former docklands. A private business venture to market Robben Island memorabilia under the label "The Original Robben Island Trading Store" provoked an outcry from former political prisoners, who regarded such crass commercialization as a sacrilegious violation of an important symbol of national resistance. Despite these protestations, the local shop on the island sells such items as "authentic prison cutlery and plates," key rings celebrating the accused in the Rivonia Treason Trial, souvenir T-shirts, and bottles of wine labeled "Robben Island Red."[142]

The Apartheid Museum

As an integral part of the cultural production, museums under white minority rule conformed to an anachronistic neocolonial and Eurocentric archetype. Museums functioned as storehouses for objects, artifacts, and assorted memorabilia that both reflected and sensationalized the power and dominance of settler colonialism.[143] This museological tradition rested on the ideology of social Darwinism, which placed indigenous people on a lower level on the developmental hierarchy, that is, as primitive people frozen in a timeless present: "static, dark, mysterious, and passive."[144]

With the end of apartheid and the transition to parliamentary democracy, the museum and heritage communities have experimented with new museological typologies that "allow for a truthful, unflinching examination of the past and creative, participatory approach to the future."[145] Opened in 2001, the Apartheid Museum in Johannesburg seeks to make a clean break from the discredited Eurocentric memory-practices that prevailed under white minority rule. Modeled on the Holocaust Memorial Museum in Washington, D.C., this museum fuses distinctive architecture, documentary film, textual narratives and commentary, artifacts, and visual displays to create an aura of authenticity in retelling the story of apartheid in the form of a didactic, linear narrative. As an alternative to conventional object-based museology, the Apartheid Museum is inventive in its use of what has been called "experiential' memory space to immerse uninformed visitors (who often have no direct experience or even knowledge of the events depicted) in a sensory-rich environment that enables them to imagine what the past "was really like." This new kind of "experiential" museum re-creates national trauma through the simulated experience of the pain and suffering of others. The construction of this sensuous engagement with the traumatic national past appeals to the emotional sensibilities of visitors in order to produce an empathetic identification with the victims of state-sponsored violence and brutality.[146]

FIGURE 15. Apartheid Museum, Johannesburg. Photograph by Joe Levy, M.D.

The Apartheid Museum was the brainchild of Abe and Solly Krok, entrepreneurs who wanted to take advantage of the post-apartheid relaxation of legal restrictions on gambling establishments to open a huge casino-entertainment complex on the premises of Gold Reef City, a popular theme park built around a *faux* mining town on the southwestern outskirts of Johannesburg. In order to secure approval for their casino, the brothers agreed to finance the construction of a museum as a requisite "social development" project. The weird juxtaposition of a purposeful museum and a mindless theme park highlights the contradictions and complexities of allowing cultural heritage to be dependent upon the crass pursuit of profit.[147] What seemed conveniently overlooked and forgotten in the rush to attach the museum to the gambling casino was the uncomfortable fact that the Krok brothers made their fortune during the apartheid years selling toxic skin-lightening cream to black women.[148]

As a form of cultural production of history, the Apartheid Museum employs the semiotics of spatial design, visual spectacle, and theatrical display to reenact the historical experience of oppression and resistance.[149] Its inventive use of photography, documentary film, and other realist displays functions as much as *aides-mémoire* as testimonies to loss. The visualization of the oppressive nature of the apartheid system transforms visitors into witnesses to atrocity who have a moral and personal stake in the outcome. These visual images are more than material objects that bear witness to the past, but they act as mnemonic devices that shape the collective memory of apartheid. In borrowing from the conventional repertoire of documentary realism, the visual displays and accompanying commentary act silently to accuse, to place blame, and to expose long-hidden secrets. In bringing to life circumstances where an objective, neutral stance simply appears immoral, the visualization of the apartheid system compels us to respond with moral outrage and indignation.[150]

Much like the Holocaust Memorial Museum in Washington, D.C., the Apartheid Museum functions less like a conventional museum that "teaches by showing" than as a kind of "exhibitionary complex" that stresses subjective experience.[151] The museum space makes use of controlled lighting, colorful banners and displays, and sound effects to create an all-encompassing environment that wordlessly conveys a sense of the realities of apartheid through a kind of "simulated experience." This "simulated experience" is to impart "to the visitor a bodily sense of discomfort and brutality irrevocably associated with the events detailed in the displays themselves."[152] The windowless spaces, narrow passageways, and enveloping walls produce what John Matshikiza has referred to as "claustrophobic panic,"[153] where "senses of alienation, dehumanization, restriction and control prevail."[154] The museum fashions an engagement with the past that moves almost seamlessly along a chronological arc of historical time, chronicling the linear story of the apartheid policies of segregation and discrimination.[155]

Like the Hector Pieterson Museum, the Robben Island Museum, and other post-apartheid sites of memory, the Apartheid Museum seeks to appropriate the bitter memories of white minority rule in the service of nation-building and the forging of a new common identity. The goal is to incubate a post-conflict ideology of tolerance and mutual respect. But unlike other cultural-heritage sites that have been established since the end of apartheid, the Apartheid Museum has no specific historical or locational reference point. It is a constructed space in which collective remembrance "floats in the realm of pure narrative."[156]

The Apartheid Museum offers a singular, almost teleological reading of the past where oppression gave rise to resistance, which in turn yielded ultimately to a new nation reborn under the sign of tolerance and reconciliation. As a theater of collective memory, the museum focuses on the selective reenactment of the state-orchestrated violence and injustice of the past as a way of prescribing a commitment to tolerance and enlightened citizenship in the present. The conjoined stories of oppression followed by liberation suggest a clear fault line between "before" and "after," insinuating that apartheid can be relegated to the past, thrown into the dustbin of history, displayed as a ruin and relic of a bygone era, rather than conceding that its remnants—its spectral presence—still haunt the present.[157]

A Monument to the Women's Struggle in South Africa

The showering of a great deal of attention on such preeminent sites of heroic struggle as Robben Island and the Hector Pieterson Memorial has inadvertently contributed to overlooking the role of women in the anti-apartheid resistance. Thandi Modise's angry speech in 1995 at the Peninsula Technikon in front of more than a thousand former political prisoners abruptly brought into the open the tensions about the invisibility of women in the official remembrances of the liberation struggle. Modise angrily berated the organizers of the event for almost totally ignoring the role of women in bringing about the downfall of apartheid and the end of white minority rule.[158]

In 2000, the first monument commemorating the role of women in the struggle against apartheid was unveiled at the Union Buildings in Pretoria. The monument is located at the site of the historic women's march of August 9, 1956, when a multiracial crowd of about twenty thousand women converged on the Union Buildings to protest the extension of the hated Pass Laws to include black women. As the women waited to deliver petitions to Prime Minister J. G. Strijdom, they sang the hymn "Nkosi Sikelel' iAfrica" (which has become the South African national anthem). The women followed by chanting the rallying cry: *Wathint 'abafazi Wathint 'imbokodo Uzokufa* ["You have tampered with the women. You have struck a rock. You will be crushed."] The centerpiece of the monument, and perhaps the most sacred element of the site, is a grinding stone—the "rock," or the *'imbokotu* of the refrain. The designers of the monument placed the grinding stone where the two wings of the Union Buildings meet at the top of the amphitheater, the site where the women gathered in 1956.[159]

The Monument to the Women of South Africa stands as a reminder of the spirit of women's resistance to oppression. Rather than having a single focal point, the monument consists of an agglomeration of objects that collectively produce its symbolic significance. The design consists of four separate but interrelated components. Each component recalls, memorializes, or speaks through metaphor about the day of protest in August 1956.[160] The monument seeks to preserve shared memory through sight, stone, and sound.[161] Its design contains a multimedia sound and light installation. The risers of the steps leading to the top of the amphitheater contain various phrases from the women's petitions. At the top of the steps, visitors can activate a tape recording of women's voices chanting the rallying cry in the eleven official languages of the "new South Africa." A video machine projects the words around the small, domed antechamber. This historic monument reclaims a celebratory interpretation of women's contribution to the struggle against apartheid. The combination of visceral images, evocative sound

FIGURE 16. Monument to the Women of South Africa, Union Buildings, Pretoria. Photograph by Adam J. Cruise, Courtesy of Wilma Cruise.

effects and music, and a romantized commentary provides a staged experience in communal remembrance.[162] The assemblage of diverse elements enables the monument to function as a polyvalent site of memory, haunted by images and voices resonating from the past. Seen in this light, the monument showcases in a visceral way "the ineluctability of spectral returns."[163]

The artist/architecture collaborative team of Wilma Cruise and Marcus Holmes designed the Women's Monument. At a formal level, they were primarily concerned with creating a lasting tribute to South African women that would differ conceptually and aesthetically from the typical Eurocentric convention of commemorative public monuments in South Africa. This tradition, of course, is epitomized by the Voortrekker Monument, the grandiose "icon of conservative, white, patriarchal Afrikaner culture," a short distance from the Union Buildings.[164] The Women's Monument "celebrates the democratic, collaborative, and communal nature" of the 1956 protest march and "the ordinariness" of its participants. While the Voortrekker Monument is an imposing, grand structure designed to overwhelm the surrounding landscape, the Women's Monument is unobtrusive, inconspicuous, and unpretentious.[165]

In contrast to the traditional style of hero worship of key individuals, a commemorative practice common in monumental architecture, Cruise and Holmes chose a language of commemoration that stressed metaphor and symbol over figural forms of representation. This choice fits with the current trend in public commemoration. In the 1960s, artists and architects began experimenting with new design motifs for commemorative sites that moved away from the singular focus on figural forms in stone or bronze.[166] In a style similar to Maya Lin's Vietnam Veterans Memorial in Washington, D.C., Cruise and Holmes use abstract references to signal the ghostly presence of the twenty thousand women who stood in the amphitheater and proclaimed with their voices their opposition to the Pass Laws.[167]

Under circumstances where conventional monuments are dedicated to women, they usually follow a collective rather than individual mode of commemoration. Such tributes tend to conform to traditional gendered stereotypes in commemorative practices that are typically associated with group or national identity. The contributions of women are remembered largely through the trope of sacrifice—something that fits with stereotyped female roles.[168] A classic example is the Nasionale Vrouemonument, a memorial dedicated to Boer women and children who lost their lives in British concentration camps during the Second Boer War (1899–1902).[169]

The Monument to the Women of South Africa at the Union Buildings in Pretoria sets the tone for the post-apartheid interpretation of the concept of sacrifice framed in terms of political activism. As a commemorative site that serves a specific purpose, the monument "celebrates all those courageous women who took risks and accepted hardship and suffering for the collective sake of their vision of a non-racial and democratic nation."[170] By focusing on the grand metanarrative of resistance and the anti-apartheid struggle for liberation, the Monument to the Women of South Africa is intricately linked with the foundation myth of the "new South Africa." Yet despite its anti-elitist aims, the monument commemorates not all women but only those who participated in the anti-apartheid struggle under the banner of the ANC. The grinding stone symbolically privileges "traditional" rural life in ways that ignore the urban backgrounds of most women who participated in the 1956 march.[171] Critics have charged that the monument functions as a "secure alibi"—to borrow an expression from Gayatri Spivak and Sonia Gunew from another context—a kind of "patronizing, token gesture" that "conveniently obliterates the need to commemorate women and their contributions elsewhere."[172]

The introduction of new security measures has greatly reduced public access to the site, rendering it largely invisible. Some critics have suggested that the monument is "overly academic, rational, dry, and 'belabored' in its eagerness to be different." Despite the good intentions of the design team, the monument "is too obviously a textbook-like application of all the basic tenets of post-structuralist theory, postmodernism, and postcolonial discourses." While the monument represents women's experiences, however narrow and somewhat biased, and gives women a voice, however limited, it is "better than nothing."[173]

6 Makeshift Memorials

Marking Time with Vernacular Remembrance

In the aftermath of tragedy, collective memory can become attached to a specific place: sites of loss can be marked, set aside, and sanctified as "hollowed ground." Particular places—Robben Island, the Hector Pieterson Memorial, the District Six Museum, the commemorative plaque in Gugulethu dedicated to the memory of Amy Biehl, the bronze statue of Steve Biko in East London, and more—have become the fixed, externalized locations of what was once an internalized social memory.[1] As the located presence of the past, these places can be transformed into pilgrimage destinations. As spatially demarcated places set aside for public viewing, these sites of memory act as conduits, or heuristic devices, for the transmission of historical consciousness, a collective awareness that the present owes a genuine debt to the past. "[There is] nothing that memory cannot reach or touch or call back," Don Mattera has said. "Memory is a powerful weapon."[2] Erecting these formal reminders or iconic replicas of something people ought to remember represents a self-conscious, deliberate effort to preserve memory in historically meaningful ways.[3]

Commemoration is ultimately a process of legitimation. Embodied in sites of memory, commemorative acts preserve an account of past deeds that might otherwise be forgotten, securing a record for the future. Memorials, monumental statuary, commemorative plaques, photographic exhibitions, public murals, graffiti art, and museums remind people of what they know or think they know—to tell people about those things they may not know. Or the things they have forgotten or never learned. The construction of sites of memory often reflects the fear of those who want always to remember that without a material embodiment of remembrance what happened there would succumb to the culture of amnesia and gradually fade from historical consciousness.[4]

The preservation of these locations is not a single event but a long-term process, the beginning of a cycle of development rather than simply a momentary attempt to arrest the march of time. The safeguarding of places of remembrance, even if it is intended to do no more than stabilize and conserve, necessarily involves a whole series of innovations, if only to draw attention to the location itself. What may begin as a salvage operation, designed primarily to rescue the relics of the past, passes by degree into a work of preservation and restoration in which a new built environment has to be constructed in order to transform the fragmentary detritus of the past into meaningful wholes that can stimulate remembrance. The sites of collective memory are vulnerable to transfiguration because they must be altered to accommodate the visiting public and because they are often subjected to custodial modification in order to make them more aesthetically pleasing or more up-to-date in appearance. The framing of exhibitionary spaces and the narrating of histories demonstrate the power to shape remembrance. While cultural theme parks package the past in the easily digestible form of a consumable commodity, official memorialization identifies a usable past, functioning to define and fix stories of remembrance to conform to what state-approved custodians of memory would want visitors to believe. Imbricated with dominant political discourses, official memory decides which events, figures, and sites are worth remembering, and "which narratives are appropriate or authentic."[5]

Deliberate efforts to construct vehicles of collective memory in the aftermath of apartheid rule have been forced to confront the paradox of "nation-building" exercises designed to inaugurate an intelligible foundation for remembrance in a social order unsure about its political future. With the transition to parliamentary democracy, art galleries, museums, and other exhibitionary sites have undergone a fundamental reorganization in the way they display and highlight objects in order to represent more accurately the multiracial and multicultural realities of the "new South Africa." As a result, these cultural establishments have opened their exhibitionary spaces to include a more diverse range of artists and curators. In keeping with the nation-building objectives of the transition to parliamentary democracy, these cultural institutions have reoriented themselves to tell altogether different stories about the past. These places have tried "to forge a new understanding of South Africa's history," built on the conjoined themes of acknowledgment, commemoration, and reconciliation.[6]

Vernacular, Commonplace, and Everyday Remembrance

Recent scholarly literature in cultural and historical geography has directed a great deal of attention toward officially sanctioned monumental landscapes and the collective memories they are intended to foster. Yet vernacular landscapes have received only limited consideration, even though they also bear testimony to collective memory. The vernacular and monumental are intertwined at sites of collective memory, and ambiguity and fluidity mark the boundaries that separate them both analytically and symbolically. Public commemorations always involve a combination of the official or monumental and the vernacular or the popular.[7] While there are clear similarities in the way they commemorate past events, the distinction between the two modes of remembrance remains significant.[8]

Put in general terms, vernacular, commonplace, and everyday modes of remembrance refer to those social practices of memorialization that are created outside official or institutionalized sanction. These can take the form of, but are certainly not restricted to, spontaneous assemblages at sites of tragic occurrences, pilgrimages, roadside shrines, murals, plaques, and graffiti, where the range is only set by the limits of innovation.[9] Since commemorative sites are places where "memory crystallizes and secretes itself" as the material manifestations of social consciousness, unsanctioned vernacular performances of shared mourning are useful guides to understanding the ways that local communities choose to remember their pasts.[10] These modes of remembrance provide evidence of a felt need for "bottom-up" avenues through which to express grief at loss, and they reflect efforts to reclaim, or at least more properly represent, the distinctiveness of the persons mourned and the events remembered. In the broadest sense, communities of mourners—in looking for ways to express shared sorrow—make use of material objects to remind themselves of what happened in the past and to reorient themselves to the present. The most visible expressions of vernacular modes of remembrance are "makeshift memorials," "spontaneous shrines," and other impromptu physical markers that suddenly emerge at sites of an untimely death or catastrophic event.[11]

These physical markers operate on several complicated and intertwined levels. They offer at least a modest sense of empowerment to the community of mourners, bringing the act of grieving back into the personal realm of subjective experience, and away from the clinical, official realm of church services, funerals, and cemeteries. The act of constructing spontaneous memorials and shrines enables communities of mourners to symbolically reconstruct their own lives around the absence of the departed. It also allows communities of mourners to construct coherent stories around persons and events, giving structure and meaning to what otherwise might seem inexplicable or incomprehensible. Vernacular memorials come about through the synthesis of the fragments of lives cut short by tragedy and the fragments of the lives of those left behind, their own lives thoroughly disrupted by senseless death. What generates the emotive power of these memorials is the friction between the desire of mourners to reclaim the wholeness of the deceased and the inadequacy of the remnants that remain, frozen in time forever in photographs or etched in personal memories.[12]

Vernacular memorials become a focal point for the tensions created by the unfulfilled desire to properly represent what has been lost and the frustration with the inadequacy of all forms of representation. Through the public expression and display of grief, communities of mourners are able to mitigate individual and collective feelings of hopelessness and despair. In the typical case, the stories embedded in these vernacular modes of remembrance allow the spectral presence of those who lost their lives to be integrated into the mental geography of a specific place.[13]

As a number of scholars have noted, roadside memorials and other physical reminders of traumatic tragedy that focus on specific locations play a significant role in channeling mourning and grief. These places occupy a visible space in the *public* landscape and in the popular imagination. The proximic resonance of these sites enables them to function as makeshift altars, sacred sites facilitating an ongoing dialogue between the living and the dead.[14]

In the face of unexpected or untimely death, communities of mourners who participate in the creation of these vernacular sites of memory acquire a sense of regained control in response to feelings of powerlessness. The construction of such everyday memory-markers as roadside memorials and spontaneous shrines restores a sense of agency to communities of mourners who feel powerless. In addition to allowing for the public expressions of grief, vernacular modes of remembrance emphasize the individuality of those who lost their lives, affirming personal identities in the face of the anonymity of normal everyday life.[15]

The memorialization of the Trojan Horse Massacre—an incident where South African security forces, hiding in crates on the back of a railway delivery truck, ambushed and killed three young men in Athlone, a suburb of Cape Town, in August 1985—provides an exemplary illustration of how the process of remembering that initially took the form of intensely local, personal, and popular expressions of outrage and grief eventually achieved a prominent place in the public realm of official memory. Unveiled on Heritage Day, September 24, 2005, the official Trojan Horse Massacre Memorial marked the culmination of the process of the institutionalization of collective memory where monumental landmark architecture becomes state-sponsored public infrastructure. This shift away from vernacular expressions of localized remembrance at the site of the Trojan Horse Massacre to "the official design and endorsement of one coordinated, amalgamated formation is symptomatic of a wider trend of synthesizing the past and appropriating it for the needs of the present." This official institutionalization of state-sponsored collective memory "solidifies hegemonic narratives [of the liberation struggle], invalidates alternative memories, and eclipses other forms of understanding and remembering the past."[16]

Thanatourism: Pilgrimages to Sites of Inexplicable Suffering

Sometimes the personal stories behind memorials reveal the kinds of personal tragedy that unsettle the master narratives of sweeping change that typically accompany watershed historical turning points.[17] In the dying days of apartheid, when the conditions of the transition to parliamentary democracy were not yet firmly in place, political ferment on the ground seethed with

FIGURE 17. Trojan Horse Massacre Memorial, Cape Town. Photograph by Sabine Marschall.

anger. Under these unstable and volatile circumstances, tragic events become almost inevitable.

The death of Amy Biehl is an uncomfortable story to tell. Surely, if the phrase "being in the wrong place at the wrong time" means anything, it seeks to convey the sense that something should not have happened. On August 25, 1993, Amy Biehl, a twenty-three-year-old American Fulbright scholar living in Cape Town, was driving three black companions through Gugulethu Township. Her car just happened to come into contact with a throng of young men who had just left a political meeting of the youth league of the Pan-Africanist Congress (PAC). They attacked her car, pelting it with stones and smashing its windows while shouting "one settler, one bullet," the popular PAC slogan at the time. Dragged from her vehicle, Biehl was viciously assaulted. As she tried to flee across the road, she was surrounded by a large crowd who repeatedly kicked and stoned her before stabbing her to death.[18]

Four of Biehl's assailants, from among the dozen or so who attacked her, were arrested, convicted, and sentenced to eighteen years in prison. They applied for amnesty to the TRC, claiming that their actions were politically motivated. In July 1998, in the wake of the demise of apartheid, they were released from prison. The Biehl family attended the hearing. They could have objected to the plea for amnesty, but they chose not to do so.

In the remembrance of senseless, tragic death, all that is left is the vague outline of a void, "a shadow-tracing of the shape of a loss that can never serve as a proper substitute for a life." In the absence of physical presence, communities of mourners typically turn to whatever residues or reminders of the living person remain—old photographs, diaries and letters, home movies, personal effects—as vehicles to preserve memory. What acts of commemoration bring to the surface is an "almost unbearable tension between the stillness of memory and the vibrancy of life."[19]

Social memory leaves its marks on the social fabric of the city. But why are some places where tragedy occurred forgotten by all but eyewitnesses, whereas others become the hallowed sites of public commemoration is a complex question without a simple answer. What seems to be commonplace is that few places bear the traces of their past without some kind of assistance.[20] In the case of Amy Biehl, her family and friends refused to allow her memory to simply fade away. In their act of creating a memorial, they attempted to piece together the fragments of a young life. Certainly for the mourners close to the Biehl family, dedicating a monument played an important and therapeutic part in managing their grief. From the start, a simple, nondescript plaque marked the site. On August 25, 2010, seventeen years after her death, a memorial stone was dedicated to Amy Biehl's life and legacy at a place close to where she perished. This modest memorial marks a haunted site that is both intensely personal and local. There is a sense of spiritual mystery about these places of tragedy. It is as though something of the essence of the deceased might linger in the area, imparting a hierophantic aura to the monument itself. These memorials often serve symbolically to cleanse the site of death by creating an uplifting story of the life that has been lost.[21]

Pilgrimages to sites of suffering, violence, and death exemplify what some have called "dark tourism."[22] Like the memorial erected to the Cradock Four (Mathew Goniwe, Fort Calata, Sparrow Mkonto, and Sicelo Mhlauli), the Amy Biehl memorial conveys a message of hope: out of tragedy comes reconciliation and rebuilding.[23] In *The Ethics of Memory,* the philosopher Avishai

FIGURE 18. Amy Biehl Memorial, Cape Town. Photograph by Edward Schonsett.

Margalit has suggested that one role of the moral witness is to deliver a testimony to an imagined future.[24] Perhaps memorials to senseless deaths can stand as a kind of witnessing that anticipates a future in which these hallowed sites will no longer have to carry the entire burden of grief for the family and friends of those who perished. Custodians of memory have crafted a peculiar kind of memorial: "one that preserves the memories of the events while, at the same time, anticipating a day when those who enter into the memory space it creates will be freed from the compulsion to remember everything."[25]

Counter-Memory: Popular Responses to the Culture of Amnesia

Acts of official commemoration have not deviated far from the conventional aesthetic principles and visual strategies, including predictable iconic references, stylistic formulas, and symbolic coding, in the use of traditional building materials like bronze, steel, and concrete.[26] In contrast, gestures toward vernacular and unofficial memorialization typically rely on a variety of different experimental forms of artistic expression that are uniquely suited to local circumstances.[27]

Faced with a commemorative landscape already inundated with ponderous, colossal monuments to British and Boer triumphs over adversity, memory-makers in the "new South Africa" have struggled to create space for their own versions of collective memory. While officially sanctioned preservation of collective memory typically takes place in such easily recognized sites as museums, monuments, memorials, and public statuary, popular memorialization is more often than not rooted in vernacular, and sometimes intangible and ephemeral, expressions such as festivals, songs, performances, rituals, photography exhibits, drawings, and painting.[28] Ethically certain of their moral duty to remember but aesthetically skeptical of the assumptions underpinning conventional artistic forms, a new generation of contemporary memory-makers, including graffiti artists, musicians, muralists, and filmmakers, have begun to probe the limits of both their means of artistic expression and the official versions of collective memory.[29] They are heirs to a double-edged post-apartheid legacy: first, they maintain a profound desire to keep alive the memory of those who suffered and died at the hands of the apartheid state; and second, they harbor a deep distrust of state-sanctioned official memory, ever-mindful that "top-down" acts of remembrance often fail to capture local experiences.[30]

As a general rule, state-sponsored memory "aims to affirm the righteousness of a nation's birth," where the assemblage of monuments and memorials typically "emplots the story of ennobling events," the triumphs over oppression and adversity, and "recalls the martyrdom of those who gave their lives in the struggle for national existence."[31] While official memory in the "new South Africa" has tended to follow the conventional path, unofficial expressions of popular remembrance have produced entirely different ways of seeing and acting in relation to the historical past. Such visual expressions as graffiti art and popular murals are "antimonuments"—they do not celebrate individuals as heroic figures but instead reveal the lived experience of ordinary people.[32] These forms of expression offer a kind of documentation of popular temperament.[33] In her surreal, dreamscape mural that adorns the lobby of the Civic Theatre in the heart of downtown Johannesburg, Reshada Crouse constructs a visual montage of television personalities, actors, and playwrights as a lasting tribute to the active role that theater people played in the anti-apartheid struggle. The visual images that Crouse fashions have numerous layers of significance that only those well versed in the intricacies of South African theater can readily grasp. Purposefully constructed as an almost kitsch-like knockoff of Delacroix's *Liberty Leading the People,* this work is at once romantic and celebratory, whimsical and playful.[34]

Artists are often at the forefront of initiating projects to publicly remember trauma, that is, to combat "institutionalized forgetfulness."[35] Rather than merely visualizing historical events, artists such as Willie Bester, David Koloane, William Kentridge, Jane Alexander, and dozens of others seek to activate memory by staging their scenes like a theatrical performance. This method of dramaturgical storytelling is a means of intensifying and deepening the horror of a historical event that is alive in popular memory.[36] For example, Willie Bester uses the approach of a *bricoleur* in his collage entitled "Homage to Steve Biko," which invites us to question the official version of events surrounding Biko's death at the hands of the security forces. In a similar vein, the artist Jane Alexander has used a variety of brazen, painful images that are irreverent, mocking, and even shocking in her sculptural practice.[37]

Neglected narratives and counter-memories have survived in the most unlikely places. For example, the Mayibuye Centre, located at the University of the Western Cape in Belleville near Cape Town, is an exemplar of museology from "the bottom up." Politically conscious custodians have collected, stored, and catalogued collections of artifacts and memorabilia, including photographs, printed ephemera, and posters, from the anti-apartheid "struggle days." These remaining artifacts are the living signatures of oppression and exploitation. Operating within an abiding culture of amnesia, the Mayibuye project has sought to fuse two goals: to preserve a particular understanding of the past, and to influence the way future generations remember the past.[38]

Festivals of Equality: The Pageantry of Democratic Elections

Broadly speaking, public drama is an ambiguous, generic category that embraces events as diverse as pageants, civic processions, popular celebrations, Remembrance Day ceremonies, parades, carnivals, and large-scale festivals. All these activities engage the public in a performance, either as active participants or as interested spectators. Historically, dominant groups have used various methods of public dramatization in order to establish, confirm, and legitimate the social and political order, especially during and after times of turbulence. As an exercise in legitimization, public drama combines elements of ritual, spectacle, and carnival. As ritual, public drama typically involves rule-governed activities of symbolic character, the aim of which is to create a sense of commonality among the participants. As spectacle, public drama resembles a theatrical engagement, or an elaborately choreographed exhibition, that conveys its message through such means as visual display, sound, music, speech, and costume. Communal events "naturalize" a collective identity through physical enactment of what is considered normal, appropriate, or even possible in public settings.[39] Finally, as carnival, public drama may create the kind of liminal space that invites participants to transgress or subvert conventional boundaries by the blurring of social roles, or even enabling them to act out role reversals.[40]

The pageantry, ritual, and ceremony that surrounded South Africa's first nonracial elections—held on April 26–29, 1994—illustrates the powerful political and symbolic force of public dramatization in shaping political values, instilling civic pride, and fostering collective remembrance in the "new South Africa." These "liberation" elections, as they were popularly known, were the pivotal moment of the transition process: as the culmination of the anti-apartheid struggle, they marked the end of white minority rule; and, as the inaugural event denoting the onset of nonracial democracy, they signaled the beginning of political normalization that allowed South Africa to rid itself of its unwelcome "pariah" status. For millions of black South Africans, the act of casting a secret ballot for the first time assumed enormous significance. South Africa's first nonracial elections became an occasion for popular celebration. The kinds of lasting images generated by the electoral process—the photographs of long lines of voters queuing for hours at polling stations all over the country, waiting patiently to cast their ballots, is perhaps the most enduring one—illustrate how collective remembrance can be aroused through activities that are typically taken for granted in countries where civic participation is an ordinary feature of political life.[41]

As a ritualistic civic ceremony, the public drama of elections in the "new South Africa" has become an important vehicle through which popular identification with "nation-building" is secured and reaffirmed. Elections create partners in democracy. The performative act of voting transforms atomized individual citizens into members of an "imagined community." The regenerative power of this ritual observance comes with its ability to symbolically breathe new life into the body politic. As an integral part of the discourse of citizenship, popular participation in elections instills civic pride, fosters a sense of patriotic duty, and offers the promise of a bright future. The carnavalesque attraction revolves around the allegorical, ephemeral image of the "equality of citizens," where the act of voting momentarily abolishes the distinctions of wealth, status, and rank.[42]

Township "Struggle" Tours and the Creation of Collective Memory

The advent of "struggle tours" in the post-apartheid era represents the convergence of the politics of memory, the practice of historical production, and theatrical performance. As mnenomic devices, "struggle tours" consist of guided excursions where knowledgeable "insiders" transport visitors to sites of memory and places of mourning.[43] Because they are a kind of historical production, they fall under the general rubric of travel narratives, where the visual experience of spatially dispersed exhibitions is translated into "authentic" knowledge. The aim of this kind of engaged tourist experience is to reveal forgotten stories and hidden places, rescuing them from possible oblivion. As didactic exercises that rely on a kind of visual rhetoric, "struggle tours" transform locations into real-life destinations, sightseeing tours into (quasi-religious) pilgrimages, cultural into economic capital, and discarded "ruins" into meaningful "sights." These mapped destinations signal points of significance that politically- and socially-conscious tourists can visit in their search for an "authentic" experience of the historical reconstruction of a concrete slice of the anti-apartheid struggle.[44]

Rather than conceiving of tourism as a passive spectacle, "struggle tourism" encourages a distinctive kind of active engagement, a tactical intervention into the seams and crevices of tucked-away urban space, to use the language of Michel de Certeau.[45] These excursions into the politics of yesteryear seek to reconnect the present with what is perceived as the rapidly vanishing past.[46] In its active entanglement with the ghostly presences of the political past, "struggle tourism" seeks to disrupt the conventional "tourist gaze" and, at the same time, subvert the consumerist impulses of the "experience economies" that characterize the neoliberal Entertainment City.[47] Placed in a larger comparative framework, "struggle tours" constitute an alternative travel experience that has been called "reality tourism" because of the type of authentic encounter it promotes.[48] As a distinctive subgenre of reality tourism, "social tourism" provides visits to off-the-beaten-track destinations that offer a participatory experience and interactive engagement with local residents as a counterpoint to the mass-produced, voyeuristic experience of the conventional tourist gaze.[49] Framed as exotic adventure, "reality tourism" can easily fall prey to a kind of atrocity as entertainment.[50]

In the deterritorialized mind-set of the tourist imagination, Soweto has become an iconic brand that symbolizes the "Other South Africa": poor and black, dangerous and exotic. In the visibility politics that defines the "new South Africa," it is a preferred destination for visitors who want to experience everyday life in a "real township." Soweto—Johannesburg's "shadow city"—has become South Africa's fourth largest tourist attraction, more popular than such venues as the Wild Coast, Sun City, or the Mpumalanga and Pilanesberg game parks. The steady expansion of "township tourism" has widened the market with the increasingly professional packaging of "authentic" "interact-with-the-locals" walkabouts, sanitized "stopovers" at a real shebeen (drinking establishment), and home visits. This new kind of theatrical staging has reduced the attraction of pioneering adventure into a potentially dangerous area.[51]

The Soweto Heritage Trust, which has Standard Bank as its largest benefactor and is chaired by Nthato Motlana, has embarked on an ambitious preservation scheme designed to acquire old school buildings, hostel blocks, and former pass offices. By leaving these facilities in their current dilapidated state, the custodians of collective memory hope to exhibit the past as "it really was." A key feature for tourists is Freedom Trail, a designated route that takes visitors from Hector Pieterson Square, with its small church and modest community center, to such venues as the residence of the late Pan Africanist Congress leader Zeph Mothopeng, the home of ANC leaders Albertina and Walter Sisulu, and to Vilakazi Street—the only street in the world, tourist guides proudly boast, with the homes of two living Nobel Peace Prize winners (Nelson Mandela and Bishop Desmond Tutu). Other popular "heritage venues" include Baraganith/Chris Hani hospital, frequently described as "the largest medical facility in Africa"; and Regina Mundi, the largest church in Soweto and the site of countless protest rallies, prayer gatherings, and choir festivals. Freedom Square in Kliptown marks the location where the 1956 Congress of the People was convened and the Freedom Charter ratified.[52] Nearby is Avalon cemetery, where resistance luminaries, including Lilian Ngoyi, Joe Slovo, and Helen Joseph, are buried.[53]

Multiple meanings are embedded in such cultural-heritage sites. These meanings are at once significantly different, intensely contested, and mutually constitutive. Township tours have become increasingly popular among casual tourists, international visitors, and curious white suburbanites. In Cape Town, for example, tour guides take visitors to the older, settled ("African") townships of Langa, Nyanga, and Gugulethu, as well as the newer townships and squatter areas, such as Mitchell's Plain and Khayelitsha, located in the Cape Flats.[54] Black travel operators have complained that white companies with little knowledge of the Cape Flats townships have used their superior resources to muscle in on local initiative, organizing whirlwind tours that "turn out to be more like a visit to the zoo in which a visitor gets off the bus, takes a few pictures of the locals and within minutes is out of the area."[55]

The Theatrics of Collective Memory: The Mandela House

Cultural heritage should not be confused with history. As a scholarly discipline, history "seeks to convince by truth, and succumbs to falsehood." In contrast, cultural heritage "exaggerates and omits, candidly invents and frankly forgets, and thrives on ignorance and error."[56] As Rafael Samuel observed, "Heritage is a nomadic term, which travels easily." It is a term that is capricious and malleable enough to accommodate multiple and widely discrepant meanings.[57] Heritage uses historical traces and residues to fashion stories about the past. But these traces and residues "are stitched into fables closed to critical scrutiny." Heritage is neither an empirically testable or verifiable version of the past. Instead, it is a declaration of faith in a contrived past.[58]

The Winnie Mandela and Family Museum, located on Vilikazi Street in Orlando West at the modest house where Winnie Madikizela-Mandela and Nelson Mandela once lived, has become a popular tourist attraction. The Mandela house enjoys its symbolic catchet because it is a place where private memories and public histories intersect. By the late 1990s, it was estimated that the museum was able to draw around a thousand visitors a day and earn between $20,000 and $25,000 per month.

Nelson Mandela and his first wife, Evelyn Ntoko Mase, lived in the house in the early 1940s. The matchbox home, at 8115 Ngakane Street, was Mandela's first house. He and Evelyn moved there in 1946; she moved out after their divorce in 1957. From here, Mandela began his leadership work in the ANC, first as leader of the Youth League, through the 1956 Treason Trial, and then as commander-in-chief of *Umkhonto we Sizwe*. Mandela brought Winnie Madikizela to the house after they were married in the late 1950s, and their two children were born there. It was from this home that Mandela went underground before he was arrested and jailed in 1962.

While Nelson Mandela was incarcerated, Winnie Madikizela-Mandela continued to live in the tiny house with her two daughters, Zeni and Zindzi. After his release from prison on February 12, 1990, Mandela returned here before he and Winnie went to live in the larger Orlando West mansion she had built while he was still imprisoned. However, after his release, he stayed there for a mere eleven days because he was moved from one secret location to the next until he settled into his present Houghton residence. Mandela

FIGURE 19. Winnie Mandela and Family Museum, Orlando East, Soweto. Photograph by William Cobane.

separated from Madikizela-Mandela in 1992 and the couple was divorced in 1996. Although her ex-husband bequeathed the house to the Soweto Heritage Trust to be used as a cultural-heritage site, Madikizela-Mandela refused to relinquish it. Instead, in 1997, she turned it into the Mandela Family Museum and set up a pub and restaurant across the road. Under the guiding hand of crass commercialism, the self-appointed custodians of collective memory who managed the Mandela House adeptly marketed it as an interesting stopover for tourists wanting to experience a "slice of authentic history" about the world's most famous former prisoner.[59]

Officially opened by Deputy Minister of Environmental Affairs and Tourism, Peter Mokaba, in November 1997, the Winnie Mandela and Family Museum epitomizes in a particularly egregious way the nexus between cultural heritage, national identity, and commercialism. The museum exhibit illustrates how an idealized, sanitized version of the past can be turned into a cultural theme park—a commodity for mass consumption. Visitors who come to see where Nelson Mandela lived in Soweto before his imprisonment pay an entrance fee to inspect personal items ranging from a pair of his shoes and his academic gown to gifts from foreign dignitaries and organizations. The souvenir shop peddles memorabilia that range from such kitsch items as key chains and flags to small vials of "Mandela garden soil" extracted from the yard.[60]

In 1998, Winnie Madikizela-Mandela was forced to flee when Soweto youths set the house on fire following allegations that members of the Mandela United Football Club, who acted as her bodyguards, had kidnapped several youths and killed a fourteen-year-old ANC activist named Stompie Moeketsi.[61] As Andreas Huyssen reminds us, formal construction, aesthetic appeal, and persuasive execution remain the *sine qua non* for a memory site to maintain a viable, visible presence in the urban public sphere.[62] By 2004, Soweto Heritage Trust had wrestled back control of the house. After undertaking a significant R9-million restoration (with donations from Standard Bank and Anglo American Corporation) as part of a greater Vilakazi Street heritage project, the museum reopened in March 2009. Besides enclosing the premises behind a high wall, the restoration included the addition of a visitors' center. The restoration of Mandela House is only a small part of a much bigger cultural-heritage intervention in Orlando West. The Vilakazi Street precinct, which has been described as an "outdoor living museum," has become a visitor-friendly tourist destination. The cultural-heritage precinct includes Bishop Desmond Tutu's house on Vilakazi Street, and the Hector Pieterson Museum and Memorial nearby.[63]

7 Textual Memories

Autobiographical Writing in a Time of Uncertainty

The birth of the "new South Africa" brought with it a proliferation of commentaries and essays, autobiographies, memoirs, personal reminiscences, and realist documentaries that explore the quandaries of social institutions and individuals as they attempt to deal honestly and forthrightly with the multiple legacies of tyranny, repression, and rebellion. As Athol Fugard argued, "[After 1994] I felt free to tell personal stories that I would have thought of as an indulgence during those years of apartheid.[1]As a kind of first-person narrative convention, these "mementos" have entered the public discourse as fact-based stories that reflect their particular time and place in history. Autobiographical writing in the aftermath of historical trauma is a cultural manifestation of the personal need to rid oneself of the burden of history, or a kind of therapeutic undertaking designed to reconcile oneself with the past.[2] Yet individual memories only become meaningful when they become social, that is, when they are shared and cross over into the realm of collective-cultural remembrance.[3] The truth-telling impulse inherent in such witness literature reflects the collective engagement of writers committed to the process of putting the past into proper perspective in a "drama of self-definition," or the textual creation of the "new South Africa" through first-person testimonials.[4]

One of the great attractions of all writing—fictional, historiographical, autobiographical—is its ability to resist the temptation to conform to current fashion. Writing provides an imaginative space for the freedom of expression where it is possible to entertain alternatives to the status quo. Thus, literature and other kinds of creative writing can sometimes lead, rather than follow, historical trends, introducing new ideas and ways of thinking from which subsequent political developments can emerge.[5] This prescient quality of imaginatively producing the future before it actually comes into being is present in fiction writing, plays and theatrical performances, visual arts and film.[6]

If national state-crafting occupies the center stage in mapping the transition to parliamentary democracy in post-apartheid South Africa, then autobiographies and personal memoirs are located on the margins. Autobiographies occupy the uncertain "in-between" place between the "self-fashioning" and "truth-telling" built into personal narratives. They offer a glimpse at the human geographies of storytelling. The power—and hence the value—of autobiographies is that they work to recuperate hidden voices, whether pushed out of sight or erased. Personal memories cut through place and take unexpected detours. They can escape memorialization and ossification. Autobiographies can be the residue that remains after official memory has obliterated alternative histories.[7]

Yet valorization of autobiographical writing is not without its limitations. One must take care in looking to personal, "I-witness" accounts to provide a privileged route to the recovery of historical truth. There is a difference between autobiographical remembrance and historical memory. One way to grasp this distinction is to distinguish between the personal act of remembering (autobiography) and the shared activity of memorializing (writing history). Autobiographical writing exemplifies the uncertainty of memory. As a particular type of recollecting the past, it only offers fragments of a dispersed memory, condensing time into memorable episodes, imposing silences on uncomfortable truths, and erasing that which is deemed irrelevant. If sites of memory evolve with the passage of time despite our expectations of durability, autobiographies that valorize, commemorate, or celebrate events and places prove even more porous. "I-witnessing" dispenses with the conventional protocols of truth-telling, substituting instead subjective remembrance for historical accuracy, anecdote for empirically grounded evidence, and opinion for analysis.[8] Because it is constructed by looking backward, memory is always open to revision and embellishment. Because "I-witness" accounts about "what really happened" can easily slip into what *might* have happened or what *should* have happened, one must remain vigilant about the reliability of autobiography as a key to "truth" and historical accuracy.[9]

The idealized formulation of the classic autobiography—the retrospective, chronological narration of a coherent subject reflecting on past events with which the writer was intimately connected—has come under intense scrutiny in recent years. The theoretical debates surrounding life-writing as a literary form have resulted in a destabilization of the categories of fact and fiction, thereby calling into question the reliability and accuracy of autobiographical memory.[10] On the one hand, some argue that memory and history almost always stand in an adversarial relationship to each other. For example, poststructuralist theorists such as Paul John Eakin have gone so far as to argue that all self-narration, including autobiography, is a kind of fabrication or fiction.[11] Because it is socially constructed from the vantage point of hindsight, memory is always open to revision and manipulation, embellishment and deliberate forgetting. This exposure to outside influences makes it an instance of fiction rather than imprint.[12] On the other hand, for scholars like Marita Sturken, history and memory can be more accurately described as "*entangled* rather than oppositional."[13] However they are intertwined and mutually constructed, history and memory certainly have two different modes of address. Memory always implies a subjective, affective relationship with the past. In contrast, history strives to "maintain a sense of distance from the past," that is, to dispassionately, objectively recover what happened and why.[14]

Creative Writing in Uncertain Times

Broadly speaking, literature and other writing practices cannot properly be understood without examining the social conditions of their production and the historical context of their reception. Over the course of more than four decades of apartheid rule, creative writers, artists, filmmakers, and cultural workers of all kinds were invited to lend their voices, to harness their special talents, and to direct their energies to the "cause" of liberation. Without a doubt, the urgency of political opposition to white minority rule encouraged writers to favor certain stylistic modes of presentation over others, to arrogate an up-front, uncompromising mimetic aesthetic capable of faithfully documenting apartheid wrongs, and therefore to attach little importance to the formal dimensions of writing as such, and to minimize experimentation, nuance, and the lighthearted play of ambiguity for its own sake. The moral imperatives of "resistance politics" enjoined writers, including political commentators and essayists, to express their message as directly, unequivocally, and realistically as possible. The call was for "rapid-fire art," where artists, cultural performers, and playwrights were encouraged to produce committed, inspirational work that contributed to the formation of a unifying national culture defined by opposition to white minority rule and resistance to apartheid.[15] It was *de rigueur* for writers, novelists, and poets to incorporate uplifting political themes into their literary works and to express moral outrage at censorship, legalized white supremacy and everyday racism, and the prevailing cultural backwardness.[16] Viewed retrospectively, what is remarkable is the extent to which artistic achievements of such scope and depth were able to come into existence and even flourish in such a "parched place," as Elleke Boehmer put it at the time—a highly regimented, racially compartmentalized social order consisting of stultifying "dead-ends, closures, multiple restrictions on speech and movement, blockages of every kind, spiritual and political."[17]

The collapse of white minority rule and the end of apartheid fundamentally altered the conditions under which creative writing and other forms of cultural expression were produced and received. The relaxation of the moral imperatives of the "liberation struggle" opened up vast new opportunities in literature, art, and theater to explore themes and subjects that were marginalized or censored during the apartheid years. The replacement of "liberation" discourse with the forward-looking language of reconciliation and nation-building has created the imaginative space for open-ended, free-floating experimentation with what Boehmer calls "narrative uncertainty."[18]

Yet, ironically, without the moral compass of the anti-apartheid struggle to guide their work, many politically-conscious writers, artists, and playwrights were cast adrift, searching for vantage points and perspectives around which to center their creative energies.[19] As Njabulo Ndebele put it so eloquently at the time, "With the demise of grand apartheid now certain, what are South African writers now going to write about?"[20] No longer umbilically tied to the distinctive oppositional mode of thinking—the "us-versus-them" binaries of "resistance aesthetics"—that had taken on a life of its own during the apartheid years, writing in the "new South Africa" has sometimes suffered from a "suspension of vision," as one critic put it, a "hemming in as opposed to a convinced and convincing opening up or testing of options," a "cultural or artistic pessimism," and "loss of will."[21] In a particularly provocative essay, Lewis Nkosi suggested that during the transition to parliamentary democracy there existed "an unhealed—I will not say incurable—split between black and white writing, between on the one side an urgent need to document and bear witness and on the other the capacity to go on furlough, to loiter, and to experiment."[22]

Rediscovery of the Ordinary: Creative Writing in Post-Apartheid South Africa

What distinguished the apartheid system from other, more subtle forms of oppression was, as the South African writer and literary critic Njabulo Ndebele put it, "its brazen, exhibitionist openness."[23] For black writers in particular, the imaginative engagement with this "mind-boggling spectacle"—characterized by the violence and brutality of everyday life for most black people, recurrent displays of racial intolerance, and conspicuous consumption in the midst of grinding poverty and degradation—engendered a distinctive manner of thinking that, epistemologically speaking, conceived of the sociopolitical realities of apartheid South Africa "purely in terms of a total polarity of absolutes."[24] This mode of perception gathered momentum over the years and in time crystallized into what came to be called "protest literature." For the most part, the stories of James Matthews, Ezekiel Mphahlele, Alex La Guma, Can Themba, Webster Makaza, Bessie Head, and others fall into this category.[25]

Motivated by outrage and anger, "protest writing," joined together alongside with other forms of cultural and artistic expression, sought to validate itself through the "spectacular dramatization" of the odious, repressive nature of apartheid. In order to achieve its desired effects, this kind of writing represented the victims of the oppressive system in starkly realist terms.[26] As Ndebele put it, "The more the brutality of the system is dramatized, the better; the more exploitation is revealed and starkly dramatized, the better. The more the hypocrisy of liberals is revealed, the better."[27] Similarly, plays—

from *Sizwe Bansi Is Dead* (1973) and *Survival* (1976), to *Woza Albert* (1981), *Asinamali* (1985), *Born in the RSA* (1985), and *Have You Seen Zandile?* (1987), to name only some of the more well known titles—"shared a thematic emphasis on bearing witness to the brutality of apartheid and the effects of state violence not only on the social and political aspirations but also on the bodies, voices, and dreams of the majority of South Africans."[28]

All in all, these various kinds of cultural and artistic expression exhibited similar characteristics: the preoccupation with certain themes, characters, and situations, welded together in a recognizable grammar, expressed in the stylized format of "aesthetic realism," and designed to convey an angry message of moral outrage.[29] The near-exclusive focus on identifying, documenting, and highlighting the evils of apartheid predisposed creative writers of all kinds to favor certain topics over others, to downplay nuance and contradiction, and sometimes to sacrifice aesthetic standards in the service of "politicizing the masses."[30] The exigencies of the "liberation struggle" dictated certain aesthetic orthodoxies, imposed rigorous standards of political relevance, and prescribed the moral responsibility to get as close to the truth as possible. Yoked to the political imperatives of the anti-apartheid struggle, "protest writing"—fictional and otherwise—operated as a front for other kinds of exhortatory communication: for bearing witness, for telling the truth about history, and for informing the world about the evils of apartheid.[31] Viewed through the narrow optic of transforming culture into a weapon of struggle, the primary goal of politically motivated writing was to stimulate a sense of solidarity among the oppressed and to "conscienticize" those not immediately involved or implicated in the freedom struggle.[32] In the counter-hegemonic paradigm of "resistance aesthetics," politically-conscious critics typically judged the literary value and social worthiness of textual and other cultural productions on their capacity to function in the service of liberation.[33] In a word, artistic works were subjected to the litmus test of political "relevance," and any deviation from these exacting standards invited the damning criticism of "fiddling while Rome was burning."[34]

In the mid-1980s, at a time when the South African landscape was still painted in stark chiaroscuro rather than the shaded hues of the post-1994 "rainbow nation," Ndebele worried aloud that the kind of creatively analytic thinking required to imagine a social world after apartheid had become entrapped in an unreflective rhetoric of protest. In suggesting that protest literature had perhaps run its course, he enjoined his fellow *belletrists* to move beyond the almost exclusive preoccupation with viewing the political situation through the narrow lens of a Manichean struggle between "the people" and "the apartheid state" and to explore instead the variegated textures, nuances, and ambiguities of the day-to-day existence of ordinary people.[35] In anticipation of the open-ended future to come, Albie Sachs raised similar concerns around the same time when he issued a carefully worded warning to the antiapartheid movement: "Our [ANC] members should be banned for saying culture is a weapon of struggle."[36] By juxtaposing the "spectacular" representation of "resistance aesthetics" with the mundane "ordinariness" of everyday life, Ndebele offered an alternative to the stylistic demands of "struggle realism" that converted artistic expression into moral obligation. Instead, he called for a mode of oppositional writing that affirmed the capacity for survival in the day-to-day ingenuity and inventiveness of township dwellers, particularly children and mothers.[37]

This prescient appeal for a genuine post-apartheid literary imagination struck a responsive chord with a wide range of well-known South African writers, academics, and cultural workers. With the collapse of white minority rule, the stylistic, aesthetic, and political orthodoxies that had influenced anti-apartheid writing appeared to lose much of their raison d'être and relevance. With these changing circumstances, the underlying premise of "resistance aesthetics"—that literature and other kinds of creative writing finds its theoretical grounding, moral value, and cultural relevance in political practice—seemed vaguely quaint and anachronistic. In questioning the continued relevance of cloistering written expression within the mimetic codes and didactic demands of "aesthetic realism," key writers and literary figures such as Lewis Nkosi, J. M. Coetzee, Nadine Gordimer, Albie Sachs, André Brink, and others insist that the novelty and aesthetic value of creative writing comes with the freedom to explore imaginary spaces unencumbered by the stultifying stylistic conventions and moral strictures of "protest literature." In their view, the defining characteristic of literature is that it brings to life and amplifies those areas of personal and social experience that political discourse generally cannot reach.[38]

The various kinds of artistic expression that came into existence and developed as a visceral response to apartheid were never so monolithic in style and unitary in purpose that they were bound together in a single, consensual paradigmatic reaction. The production of a "resistance aesthetic" at ground zero has always been a more diverse and fragmented process than those who wished to transform culture into a "weapon of struggle" would care to admit. Writers are an unruly, irascible lot, and the sheer diversity of themes, styles, and narratological strategies embedded in novels, social commentaries, essays, plays, and poetry are difficult if not impossible to classify into hermetically sealed subtypes. Even such commonplace distinctions as the difference between "white writing" and "black writing," or the dissimilarity between English and Afrikaans literature, fail to yield the kinds of meaningful differences that those who use these labels would have us believe.[39]

The "Memoir Boom": "I-Witnessing" in the Twilight of Apartheid

The collapse of oppressive regimes is often portrayed in art and literature as an apocalyptic occurrence. As James Berger has argued, such events function as "definitive historical divides, as ruptures, pivots, fulcrums, separating what came before from what came after," and reveal "the true nature of what has been brought to an end."[40] The end of apartheid and the birth of the "new South Africa" triggered an explosion of cathartic writing, ranging from autobiographies, reminiscences, and memoirs to novels, social commentaries, and journalistic *tours d'horizon.* This new alertness to introspective reflection paralleled similar shifts in scholarly fields of inquiry as well, where researchers have dared to become more intimate and familiar in their writing, interjecting self-portraiture, personal perspective, and feeling—"what it means to me"—into their otherwise empirically grounded, carefully footnoted monographs.[41]

Despite its limitations, autobiographical writing offers a particularly fertile ground for the exploration of collective remembrance. Focusing attention on autobiographical writing means seeing politics played out symbolically in metaphorical space where discourses, or those finite patterns of words and ideas that literary theorists have referred to as "scripts," shape the way writers not only understand the past but also their vision of the future. Autobiographical writing contains sets of oppositions that reveal the contradictory, ambivalent, ambiguous character of the transition to parliamentary democracy. Memoirs, personal reminiscences, and diaries supply some of the pieces of evidence that indicate how particular individuals from different backgrounds and subject positions experienced apartheid and its demise in very different ways. Taking this writing at face value, it is possible to reconstruct a sense of the multiple, and sometimes contradictory, journeys that accompanied the transition to parliamentary democracy.

During transitional periods where the eventual political outcome is far from certain, the attraction of first-person narrative should come as no surprise. For in accounting for the passage of time that connects the past to the present, this kind of storytelling enriches the imagination because it enables prescient writers to point toward possibilities for everyday life other than the one we live and to anticipate a common culture of shared understandings. By rummaging around history in search of a usable past, stories build consensus and create their own solidaristic bonds. They represent cohesion and order, convey shared understandings and meanings, dispense with ambiguity, and express widely held optimism or pessimism about future possibilities. Personal reflections, impressions, and vignettes are powerful heuristic devices that can challenge received wisdoms, subvert cherished myths, and call into question seemingly "naturalized" moral orders inherited from the past.[42] As Nadine Gordimer put it, "[The interregnum is] not only between two social orders but between two identities, one known and discarded, the other unknown and undetermined." For white writers who have declared themselves in favor of embracing that future, there exists an uncertainty about whether they "will find [their] 'home at last' in the 'new South Africa.'"[43]

The resurgence of autobiography as a distinctive form of literary expression in post-apartheid South Africa is part of a broader shift in the popular belletristic landscape of Europe and North America. Autobiographical writing is a kind of cultural cartography animated by the desire to cognitively map the past as it was experienced, to center it on a certain thematic point, to produce explanatory narratives, and to assign fixed, stable meanings to events and the persons who participated in them. Autobiographies represent the past in written text. The appeal of autobiography as a way of writing South Africa is twofold: first, by offering an insider's view of someone who "was there," it personalizes key historical events and processes; and second, by providing an intimate glimpse of personal motives, opinions, and feelings not available anywhere else, it humanizes the past. In autobiographies, the subject-position of the author figures prominently in the narrative, as "I-witnessing" inscribes an aura of authority and authenticity, and a sense of finality and closure, to the account. This kind of public rehearsal of memory provides storytellers with a public platform by which to situate themselves in history and to reconstruct their own lives as an unfolding journey—a progressive unveiling of certain truths in the past that point the way to the future.[44]

Although atrocity is often represented through the language of the unspeakable, the power of what is and can be spoken, especially through memoirs, personal testimonials, or "I-witness" literature, has continued to play a compelling role after the transition to parliamentary democracy. The overall impact of such storytelling is often understood through the lens of trauma theory, in which personal testimonials provide an important therapeutic exercise for traumatized individuals seeking to reconcile themselves with the terrible circumstances of their past experiences.[45] Those victims who have suffered at the hands of oppressive regimes tell stories that range from accounts of pain and trauma to narratives of survival and resistance. The goals of this storytelling vary from victims seeking compensation to survivors demanding justice. Often victims regard the telling of their own personal stories as essential, either in terms of bearing witness to hidden "truths" or in terms of recovery and healing.[46] For many victims and survivors of injustice, personal testimony is rooted in a struggle against oblivion, a struggle always to remember so as never to forget.[47]

With their almost fetishized fixation on verifiable facts and fact-checking, professional historians typically remain skeptical of what Susan Crane has called "the unincorporated realm of personal historical memory." As a consequence, they tend to view autobiographical writing as a possible source of almost calculated and willful misrepresentation, an ingrained stylistic feature of the genre itself, and something that follows from the "lack of understanding of the knowledge and interpretation available from competently performed historical study."[48] As a self-constructed site where the personal assumes a public form, autobiographical writing contains an "excess" of memory.[49] As numerous scholars have pointed out, the "poetics" of personal testimonies and "I-witness" accounts rest less on factual evidence of events than a meaningful interpretation of the experience itself.[50] As a distinct variety of narration, autobiographical writing is never value-free and objective.

It is a kind of "translation tool" that threads together disparate events, feelings, experiences, and relationships into coherent stories.[51]

One of the strengths of autobiographical writing is its capacity to provide a free-flowing space partially insulated from the pressures dictated by rigors of scholarly production. Autobiographical writing is a powerful vehicle that enables the raconteur—in the guise of a truth-seeking chronicler or storyteller—to sanction a particular way of seeing the past, to represent as fact what is often opinion or even hearsay, and to reconfigure existing understandings of events and people, times and places. In their haste and exuberance to "set the story straight," autobiographical accounts may contain willful prejudices and distortions and elisions of the truth. Without the rigorous rules of evidence that govern scholarly research, autobiographers may choose to ignore unsettling truths, to downplay alternative points of view, and overlook personal failures and poor judgment.[52]

Autobiographical Writing as Catharsis and Revelation

Autobiographical writing is a notoriously slippery and capricious genre.[53] As Roger Luckhurst has argued, "The memoir boom is now a vast and complicated delta region with major channels but also curious back-waters, and is treacherous to map."[54] In his novel *Sugar and Rum,* Barry Unsworth inquires: "How much of [the past] is truly remembered? How much embroidered, how much invented?" In response to his own question, he suggests: "Does it matter? Memories have to be aided by invention or they could not be formulated at all."[55]

Because of its commitment to verifiable truth, empirical accuracy, and documentary proof, autobiographical writing is "not quite fiction."[56] Correlatively, because of its refusal to be bound by the rigorous canons of objectivity, impartiality, and appropriate distance, it is "not quite history."[57] In fact, what gives autobiographical writing its distinctiveness, it uniqueness of insight, are exactly those stylistic features that are the most suspect in scholarly production: partisanship, the emphasis on personal opinion instead of critical analysis, and the reliance upon personal memory rather than archivally stored and cross-checked documentary records. The autobiographer is not a neutral medium, an innocent raconteur, through which events more or less "write themselves." Autobiography is a textual mode of expression mediated by the circumstances of its coming-into-being. Rather than reflecting the unvarnished truth of the past, autobiographical writing reflects a specific point of view and emanates from what the author wants us to hear. It is an interpretive act rather than a mimetic art. Autobiographers are active agents in shaping a narrative in which events, dramatis personae, and contexts are selected, ordered, dramatized, simplified, downplayed, and passed over in silence. Seen from this angle, autobiographies acquire their historical significance less as faithful renditions of what actually happened and more as depictions of life as lived experience. The appeal of autobiography for writer and audience alike lies in its twofold character: it is revelatory, and it is cathartic. The privileged place that autobiography enjoys as a source of reliable information lies in the insider's intimacy with the events portrayed and personalities described. The "higher truth" of autobiography rests with its claims to "I-witnessing."[58]

The stories that South Africans tell about themselves after the formal end of apartheid generally fall into five broad categories.[59] The first is the "documentary-realist" autobiography, the primary purpose of which is to reveal "hidden truths" long suppressed and unavailable elsewhere. In contrast to diaristic modes of writing originally constructed solely for private purposes, formal autobiographies of the "documentary-realist" kind are intended, as Marc Bloch pointed out years ago, for a public and frequently posterior audience. By focusing on the "inner truths" of the past as subjectively lived, this mode of storytelling often provides the most comprehensive, and comprehensible, account of the personal experience of historical events.[60] "Documentary-realist" reminiscences achieve their full political effect by taking what Georg Lukács called a "social-historical and not merely individual-biographical standpoint."[61] The second category of biographical writing is "struggle" narratives. While their aims typically dovetail with "documentary-realist" accounts, they also seek to humanize the political struggle against the white minority regime and the apartheid system. The third category is "exile" narratives. By focusing on personal lives torn asunder by the inhuman logic of the apartheid system, these autobiographical accounts retrace journeys of departure and return. What establishes the authority of these kinds of stories is the repetitive gesture of affixing meaning to a place, a particular spatial location, through the conjoined sense of longing and belonging. The fourth category is "confessional" narratives, which tell stories of conversion. Scripted as transformative explorations of the self, these are stories of redemption and hope, embodying liberal-humanist values of racial harmony that signal the triumph of the human spirit over prejudice and discrimination. Fifth, and finally, "alarmist" narratives are futurist, eschatological tales that warn of impending doom. They exemplify a dystopian, apocalyptic discourse of fear, anxiety, and disavowal. They operate as powerful vehicles for the politics of negation—a dismissive repudiation of the transformative, progressive consequences of the transition to democracy in post-apartheid South Africa.

While kinds of questions addressed and the themes considered overlap to some degree, these distinct modes of autobiographical writing diverge significantly with regard to style, tone, and purpose. The style can vary from the didactic to the revelatory. The tone can range from self-congratulatory and self-aggrandizing to the self-depreciating and apologetic. The purposes can vary from the desire to illuminate, enlighten, and inform to the desire to motivate, warn, and console.

The sheer variety of stories told during and after South Africa's transition to democracy reflects the divergence of opinion regarding the substantive and symbolic meaning of the "new South Africa." These differences reflect enduring tensions inherent in "I-witnessing" accounts and personal testimonials. Instead of reading autobiographical accounts as "genuine" (that is, factually accurate) recollections of actual events, and judging their dubious veracity accordingly, it also makes sense to interpret them as rhetorically constructed stories of the relation of narrated past to narrating present within the life history of a particular individual.[62] Seen in this light, autobiographical accounts reveal their "true" historical value less through their manifest informational content than through their rhetorical devices, their dialogic relations with the imagined past, and their discernible traces of subjectivity. To read autobiographies in this way means to interpret "I-witnessing" accounts as a kind of mythmaking exercise that connects the self to a particular place and time, that asserts a group and national identity, and that projects an imaginary future. Viewed from this angle, autobiographies become most important to understanding the transition to post-apartheid South Africa not as factually-accurate, truthful accounts of the course of events but as "indications of *projection* and *mood,* of what participants might have thought happened around them and of how they might remember feeling while it was occurring."[63]

These discourses of revelation, struggle, exile, conversion, and alarm do not produce fixed or unified objects. They do not crystallize into hermetically sealed "types." Rather, they overlap and collude as much as they operate in conflict.[64] As a subtype of narrative discourse, these "I-witnessing" accounts provide what Paul Ricoeur called "allegories of temporality," that is, different autobiographical remembrances of what it means to live in time.[65] Whatever their similarities and differences, these stories have played an important role in generating the animating myths surrounding the birth of the "new South Africa," in influencing the popular views of what the post-apartheid future might bring and shaping the dynamics between remembering and forgetting.[66]

"Documentary-Realist" Narratives

The peculiar moral appeal of the South African liberation struggle and its resonance in the international politics of late twentieth-century antiracism and decolonization amplified whatever other sociopolitical forces were at work to transform Nelson Mandela from a failed guerrilla commander languishing in prison into a modern-day folk hero.[67] The distinction conferred on him by seclusion and his absence from active politics created fertile ground for the development of celebrity status of grand, mythical proportions. The Commonwealth Eminent Persons Group, which was granted an audience with Mandela at Pollsmoor prison in 1985, described him as a "legend in his own lifetime."[68] His twenty-seven-year incarceration and isolation from public view kept Mandela in a virtual state of suspended animation, thereby ensuring that public, hagiographic narratives about his life and times were shaped by whatever words and images were available from the epic struggle that stretched from the mid-1950s Defiance Campaign to the 1962 Rivonia treason trial. Official bans on publication of his words and portraits kept the story of his life simple and pristine, investing him with the glamorous appeal of martyrdom and transforming the imprisoned guerrilla convict into a patriotic icon.[69]

Mandela's triumphant return to public life in 1990 and his subsequent election in 1994 to the office of the state presidency were marked by an overwhelming outpouring of popular adulation bordering on hero worship. Mandela is still almost universally regarded as a talismanic figure, the archetypal finder and keeper of the good fortune of the "new South Africa." Whatever his personal inadequacies or official mistakes as head of state, these shortcomings have done little to diminish the omnibus appeal of his authority or to tarnish his reputation as the chief public spokesperson of South African reconciliation.

As Raymond Williams has argued, "[It is possible for] a unique life, in a place and a time, [to speak] from its own uniqueness and yet [to speak] a common experience."[70] By using the circumstances of their own lives to shed light on universal problems of truth, justice, and forgiveness, the stories that key figures tell about themselves can sometimes transcend the conventional boundaries of autobiography and become, in the process, paradigmatic narratives of national identity and "nation-building." Mandela's autobiography, *Long Walk to Freedom,* has become perhaps the most influential force in shaping popular views of the period.[71] Reproduced in an abridged, illustrated version suitable for schoolchildren, this story of an exemplary life has been metamorphosized into official memory, a key element in the institutionalized remembrance of the heroic struggle against apartheid and the triumph of self-sacrifice and "goodwill" over evil and adversity. At a time when the old ways were disappearing fast, Mandela's account of who he was and what he became effectively operated as a fixed point of moral reference when nothing else seemed particularly stable or reliable.[72]

The myth of Mandela consists in the rather Panglossian view that his life story represents the embodiment of the roseate ideals of the liberation struggle. Some biographers of Mandela have taken on the task of replacing the larger-than-life, mythical hero preordained for greatness with a more balanced portrait of a fallible human being with all his strengths and weaknesses.[73] Yet, ironically, these efforts to separate the man from the myth have only enhanced his stature as a charismatic leader. One of the virtues of autobiography is that it furnishes a powerful and eloquent sense of the complex ways that the past impinges on the present. In *Long Walk to Freedom,* Mandela chronicles his own epic journey, which focuses primarily on his participation and leadership in the aboveground political struggles of the turbulent 1950s, the turn to armed struggle in the early 1960s, his capture and long-term incarceration, and his eventual release from prison to assume the helm of the newly unbanned ANC. He recounts those experiences that led him to make the sorts of choices that he did. The transcendent goal of freedom figures prominently in his narrative, operating as the central leitmotif against which Mandela measures the actions of himself and others.[74]

Autobiographies are a particular kind of writing that valorizes the present moment by treating the end-point of the story as the seemingly inevitable consequence of what came before. By focusing attention on choices made in contrast to those not made, autobiographers screen out alternative possibilities. In *Long Walk to Freedom,* Mandela treats his early experiences as necessary building blocks that, when pieced together with what came later, produce the man that we see before us. There is an almost teleological quality to the narrative. The end-point of the story—the collapse of apartheid and the demise of white minority rule—is treated as the inexorable, inevitable culmination of what came before.

Because of their capacity to define the terms of its engagement with the past, autobiographies can sometimes lead rather than follow historical developments, creating a language from which subsequent political developments can be enframed, conceptualized, and interpreted. It is at this juncture where past and future complement each other. One of the principal rhetorical aims of Mandela's autobiography is to convince a skeptical white audience that the ANC, as both a political movement and as the government-of-the-day, cherishes the ideals of nonracialism, multiparty democracy, and political accountability. In reconstructing his own life history, Mandela writes forcefully in the service of the political cause of national reconciliation. In its treatment of his own personal story as representative of a wider spirit of resistance, its unifying sense of calling and vocation, and its stylistic sensitivity to the art of persuasion, *Long Walk to Freedom* effectively opens a dialogue "with a still resistant white world."[75]

Documentary-realist writers usually communicate their true autobiographical selves more through shades of opinion, self-reflection, and the recounting of personal experiences than by means of objectively verifiable accounts of what happened and why. First-person narratives employ voice—both their own and that of others—not just to describe past events but also to position themselves dialogically in the process of storytelling. Autobiographers not only speak from an identifiable location in the social world, but they also "ventriloquate," that is, speak through others as a way of reinforcing their own point of view. In *Long Walk to Freedom,* Mandela makes use of a number of literary and stylistic devices to convey his message about the inevitable unfolding of freedom. By moving back and forth between the direct, anecdotal first-person singular and the first-person plural, he endows his life story with an air of authority often missing in memoirist accounts. *Long Walk to Freedom* does not rely upon Mandela's recollections alone but is the result of a collaborative effort that includes at least half a dozen personal friends and acquaintances who were consulted at various stages in writing the manuscript. Mandela's frequent use of the collective "we" enables him seamlessly to merge personal memoir with public history, a storytelling maneuver that allows biography to substitute for verifiable historical accuracy.[76]

What is often overlooked is how language, voice, and rhetoric in autobiographical writing frame the debates and shape attitudes about the future. The way that Mandela positioned himself in relation to others stands in stark contrast to F. W. de Klerk's posturing. *Long Walk to Freedom* is inundated with allusions to political struggle, sacrifice and commitment, and collective achievement. In contrast, *The Last Trek—A New Beginning* is a rather wooden exercise in self-fashioning enframed within the discourses of state authority.[77] While Mandela takes every opportunity to speculate about the advantageous fruits of victory, de Klerk is at great pains to distance himself from the tarring brush of defeat. In *The Last Trek,* de Klerk narrates himself at the center of history, as both a responsible head of state and a prescient visionary capable of "doing the right thing." While he provides a useful account of what happened, detailing the smallest minutiae of the negotiating process leading to the creation of the "new South Africa," he assiduously avoids tackling the all-important question of "why."

De Klerk looks back with little remorse or regret. Not surprisingly, he claims no knowledge of any of the "dirty secrets" of the apartheid military-security complex, including assassinations, false imprisonment, and torture that took place during his time as state president. *The Last Trek—A New Beginning* is freighted with the pious certitude of a self-serving leader of a governing political party who self-righteously continued to believe long after the fact that he singlehandedly altered the course of history, and that others—mainly those in the political opposition—owe him an enormous debt of gratitude for his vision, foresight, and initiative. De Klerk admits to the moral indefensibility of white supremacy, and he acknowledges the leading role of the National Party in pursuing racialist policies over the past half a century. But these small gestures are dwarfed by his unwillingness to offer anything more than the most vapid apology for the disastrous consequences of apartheid policies on the lives of millions of black people.

In a particularly boorish game that amounts to "one-upmanship," de Klerk is quick to point out the times where he believes that Nelson Mandela slighted him or treated him badly, a man whom he depicts as much more of an in-fighter than the official hagiographic portrait reveals. The end of apartheid was indeed the consequence of a moral struggle, but it was at root the result of political negotiation and compromise. The most fascinating features of *The Last Trek* is de Klerk's retelling of the delicate balancing act that brought an end to apartheid, including the bitter feuds, the animosity among adversaries, and the shifting coalitions.[78]

In his role as a servant of the public with a responsibility to maintain social order and a duty to protect the rights of citizens, De Klerk represents himself as an elder statesman seeking a middle road between two extremes. He accuses his opponents of exploiting the discourse of constitutional rights for their own ends and tries to demolish the various "myths" that accumulated around his role as the last white resident of the Republic of South Africa. He reduces the negotiations process to a crude simplicity and casts aspersions on those who fail to conform to his moral universe. *The Last Trek* is animated by a kind of sneering vituperation reserved for those who fail to recognize his self-styled, well-mannered *noblesse oblige.* Autobiographical writing incites narcissism. In *The Last Trek,* de Klerk wraps himself in such elaborate self-justification that he can eliminate any nagging doubt about his responsibility for apartheid rule. By attributing ungracious, selfish, and self-serving motives to his opponents, de Klerk is able to invent himself as the accommodating, selfless voice of reason and to demonize his adversaries—particularly Mandela—as unreasonable, dogmatic, and rigid. In the end, there is little new or enlightening in this story.[79]

First-person narratives are powerful vehicles through which black autobiographers challenge extant white discourses on race and racial politics and enter into public debates about setting future agendas guiding "nation-building." The act of writing becomes a public affirmation of "authentic selves secure in their individual worth, group pride, and the humanity of black people."[80] In *Crossing Boundaries,* Mamphela Ramphele, the former vice-chancellor of the University of Cape Town, provides a highly personalized, inwardly focused testimonial of her own coming of age as a black woman in apartheid South Africa.[81] For Ramphele, the act of writing becomes a public way of establishing a racial authentication of self. She uses the technique of autobiographical writing to fashion a narrative identity that subverts stereotypical portrayals of black women as submissive, powerless, and passive. The single most pronounced thread that connects the different parts of Ramphele's story is her rejection of the image of black victimization at the hands of white racism in favor of a self-empowered black female self at the center of her identity. For Ramphele, self-confidence is one of the fundamental ingredients in the recipe for engendering power on one's own person. She draws upon numerous examples of her own transgressive behavior to suggest ways that black women coming of age in the "new South Africa" might successfully navigate their own survival in a hostile environment filled with racist and gendered stereotypes.

The journey that Ramphele narrates proceeds through distinct stages. Starting from an awareness of a contingent self ("my roots," as she puts it), she recounts how participation in the 1970s Black Consciousness movement enabled her, along with a whole generation of black activists, to turn to their own resources and discover a power in their own powerlessness. Yet the liberating zeitgeist of Black Consciousness failed to shield her from the personal pain and suffering brought about by traumatic experiences of imprisonment and banning. The pivotal moment in her life was the murder of her friend and lover Steve Biko. His death set in motion an unanticipated chain of events that forced Ramphele to find ways to assuage her feelings of despondency and depression, grief and bereavement. *Crossing Boundaries* reveals black female identity as a process of ongoing reinvention of self under the pressures of race, class, and gender oppression. Ramphele's story is a narrative that speaks to coming of age as a black female in South Africa and surviving beyond the victimization of whiteness. This story shapes black female identity in such a way that the self, however fashioned, is a witness against racism and not its absolute victim. Ramphele finds solace in a faith grounded in spiritual beliefs and rejoices in her feminist consciousness.[82]

In documentary-realist autobiographies, the connection with a particular "generation" has a powerful significance. By merging their own personal stories with those of their generation, autobiographers link biography with history. Mandela's formative political identity was forged in the cauldron of ANC

Youth League politics in the late 1940s and early 1950s. The social forces that crystallized during this tumultuous period paved the way for the formation of a distinct "generation" of political activists, among them Oliver Tambo, Walter Sisulu, Ahmad Kathrada, Robert Sobukwe, Joe Slovo, and Govan Mbeki. *Long Walk to Freedom* is inundated with insightful thick descriptions of the ANC Youth League generation. In contrast, Ramphele situates her own life story within the context of the origins of the Black Consciousness movement. She carries her connection with the political activism of the 1970s and her intense relationship with Steve Biko as a badge of honor. The events surrounding the 1976 Soweto Uprising and the subsequent repression left an indelible imprint on the consciousness of politicized youth and spawned an entire generation of political activists who shared a sense of common identity.

Ramphele's story parallels the grand narrative of the crisis and collapse of white minority rule. Like Mandela, she seeks a symbolic equilibrium through a process of mourning that successfully "works through" her personal trauma and loss. The conjoined tropes of grief and bereavement, suffering and healing, enable her to tell a highly personalized, metaphorical "story" about public, metonymical "history."[83] The central place that these experiences occupy in her autobiographical account is significant not because they provide an accurate portrayal of the course of events, but because they convey a mood: the sense of belonging to a distinct political "generation" and a feeling of living through the period.[84]

In their reconstruction of the past, autobiographies are not immune from the influences of present-day political imperatives. "I-witnessing" accounts typically contain narrative discontinuities, conspicuous silences, and lapses of memory. Whether intentional or not, these gaps in the story line inadvertently privilege particular lines of interpretive inquiry over others. In *Long Walk to Freedom,* Mandela virtually ignores the Black Consciousness movement and Steve Biko. In contrast, *Crossing Boundaries* downplays whatever influence the ANC might have had during the 1970s.[85]

Like other kinds of first-person "true confessions," autobiographies and memoirs enter into public discourse as mementos, or cultural expressions, of particular times and places. Autobiographical accounts constructed during the heyday of white minority rule typically focused attention on the brutality, inhumanity, and degradation of apartheid, chronicling tales of victimhood matched by the heroism and self-sacrifice of the political opposition. In contrast, the current historical conjuncture, inscribed as it is with reconciliation, favors autobiographical accounts that stress such uplifting themes as redemption, forgiveness, and contrition. With the end of apartheid, autobiographical writing provides a public platform for "remaking" the past for the purposes of promoting the ideals of common citizenship, nonracial democracy, and human rights. Unlike those who wrote within but not beyond apartheid, Mandela, Ramphele, and others write in a historical period in which the process of personal healing mirrors the impulse toward national reconciliation. The refusal of these autobiographers to dwell on the bitter memories of the past, their focus on healing and forgiveness, and their positive outlook for the future mirror the wider impulse toward national reconciliation.

"Struggle" Narratives: Stories of Heroism and Sacrifice

One striking example of self-conscious autobiographical writing is the genre that can be called "struggle" narratives. This stylized mode of storytelling typically follows a scripted choreography that fuses documentary realism with personal, and sometimes poignant, intimacy. What gives this genre its peculiar raison d'être is that in each instance the writer-as-activist inserts his or her own personal stories as *exemplars* of a governing master narrative of political struggle that both asserts a heroic self-identity and repudiates the dismissive discourses of state power.[86] "Struggle" narratives enable activist-writers to assert the typicality of their own experiences, where the story of one's own life is an exemplary instance that reflects a common thread linking countless others in a similar predicament with shared purpose.[87] By engaging in what amounts to a romantic valorization of resistance from below, this kind of writing privileges the vision of the oppressed.[88]

Earlier examples of this kind of "life story" autobiographies, such as *Down Second Avenue* (Ezekiel Mphahlele) and *Tell Freedom* (Peter Abrahams), illustrate this genre of memoir writing.[89] These stories are filled with an assemblage of anecdotes detailing heroism, self-sacrifice in the face of hardship, and tireless dedication. In the typical case, "struggle" narratives are stripped of such individualist features as childbearing, child rearing, and leisure activities as somehow self-indulgent, and there is little room for regret, remorse, or doubt.

Moral exhortations and evocative "lessons of struggle" provide the requisite narrative cohesion. The overriding concern of these "life stories" is to demonstrate how the writer-activist triumphed in spite of adversity, tragedy, and hardship, and thereby provide moral prescriptions for *la lotta continua*.[90] The anti-apartheid struggle produced an outpouring of first-person accounts chronicling individual stories of tragedy and eventual triumph in the wholesale efforts to undermine white minority rule. Personal reminiscences like *Soft Vengeance of a Freedom Fighter* (Albie Sachs) and *Inside Apartheid's Prison* (Raymond Suttner) exemplify the poignancy and catharsis of "struggle" writing.[91]

Autobiographical writing in the "struggle" mode is a particularly expressive kind of performance art. In his autobiography, *Armed and Dangerous*, Ronnie Kasrils, former *Umkhonto we Sizwe* (MK) field commander and deputy secretary of defense in the Mandela cabinet, provides a heroic portraiture of the armed struggle against the apartheid regime.[92] What emerges in this autobiography is the dedication, self-sacrifice, and commitment of thousands of MK cadres in their battle with the state security and military apparatuses. While Kasrils is at pains to express regret and remorse about the tragic deaths of comrades-in-arms, he is rarely troubled by self-doubt. In the end, *Armed and Dangerous* all too often falls into the trap of a swashbuckling, romantic adventure story, a kind of "cloak-and-dagger" tale of intrigue, deception, and plotting.[93] Kasrils inventively cobbles together what are partly satirical, often lyrical, sometimes fantastic elements into a seamless web of heroic resistance against apartheid.[94] Yet a heavy-handed, didactic undercurrent boils just beneath the surface of the story line.[95]

In his interpretation of the past, the moral superiority of MK is self-evident, where MK military successes are spectacular, defeats strengthen resolve, and mistakes are regrettable. This particular allegorical "reading" of history enables Kasrils to find the continuity he seeks, that is, to establish the unbroken threads linking the past to the present. Yet *Armed and Dangerous* is remarkably evasive at key junctures, particularly regarding the politics of negotiation. The version of history that Kasrils offers is one that legitimates his own post-1990 political positions. The past becomes a fertile resource for locating himself within the discourse of resistance politics and the eventual turn toward a negotiated compromise with the white minority regime.[96]

The principal goal of revelatory narratives is to "set the record straight" by offering a stylized retelling of personal experiences from the inside. "Struggle" narratives carry the added freight of political commentary. These stories of heroism, self-sacrifice, and political commitment provide a convenient way for well-known political luminaries to communicate the experiences and values of a radical liberation struggle to a largely ignorant, skeptical audience that remains suspicious of the ANC's motives and ultimate goals.[97]

"Confessional" Narratives: Stories of Conversion

J. M. Coetzee identifies a particular mode of autobiographical writing that he refers to as "the *confession,*" an approach that is "distinct from the memoir and the apology, on the basis of an underlying motive to tell an essential truth about the self."[98] "Confessional" narratives are a distinctive subgenre of autobiography in which authors explicitly seek to divulge intimate and often traumatic details of their own lives, to reveal painful and often shameful memories, as a way of communicating or expressing "the essential nature, the truth of self."[99] The logic of "confessional" discourse differs sharply from that of other kinds of autobiographical writing. Whereas "documentary-realist" autobiographies enrich our historical understanding of the past by examining the connection between individual biography and history, "confessional" narratives are crafted as intensively subjective explorations of the self that are principally concerned with the ethical dimensions of personal growth. "Confessional" writing of this sort focuses attention on private memories and closely guarded secrets, responds to the impulse to bear witness, and opens to public scrutiny that which had been private. The events that are recounted invariably focus on error and transgression, narrated in the service not of memorialization but of erasure. Confession is an act of memory that seeks to annul the maleficence of the past in order to achieve absolution or to gain some kind of individual or social purification. Put in another way, this kind of autobiography seeks to neutralize memory in order "to free the future from the past."[100] This process of self-disclosure enables autobiographers to relieve themselves of the shameful burden of guilt, regret, or remorse, and to exhort others to follow suit.[101] "In confession," Richard Terdiman has suggested, "one remembers in order to forget."[102]

Confession recounts events that lead to conversion. Revealing secrets is a way of asking for forgiveness. Narratives structured around "conversion" are highly personalized stories that are typically fashioned around a mélange of anecdotes stitched together in a loosely structured mosaic. As Terdiman argues, "They narrate the process by which a defective past is transformed into an integral present."[103] These are existential exercises in dramaturgy where the central characters are initially imprisoned within their own fate but are able to wrest their way free of the constraints of culture, family, and race.

This "confessional" self-disclosure provides a useful means by which white writers in the "new South Africa" typically make use of the literary trope of an epic journey, or a vision quest, in order to explore and problematize their own racial identities. These metaphorical journeys are vehicles that enable white writers to address the ethical dilemmas of coming of age in "racist" South Africa, to explore the complexities of personal growth, and to offer spiritual, moral, and social guidance for those who may wish to follow in their footsteps. "Conversion" narratives typically assume an unrelativized first-person perspective where the structure is episodic and fragmented rather than linear and chronological, and the stories themselves revolve around self-revelatory experiences. With the benefit of hindsight, autobiographers focus on those key moments that are considered as turning points in the development of a life history. Such moments always disrupt an initial state of nescient innocence, thereby putting in motion a corrosive process of self-doubt, where one's confidence in seeing the world in one way is abruptly, irrevocably, called into question.[104] The axiological force of this "confessional self-accounting" is that it enables the storyteller to frame episodes in the language of epiphanies—those liminal moments, like Paul on the Road to Damascus—that signal a "change of heart," or a turning point in personal consciousness and understanding that brings about a sudden, unexpected shift from blissful ignorance to self-awareness.[105]

"Conversion" narratives adopt a strict hermetic code by means of which the autobiographer raises questions, creates suspense and mystery, before moving on to the inevitable "uplifting" resolution. What provides narrative coherence is a sense of problem-solving, where "working things out"—or reaching a higher understanding—conforms to what Georg Lukács referred to as "a kind of ratiocinative or emotional teleology."[106] "Conversion" narratives typically assume the characteristics of personal reminiscences, or personal memoirs, rather than autobiography in a strict sense. Whereas autobiography is writing from a beginning toward a destination by integrating scattered events into an integrated and coherent whole, memoirs typically focus on narrowly defined moments of a life—often those that symbolize victimhood, a traumatic experience, or an awakening. The persuasive force of this kind of inward-looking writing emanates less from the "freeing of memory" characteristic of "cause writing" than from the bequeathing of a "model" life.[107] Narrators want to illustrate how they have moved from an initial condition of ignorance to their present state of knowledge—unlearning what they had previously learned. For them, the process of documenting their life experiences constitutes a redemptive act whereby they forge a new identity for themselves. Such an identity requires a repudiation of the past and an assertion of a hopeful and forward-looking outlook for the future.[108]

Confessional memoirs fall under what Ross Chambers has termed "aftermath cultures," defined by a testimonial impulse to "set the story straight," but one that is nevertheless marked by a "strange nexus of denial and acknowledgement."[109] Memoirs of this sort come to life through an irresolvable tension between attraction and repulsion. "Confessional" narratives are impelled by the need to tell the truth, but they are also overwhelmed by guilt and remorse. It is here where private experience meets with, and becomes, public knowledge.[110]

Wilhelm Verwoerd's *My Winds of Change* exemplifies the principal stylistic features of a "conversion" narrative.[111] What gives this coming-of-age story during the dying days of white minority rule its wider historical significance, and what imprints it with "universalizing" authority and its broad appeal, is that Verwoerd is the grandson of Hendrik Frensch Verwoerd, the hard-line former prime minister (1958–66), who is generally regarded as the chief architect of what has been called Grand Apartheid. This story of Verwoerd's "change of heart"—gradual and painful—bears all the hallmarks of the confessional. In recalling those unsettling experiences that led him to renounce his blinkered past and to formally join the ANC in 1992, he traces the genealogy of his own awakening, conversion, and redemption. He describes his upbringing, safely cocooned within the racially coded edifice of apartheid, and recounts those key moments that resulted in self-doubt, confusion, and angst. Verwoerd anchors his story in the intense personal conflicts that he experiences in trying to reconcile the meaning of his Afrikaans heritage with the new identity he acquires by discarding the racially encoded values of his youth and by embracing the conciliatory vision of a nonracial "new South Africa." By alluding to Harold Macmillan's famous "Winds of Change" speech delivered before both houses of parliament in Cape Town in 1960, he links his own need for personal change to African decolonization. By referring to his own journey as a "little trek," he assimilates the symbolic importance of the Great Trek—the key event in Afrikaner nationalist hagiography—into his narrative.

My Winds of Change is an exemplary expression of a mode of autobiographical writing that can be called "recuperative." The defining feature of recuperative autobiographies is the intense personal conflict that eventually makes way for the inevitable redemption—the triumph of good over evil. These "moral tales" typically rely upon the placement of well-timed and deftly calibrated vignettes that operate as convenient heuristic devices for spiritual, moral, and social reflection. Infused with the Sartrean sense of engagement, "conversion" narratives operate as vehicles for moral exhortation, open-ended invitations to participate in the fashioning of a better world for the future. The conjoined themes of redemption and regeneration are woven into the story line of *My Winds of Change*. The personalized discourse of "coming home to oneself," "facing my shame," and "dealing with 'the sins of the fathers'"—couched as these phrases are in the religious idiom of guilt and remorse—parallel the grandiose rhetorical appeals in the public arena to such themes as reconciliation and forgiveness that are the building blocks for "nation-building."[112]

"Conversion" narratives are a seductive medium through which to address an audience receptive to hearing the "good news" about South Africa's miraculous journey from white minority rule to parliamentary democracy. They embody the values of liberal humanism: a belief in the perfectibility of humankind, faith in progress, and confidence in the future. The central problematic at the heart of the confessional narrative is the conviction that self-examination and self-disclosure can provide a source of truth and meaning at a time when the old is dying and the new has not yet been born. Absolution is the indispensable goal of all confessional narratives.[113] Constructed in the self-celebrating ecstatic mode, confessional accounts offer a way of narrating the self-into-being. They convey the uplifting message that a healthy consciousness can triumph over the contaminating disease of racism.[114]

Yet these stylized "confessional" narratives typically require a thematic overlay that sometimes forces old-fashioned paroxysms of angst to masquerade as meaningful social commentary, and honest soul-searching to deteriorate into pretentious self-absorption. In "confessional" stories, characters and events exist only to become part of the optimistic landscape of the hero's self-discovery. White South African storytellers sometimes embroider their childhood memories with proclamations about "the racist in all of us" and moral exhortations to "confront our own racism" in everyday life. This stylized format can sometimes lead to the florid use of the collective "we" and an overabundance of ritualized references to the pressing need for forgiveness, tolerance, and understanding. The power of "confessional" autobiographies is their ability to bring into the public arena personal stories of redemption. But this mode of writing can be marred by a somewhat simplistic and faintly anachronistic opposition between shameful moral degeneracy and redemptive ethical responsibility. White autobiographers sometimes write, with the self-righteousness of a true believer, as if sympathy with nonracialism, rainbowism, and racial tolerance were an effective litmus test for democratic sentiments, and treat such sentiments anachronistically, as an unhistoricized, decontextualized, and transcendental moral and political good.[115]

In "I-witnessing" accounts, opportunities abound for autobiographers to recast historical events through the distorting lens of personal interest and the desire to put the troubling past in a more favorable light. Despite their pretensions to accuracy and truthfulness, "confessional" autobiographies can sometimes degenerate into well-mannered parody. James Gregory's ghost-written autobiography epitomizes this style. In an account larded with self-absorption and inflated self-importance, Gregory—Mandela's warder (prison guard) during most of his years of imprisonment on Robben Island—paints a more nuanced, somber picture of the "larger-than-life" first president of the "new South Africa" than the conventional wisdom allows. Seen through Gregory's eyes, Mandela is a lonelier figure than is ordinarily acknowledged, a man whose regal bearing conceals a measure of self-doubt, ambivalence, and even regret. Gregory subverts the public image of Mandela as a larger-than-life hero-icon by exposing his not-so-glorious personal traits. He takes comfort in the discoveries of Mandela's ordinariness, for these enable him to assert his own agency as friend, companion, and helpmate. By chronicling the personal services that he provided Mandela while in prison, Gregory seeks to secure his own innocence and to relieve himself of the guilt of complicity in Mandela's incarceration.[116]

Gregory presents his personal observations in an encapsulated, virtually aphoristic form rather than as closely reasoned arguments. In recounting his own "change of heart," he tries to inflate his own rather banal, prosaic existence as an anonymous prison warder into an allegory of interracial friendship and redemption. Yet the matter-of-fact and historically weightless tone of this "I-witnessing" account belies a more calculated, self-serving purpose: in reducing Mandela's stature to that of an ordinary man, Gregory elevates his own.[117]

Skeptics have pointed to what they regard as the fundamental ambivalence of this kind of "confessional" autobiographical writing. On the one hand, "coming clean" can assist those persons who were complicit in maintaining white minority rule in coming to terms with their own culpability. On the other, it can just as easily mean *accommodating,* or establishing a comfortable relationship with the past.[118]

Writing the Way Back Home: Stories of Exile

Stories of "exile" are one of the most striking examples of self-conscious autobiographical writing. What distinguishes these tales of exodus, banishment, and imprisonment is the peculiar way in which autobiographers employ the antinomies of departure and return as narrative devices that allow for a sense of national identity and belonging.[119] In departure, we find an abrupt rupture that engenders displacement or banishment, nomadism, rootlessness, and a longing for home. In return, we find fulfillment that yields solace, stability, and hope. Taken together, these forms of expression convey the message that the idea of belonging to a nation is not simply an accident or destiny of birth, but that it is connected to the conviction and consciousness of its citizens. In the passage of time that fills in the temporal space at the beginning and the end of the tale, the storyteller recounts the traumatic experience of departure and the longing for home, a harrowing Odyssey in which the narrated journey acquires its symbolic meaning by virtue of its disparity from the promise of fulfillment on which the narration is founded. In short, the true meaning of exile, its *telos,* can only be grasped in terms of its end point, that is, the return home, a stable position where the story is essentially finished and only then can begin to be told in its fullest.[120]

"Exile" narratives form a subgenre of what has been called trauma memoirs.[121] "Life writing" of this kind is partially oriented to pivot around some intrusive traumatic event that, at a single stroke, shatters narrative coherence. As Arthur Frank has put it, "Stories have to *repair* the damage that illness [or in this case, "exile"] has done."[122] "Exile" narratives offer redemptive accounts of how "the post-traumatic self might be re-configured around" the experience of diasporic displacement.[123]

National identity requires a historical consciousness and founding myths of origin that tie subjectivity to a particular place and link it to the mythical past.[124] As a subgenre of autobiographical self-disclosure, "exile" writing relies on particular kinds of mnemonic devices to evoke the pathos of national identity. Chance encounters with old acquaintances, anniversaries, photographs, and news reports from home trigger nostalgic memories of the past, undermining the false security of exile and setting in motion a renewed longing to return. Navigating the trope of enforced exile enables autobiographers to enframe their stories as travelers' tales. "Exile" writers typically invite their audience to extrapolate universalizing moral lessons from these highly personalized stories that begin with expulsion and exodus but eventually give way to triumphal return. To feel the pathos of home, it is necessary to experience the loss of one's place of origin, whether through exile, banishment, or imprisonment. By counterposing the aimless, nomadic existence of exile with the stable sense of belonging linked to home, storytellers are able to convey the message, and reinforce the idea, that the subjective experience of national identity can only find fulfillment in a particular place. This autobiographical mode of "writing from exile" reveals the schizophrenic vision that these nomadic writers have about coming home: a "re-creation" myth acts as a counterweight to pessimistic visions of doom, opening up space for valiant citizens of the "new South Africa" to conquer the dark forces of racism and ethnocentrism in the name of the "rainbow nation."

In *The Future of Nostalgia,* Svetlana Boym distinguishes between two types of nostalgic recollection: restorative and reflective. Where restorative nostalgia attempts a "transhistorical reconstruction of a lost home" and "protects the absolute truth" of being against nothingness, reflective nostalgia "dwells on the ambivalences of human longing and belonging," calling into doubt constructions of absolute truth or tradition.[125] Boym argues that both modes of nostalgia can share a deep sense of longing and loss, but the narratives they produce differ fundamentally: "If restorative nostalgia ends up restoring emblems and rituals of home and homeland in an attempt to conquer and spatialize time, reflective nostalgia cherishes shattered fragments of memory and temporalizes space."[126]

During the apartheid years, the conjoined themes of forced removal, banishment from place, and internal exile long figured prominently in fiction writing, political commentaries, and theatrical performances. Well-known writers like Bessie Head, Richard Rive, Alex La Guma, Lewis Nkosi, Don Mattera, Athol Fugard, Malcolm Purkey, Can Themba, and Bloke Modisane discovered in the destruction of celebrated places like District Six and Sophiatown a cause for lamentation and an opportunity to mourn the loss of home. Post-apartheid memoirists like Cloete Breytenbach, Yousuf Rassool, and Linda Fortune fondly recall their childhood memories of growing up in District Six. In trying to capture what they regard as the lingering spirit, the vibrant atmosphere, and the vitality of this now-lost place that they once called "home," they metonymically invoke a nostalgic fidelity to what once was.[127] Similarly, in recalling the destruction of the community that he called home, Bloke Modisane exemplifies this mode of restorative nostalgia when he writes "Something in me died, a piece of me died, with the dying of Sophiatown."[128]

Autobiographical writing about places like District Six and Sophiatown reflects a kind of restorative nostalgia where "the past is not a duration but a perfect snapshot" of what once was.[129] This type of longing does not think of itself as nostalgia but rather as the "recovery of what is perceived as an absolute truth" from the past. In contrast, reflective nostalgia stresses "historical and individual time, with the irrevocability of the past and human finitude."[130]

In writing about the loss of what is nostalgically recalled as home, attachment to place—along with that particular "moment" in South Africa's sociocultural history that it synecdochically locates—has been rediscovered and sometimes fetishized. In the popular mind, long-lost places like District Six and Sophiatown are sites of memory that have become cultural artifacts, imaginary worlds of built space and remembered vibrancy, valued less as "actual localities" in themselves than as mnemonic devices that enable us to recall a time of "colorful" bohemian living and an oasis-like refuge harboring racial tolerance. In fondly recalling lost objects of desire, these writers make inventive use of such figural tropes as attachment, loss, and mourning in order to animate what V. S. Naipaul in an unrelated context has called a "feeling of wrongness."[131] Allegorical narratives of loss and redemption are vehicles that endorse an injunctive politics of return—a moral imperative to recover the familiar.

In *A Long Way Home,* Annemarie Wolpe traces her family's journey into exile from the land of their birth and their eventual triumphant return a quarter century later. This autobiographical account is a particularly poignant example of "exile" writing because of the creative strategies Wolpe employs in seeking to achieve the calculated effect of linking "home" with a sense of belonging and connecting national identity to a particular place. By not following "a single plot line and instead exploring many ways of inhabiting the past at once," *A Long Way Home* engages in the reflective mode of nostalgia that Boym so carefully describes.[132] Wolpe uses the occasion of the unbanning of the ANC in February 1990 as the pivotal moment around which to frame her narrative account of exile and return. Yet instead of following a direct, sequential unfolding of events where past yields to present and ultimately to future, she orders her story according to an inverted chronological system that interrupts the continuous, linear progression to reach backward in time to a point earlier than where she began to tell the story. This break with chronological order—what Gérard Genette terms "anachrony"[133]—enables Wolpe to incorporate past events into the overall temporal framework and, as a consequence, eliminates gaps in the reader's knowledge of those earlier episodes to which the main characters and their respective stories are linked.

The centerpiece of Wolpe's story is a journey (or retreat) backward in time, where she focuses primarily on the events surrounding the arrest of key ANC leaders at Rivonia in 1963, particularly the dramatic jailbreak of her husband Harold (ANC lawyer and SACP member) and his narrow escape—disguised as a woman—across the Swaziland border.[134] This retrospective disruption of narrative continuity provides information bearing "regressive relevance," thereby allowing the reader to comprehend more fully what is yet to unfold.[135] By accounting for the circumstances that led to her family's hasty departure and their long ordeal in exile, Wolpe is able to infuse the post-1990 sequence of events that culminate in their return with a great deal of historical significance and poignancy.[136]

The pathos of national identity embedded in stories of exile and return typically unfolds through the spatiotemporal coordinates of an exodus or an odyssey where the prospect of returning hope activates hope. Arrayed along the spatial axis, home becomes meaningful from a distance. Viewed along the temporal axis, fulfillment is the promise that beckons at the end of the story. Longing to return home can only be comprehended when projected onto a past tainted with suffering, anxiety, and uncertainty and a future that must be imagined as one of hope. The animating force that holds the story in motion, that maintains the origin and the destination of the narrative in polar opposition, and that keeps the beginning and the ending apart long enough to justify the anguish and suffering is the awareness that the prevailing state of injustice is only temporary. The longing for home finds its most powerful expression not in the desire to return to a specific place but in the hope for a future without suffering.[137]

For Wolpe, the "home" to which she and her family return after leading such a long peripatetic existence in exile is not the place they left. In searching for the old and familiar, they find the new and the strange. On returning home, Wolpe, like other exiles, comes to understand that for so long she had been operating under a romanticized illusion. In a real sense, nostalgia, or longing for a lost home, is a cruel hoax. Time never stands still, and one cannot return or restore what was left behind. In the end, Wolpe and her family can return to South Africa only as outsiders. They cannot seamlessly take up where they left off: they must begin again.[138] This ironic tease of an ending ensures that her story, like "exile" writing as a whole, remains incomplete and without closure.[139]

In *Return to Paradise,* Breyten Breytenbach, self-proclaimed "albino terrorist," itinerant wanderer, transgressive maverick, and Afrikaans-language writer, also addresses the complex issue of homecoming as unfinished journey.[140] *Return to Paradise,* the third installment of an ongoing autobiographical reflection, mixes the anthropomorphic invention of magical realism with the searing political commentary of a returning Prodigal Son.[141] Because it acts as a "meditation on history" that marks the passage of time, autobiographical writing of this sort exemplifies a reflective nostalgia that "does not pretend to rebuild the mythical place called home," but instead revels in the journey itself.[142] In seeking to discover a redemptive identity for himself in the polyglot landscape of the "new South Africa," Breytenbach offers an alternately humorous and serious, affectionate and captious, tableau of "exhilarating sights, eccentric dreamers, displaced communities and bizarre racial myths." "Coming home" signifies the possibility of starting over and, metaphorically, a Lazarus-like return from the dead.[143]

Return to Paradise echoes themes that Breytenbach considered at length in his early autobiographical works. For him, exile signifies a liminal state of permanent displacement. He does not belong where he lives, and he does not live where he belongs. His center of gravity is always somewhere else. For Breytenbach, "coming home" serves not only to crystallize everything that "belonging to a place" represents but also to bring into sharp relief everything that it did not represent.[144] As is the case with most "exile writing," there is the paradoxical disjuncture between the mythical idea of "home" and that of the actual "South Africa." On the one hand, Breytenbach offers dreamlike, lyrical impressions of a "beautiful Paradise." On the other, he provides grim reminders of racial intolerance, callous indifference, and denial of responsibility, where the "new South Africa" is somewhat akin to a metaphorical Tower of Babel, with everyone talking but no one listening.[145]

Return to Paradise suffers from the same stylistic flaws as Breytenbach's earlier autobiographical excursions into self-doubt, cultural ennui, and personal alienation from the place he once called home. "There is something self-indulgent, something inescapably *privileged* about these ruminations," the critic Neil Lazarus remarked in his critical commentary on an earlier memoir called *A Season in Paradise.* These comments apply equally to *Return to Paradise.*[146] These excesses—melancholic, overly indulgent, self-pity coupled with an uncritical romantic sentimentalism—clouds his normative judgments and seriously compromises his self-appointed role as political gadfly, a critical critic who speaks the omniscient Truth.

Personal reminiscences of this kind are cultural artifacts of the post-apartheid era, ones that reveal the salience of reconciliation and rapprochement in the contemporary South African experience. In providing a highly personalized account of a journey into exile that ends with the return home, "exile" narratives are parables that stand as beacons of hope. They operate as the symbolic embodiments of the conciliatory moral imperative of coming to terms with the bitter memories of the past. This forgiving attitude toward the past, however, is only conceivable from the perspective of the post-apartheid present, where the enchantment with possibilities of a better future remains strong. The trope of "homecoming" embedded in stories of exile and return is a metaphorical reminder of the place of South Africa in Africa. The idea of South Africa as a white outpost on the African continent has long figured prominently in historiographical writing. Stories of coming home form part of a grand narrative that culminates with the reconciliation between post-apartheid South Africa and the rest of the African continent.

Yet "exile" narratives also display a certain amount of unavoidable discontinuity. For example, Gillian Slovo recounts with a mixture of anger and sadness her life in exile as the daughter of stalwart South African Communist Party (SACP) members Joe Slovo and Ruth First. In her much-acclaimed account of life in exile, *Ties of Blood,* she chronicles how the inevitable intrusion of public events into the private lives of her family denied her the possibility of a normal childhood.[147]

Returning after an extended absence, exile writers typically search in vain for the familiar, comforting signs of what once was and has since passed out of existence. "Exile" writing relies on a kind of reflective nostalgia where, because "home" is in ruins, the aim of homecoming is forever deferred.[148] Ironically, the desire to grasp the familiar underscores just how unbridgeable the gap between the past and the present can become. Memories are always bittersweet. Faced with so much newness and strangeness, they recoil with bewilderment and unease. Under these circumstances, it should come as no surprise that "exile" narratives sometimes fall victim to the siren song of melancholic nostalgia, or what one acerbic critic has called a "strangely powerless emotion, a sweet sadness."[149] As a backward-looking, pessimistic, and obsessive approach to exile and return, nostalgic attachment to home—or the "mourning for the impossibility of mythical return"[150]—can produce a kind of stasis and inaction that can result in a debilitating paralysis.[151]

Cautionary Tales of the Future Unwanted: Nightmares of Armageddon

In contrast to those lyrical, uplifting stories that focus on national cohesion and hope for the future, self-styled "alarmist" narratives are guarded, cautionary tales laced with doomsday thoughts, endgame scenarios, and apocalyptic visions. "Alarmist" narratives warn of imminent danger and impending doom. The animating tropes of fear, anxiety, and disillusionment propel these angst-driven stories along their trajectory from ominous present to dystopian future. Generally speaking, they are future-directed accounts—what Gérard Genette termed "proleptic tales"[152]—where the autobiographer treats events, episodes, and incidents as disturbing symptoms of what is to come, presenting them as the prefigurative embodiments that anticipate the future imperfect. In the typical case, "alarmist" writers fill their narratives with the kind of mordant nihilism that allows them to read into virtually every circumstance or chance encounter the inchoate warning signs of the coming breakdown in the order of things, incipient social decay, the early warning signs of moral degeneracy, and the ongoing downward spiral toward inevitable decline. "Alarmist" writing tends to describe the present as a tendency with a concealed agenda that prefigures the future rather than an open-ended contingency pregnant with multiple possibilities.

In seeking to achieve their desired effects, cautionary tales enlist a number of distinctive narrative strategies that distinguish this subgenre of writing from other kinds of autobiographical or semi-autobiographical truth-telling. Unlike "conversion" narratives where autobiographers as experiencing subjects are active participants in their own awakening, "alarmist" writers seek deliberately to detach themselves from that which they observe and to place the blame anywhere but upon themselves. This pretense of impartiality and distance enables them to script their stories as unsentimental, realist accounts committed to telling unvarnished truths. Whereas "conversion" narratives are introverted and soul-searching investigations of the self, "alarmist" stories focus attention on external events and the heightened presence of inanimate entities that seem to assume autonomous lives of their own. By focusing attention on the hostile power of things, these cautionary tales reinforce the conviction that human subjects are helpless victims of forces beyond their control. This mode of writing typically treats historical subjects as more or less imprisoned by human nature, where sociocultural differences are often regarded as organic, natural, and immutable. By abandoning faith in the liberal-humanist belief in social progress and the perfectibility of humanity, these writers are profoundly skeptical of the possibilities of remedial action to cure South Africa's ills.

This mode of apocalyptic storytelling generally conforms to a certain formulaic, predictable scenario. "Alarmist" narratives typically string together a concatenation of scattered vignettes, or microstories, that, laid out in linear progression, leave an impression of impending doom, or the coming Apocalypse. The guiding metaphors of collapse, disintegration, and chaos suggest a pessimistic vision of the future, with little possibility of redemption. This entropic zeitgeist is sustained in part by what Elleke Boehmer has referred to as "suspended endings," that is, stories that are cut short by "social breakdown, exile, leave-taking."[153]

Despite their differences in style and substance, Rian Malan's *My Traitor's Heart,* Graham Boynton's *Last Days in Cloud Cuckooland,* and Lester Venter's *When Mandela Goes* epitomize this subgenre of "alarmist" writing. Each in its own peculiar way echoes these millenarian themes of social breakdown, disorder, and dislocation. The common thread that holds these autobiographical and semi-autobiographical accounts together is the desire to forecast future scenarios through the prism of the present state of heightened anxiety that has accompanied the birth of the "new South Africa."[154]

In *My Traitor's Heart,* Rian Malan paints a rather gloomy portrait of South Africa in the dying days of apartheid. He begins his story by recounting his own white middle-class Afrikaner upbringing in a suburb of Johannesburg, a blissful time filled with youthful transgressions of the racial divide cut short by the threat of conscription. The bulk of the loosely structured account focuses on his erstwhile career as a journalist, an occupation that provides him with entry into a black world that few whites ever experienced.[155] Malan organizes his narrative around a repetitive litany of disconnected "horror stories" that—as they grimly parade across the text—chronicle the numbing, senseless brutality that, in his hands, becomes emblematic of the tumultuous transition to democracy in South Africa.[156] These haunting images of wanton cruelty evoke revulsion and contempt, despair, and cynicism. Malan portrays random violence as something commonplace, endemic, and gratuitous, a seemingly natural condition that reflects a Hobbesian-like "war of all against all." As white and black people "spiraled down toward mutual annihilation," he suggested, "We always seemed to miss each other in the murk of our mutually baffling cultures and our mutually blinding fears."[157] This reciprocal unintelligibility suggests that race and racism are so enigmatic, indecipherable, and opaque that challenging their foundation is literally impossible. Malan enframes his autobiographical account within an alarmist discourse clouded with entropic anxieties. "Sometimes the racial conundrum sat in my brain like a gnarling, malevolent octopus, but at others it was very remote, as remote as the threat of earthquakes in Los Angeles," he argued. "We all knew disaster was coming, but we didn't know when."[158] Malan perceives random violence as a natural condition whose centripetal force is associated metaphorically with a social order veering toward chaos and a social system sliding into decline. "I wish I could say this will end well," he concludes with what seems to be only the slightest hint of regret, "but I find it hard to have faith."[159]

Graham Boynton borrows his title from Margaret Thatcher, who in 1987 cavalierly announced that "anyone who thinks that the ANC is going to run the government of South Africa is living in Cloud Cuckooland." By weaving together personal reminiscences recounting his upbringing as a white Rhodesian with the political commentary of a putatively impartial observer, he constructs a rich and troubling tableau of disturbing images laced with farcical overtones. Boynton provides furtive, almost carnivalesque glimpses of several individuals who, in his mind, symbolize the kaleidoscopic array of white Africans inhabiting the African subcontinent at a time when settler colonialism lurched toward its tumultuous demise. These emblematic figures include Rick Turner, the anti-apartheid activist who was killed under mysterious circumstances in Durban in 1978; the "Bonnie and Clyde" couple, Pieter Grundlingh and his girfriend, Charmaine Phillips, pathetic drifters living on the margins of white respectability when they committed a gruesome murder; and Alwyn Wolfaardt, an uncompromising white supremacist and self-styled Afrikaner *Weerstandsbeging* (AWB) colonel who lost his life in an ill-fated "invasion" of Mmabatho, the *faux* capital of Bophuthatswana, in March 1994. Boynton uses these tales of senseless violence to reflect on the dilemma of many white South Africans who, faced with they perceive as the disruptive encroachment of sense violence and social disorder threatening the placid normalcy of their everyday lives, consider their options. For Boynton, white colonialists may have ruled Africa badly, but black Africans in power have not fared any better. By extrapolating this somber message of stagnation and decline to post-apartheid South Africa, Boynton obliquely suggests that there is a strong likelihood that the ANC-in-government may well suffer a similar fate.[160]

Lester Venter's *When Mandela Goes* exemplifies the "magical realist" undertones that characterize much futurist writing. Venter frames his "cautionary tale" entirely in an imagined future where he entertains various alternative "historical possibilities," which he forecasts will be the most likely political outcomes once Nelson Mandela leaves office. In his view, Mandela's powers of persuasion and moral authority remained undiminished during his term in office. His high-profile presence was a powerful centrifugal force that holds together rival interest groups in an uneasy alliance. In all likelihood, in Venter's prognosis, Mandela's departure will unloosen this delicate balance of power, unleashing an intense and debilitating competition for diminishing resources. His forecast of a post-Mandela intensification of political rivalries is a seductive one, and its appeal is strengthened by alarmist fears over rising crime, increasing unemployment, and growing despair amongst the under classes. While Venter proclaims his impartiality, critics interpret his dire warnings as a convenient facade disguising nostalgic yearnings for a simpler time.[161]

These pessimistic forecasts of impending doom are marked by what James Atlas has called "endism," an approach that reads the future almost solely in terms of the present and, as a result, finds itself unable to offer coherent insight into either time frame.[162] In "alarmist" writing, individual destiny becomes subordinated to overpowering forces that appear at once natural and immutable. By abandoning faith in social progress, "alarmist" narratives reduce temporality to a hopeless circularity. Without hope for the future, there is no exit from the seemingly endless cycle in which all is in vain. While "conversion" narratives offer diagnoses of the disorders afflicting post-apartheid South Africa, "alarmist" writers are quite skeptical of the possibility of remedial action capable of curing social ills.

"Alarmist" writing has a particular interest in themes related to violence, mayhem, and callous brutality. Random violence symbolizes the most typical allegorical topos in this kind of writing. Stories of violence are grim reminders of the limits of human subjectivity, thus negating any firm belief in the perfectibility of humankind. The disruptive force of violence, the insouciant indifference of onlookers, and the callous disregard of perpetrators for victims are seamlessly linked in a metaphorical circle from which there is no exit. While this subgenre of autobiographical writing prides itself on unsentimental truth-telling, "alarmist" narratives are actually highly selective (in an *a priori* deductive way) in their choice of illustrative vignettes, displaying only those that lend support and credibility to their somber, pessimistic view. In "alarmist" writing, the meaning of assembled anecdotes is inferred from an essentially ahistorical, decontextualized analysis of the episodes themselves. But the problem with this kind of one-dimensional interpretive strategy is that isolated events cannot be understood simply in terms of their internal structure, separate from their cultural milieux and historical setting. The meaning of events can change profoundly, depending upon the historical context and the frame of reference.

Forecasts of impending collapse, social breakdown, and decline are themes that are as common in current writing as they were in autobiographical accounts half a century ago. One must question current readings that attempt to causally link anticipated moral decay and social breakdown with the birth of the "new South Africa." Gloomy predictions of impending apocalypse haunt every transitional period in South Africa's past. The enduring quality, the persistence, of these sociocultural jeremiads problematizes those attempts to identity anticipated breakdown and expected decline as specific manifestations, or precise expressions, of the end of apartheid and the birth of the "new South Africa." The transition to parliamentary democracy emerges an unavoidable process of disintegration from which nobody can escape. From this perspective, the fear of immanent decay and social collapse in the post-apartheid era can be seen to depend more on *a priori* perceptions than empirically grounded analysis of historical realities. The lure of millenarian thinking is potent enough to create a proliferation of discourses, but efforts to link these discourses to material conditions are invariably problematic. Every age, it seems, bears witness to its own decline and, as a result, fearful forecasts of impending breakdown and inevitable crisis need to be treated with skepticism, especially when looking for ways of explaining the transition to parliamentary democracy and the birth of the "new South Africa."

Faced with uncertainties about the future, alienated white autobiographers typically seek solace in a sentimentalized past. This trope of nostalgia appears sometimes as a response to perceived decline (real or imagined), as figurative device for coping with fear, or as a symptom of exhaustion and distain for the present.[163] Melancholic discourses of nostalgia can sometimes yield to obsessive fixations with romantic ideals and mythical locations, evoking sentimental longing for a particular past, or a sense of belonging to a particular time and place.[164] The heightened sense of cynicism, pessimism, and personal anomie embedded in "alarmist" writings sometimes masks a hidden sentimentalism, an insatiable longing to return to a putative Golden Age of order, coherence, and harmony that supposedly prevailed under white minority rule. Burdened with disenchantment with the present, nostalgia is the handmaiden of escapist fantasies that signal retreat into an imagined past, an age of lost innocence, a bygone time and place in a mythical, idealized past. While the turn to nostalgia sometimes signals a longing for a bygone time or an age of lost innocence, it can also be animated by guilt and remorse, regret for paths not taken and choices not made, promises not kept or opportunities lost.[165]

Epilogue

History and Heritage

Heritage and history are like twins separated at birth: while their origins are identical, the trajectories of their distinct life-courses are quite dissimilar. As communicative devices, history and heritage rely on antithetical modes of persuasion. Heritage does not pretend to present a genuinely authentic, and reasonably plausible, account of some past but is a declaration of faith in that which came before.[1] While some observers celebrate heritage as a complementary or alternative way of mediating the past to popular audiences, critics dismiss it as little more than counterfeit history, packaged for commercial consumption.[2] "While it looks old, heritage is actually something new," Barbara Kirshenblatt-Gimblett has argued. "Heritage is a mode of cultural production in the present that has recourse to the past. Heritage thus defined depends on display to give dying economies and dead sites a second life as exhibitions of themselves."[3]

To the extent that it is embedded in the consumer-led milieux of commerce and markets, the heritage industry operates as an integral part of the leisure and tourist business. In the hands of vulgar commercializers who invent transparently essentialist fantasies of past glories, innocent times, and freewheeling adventure, the heritage industry "traffics" in *faux* history and, as a consequence, commodifies the past.[4] In contrast, history is above all a truth-seeking exercise, a theoretically informed and empirically grounded undertaking that aspires to closure by weighing alternative explanations in a ceaseless quest to best approximate, in the most convincing way, what actually happened and why.[5]

The relationship between history, heritage, and memory has been subject to intense discussion and debate.[6] Heritage makes the new seem old and the old feel new, creating a sense of continuity where none necessarily exists. It provides comforting, though distorted, impressions of both the past and the present, which cannot be dispelled by appeals to historically grounded truth because, like any system of myth, they are rooted in a powerful will to believe.[7] As David Lowenthal has argued, "Heritage distils the past into icons of identity, bonding us with precursors and progenitors, with our own earlier selves, and with promised successors."[8] As such, heritage offers a "bogus" history that ignores complex historical processes and relationships and sanitizes the less savory or uncomfortable dimensions of the past.[9] Unlike the regulative principles that govern historical accuracy, cultural heritage allows objects to "transgress upon one another" and temporal sequence to collapse into a collage of multiple temporalities that collide and merge. Heritage is intrinsically a place-based activity that uses specific place-images, whether symbolic or material, to aid in the "recovery" of the past. What is central to heritage tourism is the relationship between space and time, that is, "the awarding of space a past."[10] Cultural-heritage landscapes thus become "jutapositions[s] of asynchronous moments where space forms a container for different eras producing a depthless world where time as process is erased." This process of abandonment of spatial and temporal integrity "can be read as a metaphor for commodification, bringing different times into one homogenized (and marketable) field."[11]

As a didactic exercise that takes a partisan approach to history in order to establish moral authority, the heritage industry transmits historical narratives in a highly selective, partial, and distorting way, with the result that it often falls prey to the production of myth, a simulacrum, a copy of something that never existed or actually happened. By literally materializing this fictionalized image through monuments, memorials, and image-laden promotional materials, myths appear real and, as such, take on a life of their own.[12]

With the end of apartheid and the transition to parliamentary democracy, the new custodians of memory sought to undo and unmake the falsified monumental history of the racially coded past and to elevate popular resistance to white domination as the new national narrative. Yet in the "new South Africa," sites of memory have to compete with the rejuvenated tourist industry. Tourism is not just a commercial business; it is also a social practice engaged with the framing of history and identity.[13] Put more broadly, tourist entrepreneurialism is firmly embedded in the packaging of place-images that can evoke feelings of adventure, excitement, and relaxation just as easily as they can provoke nostalgia, grief, and anger.[14]

The Tourist-Entertainment Machine and Cultural Heritage: Giving the Past a Future through the Production of Collective Memory

As a mode of cultural production, the tourist industry is a powerful social force, exerting influence over the type of "experience" that it seeks to sell. The relationship between heritage and tourism is both collaborative and synergistic. Heritage converts locations into destinations, and tourism renders them economically viable as "exhibits of themselves."[15] As an enterprise with a global reach, the tourist industry has evolved from marketing landscapes, natural beauty, luxury accommodations, health, and leisure vacations to the packaging of the experience itself as something real and authentic, while at the same different and adventurous.[16] Functioning as global place-makers, corporate enterprises in the business of tourism and entertainment seek to transfer the logic of commodity production to the production of tourist places. This reconfiguration of localities or sites into marketable objects invariably replaces a commitment to a genuine authenticity with an appeal to a "staged" authenticity in which local histories and cultural heritage become manufactured or simulated for tourist consumption.[17] The creation of the tourist experience typically involves the postmodern blurring of leisure boundaries where travel to exotic locations blends cultural-heritage sites with retail shopping and other modes of consumption.[18] The practice of tourist consumerism reaches its low point with the global production of nonplaces (Disneyland), nonthings (mass-manufactured souvenirs and the serial reproduction of kitsch objects), and nonevents (myths and make-believe).[19]

Real-estate developers have increasingly enlisted local histories—merged with local folklore, legend, and myth—to define, package, and brand their building projects. In promoting these places, city boosters are asked to interpret local histories in contradictory ways. On the one hand, they are called upon to valorize local identities and histories as authentic illustrations of past achievements. On the other, they require that selective parts of the past be devalued in order not to draw attention to uncomfortable truths about the past. Typically, the selling of the local past involves a selective embellishment, or a kind of purposeful exaggeration, in order to draw attention to particular places. At the same time, tourism boosters engage in "organized" or "deliberate forgetting," to use phrases coined by Paul Connerton, where unwanted aspects of local history are downplayed, ignored, or effaced.[20] In this way, local histories, traditions, and cultural heritage become saleable products that city boosters exploit for their own advantage.[21]

Put at the service of the tourist-entertainment industry, collective memory is transformed into ideology "when space and time are produced as cultural commodities" in the form of nostalgic images or repackaged cultural-heritage sites.[22] By outfitting the past with backward-looking and romantic dramatizations of place, tourism boosters reclaim and represent a "usable history" in one-dimensional ways. In the typical case, these new custodians of manufactured memory ignore uncomfortable moments, rearticulating them in comforting sepia tones that integrate them as integral elements of the "good-old-days."[23] Equally important, tourism boosters typically rely on historicized discourses that stress the continuities between past and present, and between older uses and meanings of places and newer ones, as a way of tying into a linear and teleological version of history. The constructed stories told about these places transform complex lived histories into melodramatic folktales through an emphasis on seemingly universal themes of triumph, romance, and adventure.[24]

Business coalitions have increasingly viewed cultural heritage through the lens of commercial development, tourist spending, and popular entertainment.[25] Nostalgia for an imagined past is a powerful memory-marker. Tourist entrepreneurs seek to harness places such as historic neighborhoods, reclaimed waterfront districts, and famous old buildings as vehicles for expressing civic identity, shared values, and hopes for the future. Yet put in the service of the entertainment industries, what might be called sepia-tinted memories are routinely offered for popular consumption in the postmodern nostalgia market. Debates over how to "decolonize" museum displays, archaeological sites, "traditional" villages, and national game parks have provoked a great deal of controversy over what it means to promote public culture and heritage.[26] To the extent that collective memory is brought into line with crass commercialism, it loses its in-depth qualities as in integral component of history, and it appears more like "a staged costume drama and re-enactment."[27]

The Place of Collective Memory in the "New South Africa"

One of the more perplexing ironies of negotiated political transitions—like the one that gave rise to the "new South Africa"—concerns the connection between history and memory. Leaving the grim past behind involves a great deal of willful forgetting, and this process of "letting go" can engender social amnesia. In the "new South Africa," the promotion of the aesthetic pleasures of everyday life for the leisurely classes—festival marketplaces, gambling casinos, game parks, and the like—has a way of cutting South African citizens off from their own history. "For those without memory, nostalgia fills the void," Ada Louise Huxtable has said. "For those without reference points, novelties are enough."[28] This promotion of a "happy consciousness"—to borrow a phrase from Herbert Marcuse—ironically loosens the ties that the "new South Africa" has with its sordid past, but, also ironically, it promotes a certain amnesia or purposeful forgetfulness.[29]

While enterprises dealing with upscale accommodation and entertainment, airline transportation, and prepackaged "sightseeing" holiday tours are firmly ensconced within the ambit of corporate South Africa, the bulk of what constitutes the heritage industry consists of small-scale entrepreneurs, family businesses linked to fixed sites, and small-time operators selling personal services. "Heritage" is largely kept alive by a phalanx of small retailers in out-of-the-way places, selling "traditional" crafts and handmade curios, and a formidable army of flea-market stallholders specializing in mementos, bric-a-brac, and souvenirs.[30] Commodity chains stretch backward from the visible points of consumption that straddle the tourist routes, large and small, to the generally invisible points of production, typically small-scale workshops located in remote rural redoubts that include isolated villages in South Africa to places as far away as the Congo, Mali, and Côte d'Ivoire.[31]

Taken at face value, "heritage" is a serviceable idea upon whose bandwagon all manner of erstwhile promoters have climbed aboard in order to secure funding, whether from private or public sources. Using the persuasive rhetoric of "national treasures," conservationists call for protection of wildlife habitats, aviary sanctuaries, seashores, wildernesses, and virgin forests in order to maintain these places in their original state of nature.[32] Preservationists urge the protection of valued historic landmarks, ranging from railroad memorabilia to the original headgear at some of the earliest gold-mining operations, and from "Bushman" rock paintings to famous battle sites of the Anglo-Boer War (1899–1902).[33] Exhibiting places like these creates objects of display—"set[ting] the world up as a picture," to be "viewed, investigated, and experienced."[34]

The intersection of historical perservationism and commercialism has created an uneasy tension that the custodians of collective memory struggle to resolve in theory and to redeem in practice. Real-estate developers and perservationists have joined forces to urge the restoration of historical landmarks and to save old buildings from the wrecking ball, the former to promote commercial development and the latter to create an aesthetically pleasing built environment for future generations. Municipal and provincial authorities have also latched onto the renewed enthusiasm for cultural heritage. Faced with limited prospects for economic growth and burdened with high levels of unemployment, local government officials have resurrected local heritage as a way to compete for specialized niches in the tourist trade. In many localities, tourist promoters have cobbled together partnerships between local authorities, the central government, and private enterprise that they hope will create the requisite synergy to lure increasing numbers of sightseers, heritage enthusiasts, and itinerant travelers to their area.[35]

Tourist entrepreneurs typically promise travelers idyllic escape from the routines of daily life to destinations where time "stands still" or the past lives on, uncontaminated by modernity.[36] In Cape Town, Robben Island has become a major tourist destination—marketed alongside Table Mountain, the Victoria and Alfred Waterfront, local beaches, and the nearby wineries of Stellenbosch, Franschhoek, and Paarl. In scores of small towns scattered throughout the languid "wine country," refurbished wine estates, sprawling manors, historic buildings, and picturesque rustic villages—all conforming to the distinctive Cape Dutch architectural style—exude a comforting aura of timelessness, a sentimentalized nostalgia for a simpler way of life. In the Western Cape, quaint seaside villages offer the promise of leisure and relaxation.

The protection of national heritage sites includes the "historicization" of small towns, where local civic pride and municipal idealism dovetail neatly with commercial impulses to tap into the tourist trade. In the Northern Cape, tourist promoters have trumpeted the informative value of the Kimberley Mine Museum and the visual experience of the Big Hole—the original site of the Kimberley diamond diggings and the largest human-made excavation in the world, with a one-mile circumference and a surface area of thirty-three acres. In Mpumalanga, the restoration of derelict buildings at Pilgrim's Rest has created a contemporary replica of what the old mining town looked like during the "gold rush" at the end of the nineteenth century. Tourist entrepreneurs tout their location as a site of memory of one sort or another. All in all, marketing "heritage" entails the selective reification of such places as disused mining operations, abandoned industrial sites, and original homesteads as exemplars of a bygone age. Branded as an "authentic" window onto a glorious past defined by greatness and success, these heritage products create a serviceable past reconfigured as a commodity for present-day consumption.[37]

Confronted with the onslaught of entrepreneurial tourism, those custodians of collective memory who hope to foster a genuine appreciation of the untold sacrifice, heroism, and determination of those millions of political activists who struggled, Lilliputian style, to bring down the apartheid system face an uphill battle in countering obliviscence, or the state of having forgotten. The gratitude owed for the gift bestowed is dwarfed by the headlong rush for amnesiac entertainment. The new genre of tourist guidebooks that shapes the tourist experience of the South African past stresses upbeat themes, travel adventure, and exotic locations. Ironically, many of those who participated in the struggle against apartheid have become avid promoters of the tourist industry. Yet all of these local initiatives aimed at luring the tourist trade pale in comparison with large-scale efforts to sell access to tourist destinations. The giants of the corporate tourist industry package a voyage to the "new South Africa" as a Riviera-like Mediterranean holiday on the southern tip of the African subcontinent.[38]

Marita Sturken coined the term "tourists of history" to denote a particular mode of travel through which visitors vicariously "experience" the historical past through journeys to sites of memory. This mode of tourism enables visitors to acquire "mediated experience" of trauma reinforced through the consumption of visual images, souvenirs, and reenactments. The idea of tourism is deeply implicated in questions of authenticity and inauthenticity. A site like Robben Island, for example, embodies powerful meanings of authenticity: an actual place that once housed real prisoners. Visits to these tourist destinations are intended to create a connection between the tourist and the site of trauma by providing authenticity by the simple fact of "being there." But the commercialization of heritage often transforms the traces of an "authentic experience" into inauthentic spectacle. The heritage industry relies upon nostalgia, but nostalgia that is subjected to the pressure of marketability. The marketing of heritage easily falls prey to a kind of derivative pathos that reduces memorial sites to vehicles for commercial gain.[39] Reduced to the contrived innocence and playfulness of kitsch, memorabilia, and souvenirs as well as other tokens of remembrance embrace the emotional register of sincerity by drawing on the clichés of prefabricated sentimentality.[40]

Crafting Nature: Commodifying the Game Park Experience

With its expanding international airport and its grid of interconnecting arterial highways, Johannesburg is the gateway to the nature preserves, game parks, and wildlife sanctuaries of southern Africa. "There are few things in life that conjure up more excitement or uncontrollable wanderlust than the thought of a safari through some of South Africa's most notable game parks and reserves," Jan Baumgartner has suggested.[41] Entrepreneurs promoting the tourist trade have attached themselves to the exotic lure of animals in the wild as a way of "Africanizing" South Africa. These efforts to carve out a specialized niche in the ecotourism market dovetail with the emphasis of global tourism on specialization and off-the-beaten-track realism.

The tourist industry in the "new South Africa" has set its sights on globe-trotting travelers who, with the collapse of apartheid, no longer attract the opprobrium of their politically conscious acquaintances if they include South Africa as one of their leisure destinations. From offering champagne-laced luxury lodges to no-frills campsites in the bush, tourist entrepreneurs cater to the varied tastes of travelers who want to experience the untamed wilds of the South African game parks and private reserves. Safari tours are local adaptions aimed to satisfy the seemingly insatiable demands of foreigners, mainly North Americans and Europeans, to experience "the real Africa" in its "primitive and natural state" before it is erased by the march of civilization. "Having fought to defeat the Old South Africa, I found myself an unapologetic evangelist for the New One," Peter Hain proclaims. "The people are hospitable, the weather warm, the food and wine a delight. Nowhere else in the world can such a rich variety of animals, birds and flowers, and such breathtaking variations in landscapes be found, with an infrastructure that makes visiting so effortless."[42] Tourist entrepreneurs and travel operators have learned to produce and sell safari excursions as highly selected and carefully choreographed images of South African nature that are attractive and romantic stories of "wild adventure into a savage land" with danger lurking everywhere.[43]

South African tourism is an embedded set of visual practices that set out to capture "authentic" nature unspoiled by modernizing or civilizing influences. As a kind of theatrical performance, most tourist productions play on the thematic image of Africa as an exotic wilderness in which wildlife, landscape, and native peoples form a seamless web, and, collapsed into a single, all-encompassing category, are rendered as timeless, unchanging, and primitive.[44] The safari simply repeats these themes and images of wild and exotic Africa where tourists "experience an exciting journey into the distant past." Tourists come to Africa with a ready-made perspective and a story already in mind, and they try to find scenes that resemble their preconceived images that evoke a comforting sense of familiarity.[45]

The operational mode of the tourist experience is scenographic, or what W. J. T. Mitchell has called the "visual construction of the social."[46] The metaphor of seeing—the tourist gaze—enframes and valorizes the "wild" and the "primitive," on the one side, and the "civilized" and the "modern," on the other, as opposing poles of visual production. The production of the tourist experience relies upon a staged setting whereby "expectant visitors" are allowed to "see" the animals in their natural habitats, "explore" untamed landscapes, and "observe" the indigenous peoples. "Guns have metamorphosed into cameras in this earnest comedy, the ecology safari, because nature has ceased to be what it always had been—what people needed protection from," Susan Sontag has noted. "Now nature—tamed, endangered, mortal—needs to be protected from people. When we are afraid, we shoot, but when we are nostalgic, we take pictures."[47] As prepackaged cultural performance, the safari offers a journey back in time, holding out the promise of seeing the world as our primitive ancestors saw it, in its natural state, without the influences of modern civilization. The experience of being there gives the safari the aura of authenticity and the appearance of realism.[48]

Official tourist guidebooks do not simply provide engrossing details about places of interest but also actively shape the discourse of travel, provide rules of etiquette for the inexperienced traveler, offer cautionary tales on crime and disease, and present sentimental and romanticized views of the timeless and untamed wilderness. In short, these guidebooks "instruct" tourists in how to remember their journey. Tourist production rests on the premise that "visitors" experience the exotic by trying to grasp the "real thing"—the vast "otherness" of primitive nature—as a pictorial image, an authentic record that "I was there."[49] What makes the tourist experience work is the juxtaposition between "culture" (civilization) and "nature" (primitive, timeless). In the tourist gaze, nature in all its manifest forms—the animal kingdom, mountains and forests, savannas, topography, rivers and rain—is elevated to the status of exotic and mysterious, magisterial and awe-inspiring, unforgiving and raw—in other words, a visual spectacle. Those who gaze upon this spectacle of timeless beauty are themselves dwarfed, reduced to the role of passive spectators.[50]

Kruger National Park, a travel enthusiast's dream, is home to more species of wildlife than any other park or reserve in southern Africa. Slightly larger than the state of New Jersey, the park is a maze of rough-hewn roads that crisscross the variegated animal habitats, with only scattered bushveld camps and rest areas to accommodate visitors. The custodians of Kruger National Park promote the visceral excitement of seeing one or more of the "Big Five"—lion, rhinoceros, elephant, leopard, and Cape buffalo—in their natural surroundings. Kruger National Park is meant to be experienced as a wild and primitive journey to a timeless place, but it is also meant to be safe and luxurious entertainment.[51] In the language of nature conservancy, heritage is embodied in unspoiled wildlife habitats, wetlands sanctuaries, and the untamed bush. State-sponsored efforts to maintain and sustain game parks reflect both an environmental consciousness and sensitivity and an ecotourist attraction.[52]

As an integral element of tourist realism, game parks allow wild animals in their natural habitat to represent timeless nature, or "primitive Africa" as it has always been. Wild animals serve as an "effect of the real."[53] This process of objectification of the gaze, or this creation of "tourist realism," is part of a larger story of transforming the exotic world of nature into an exhibition, that is, reconfiguring the "natural" world as spectacle.[54]

The Power of Amnesia

Transitional conjunctures—radical breaks with the past and the beginning of something new—are invariably accompanied by crises of collective memory. Ruptures in historical time give rise to calls to forget, eradicate, and repress everything in the recent past, to treat what came before as moribund and unthinkable, in order to create a foundation for starting afresh.[55] As Michel de Certeau has argued, every "new time" finds its legitimation in what it excludes and denies. Yet this new time always proves to be porous and malleable, providing plenty of room for slippage and contestation. Remnants of the past, thought to be discarded into the dustbin of history, reappear in distorted and truncated forms, seeking to embed and insinuate themselves in the new order.[56]

If the decade or so after the end of apartheid was a time of setting the record straight, exposing the "dirty secrets" of the past, then what followed seemed to be a fixation on the return to normalcy. The fields of force pull in opposite directions: memory against forgetting, transparency against erasure, rooted-in-place against moving-forward-in-time. The paradox is that memory-markers themselves partake in the de-temporalizing processes that characterize the contemporary culture of consumption and obsolescence. Strictly speaking, memory-markers that identify the apartheid system and white minority rule as the single source of oppression contribute to a kind of social amnesia. In his speech to Parliament on June 3, 1998, then–deputy president Thabo Mbeki pointedly argued: "The only escape for those who seek the absence of turbulence, and strive to maintain their positions of privilege by stealth, will be the artificial imposition of a social amnesia, until the next conflict emerges above the gentle waves. I do not believe that anyone of us want to live in this fake and unreal world peopled by ostriches with heads hidden in the sand of the Kgalagadi."[57] To a certain extent, apartheid has become the symbolic marker for the inability to achieve racial harmony, for the failure of the nation to incorporate otherness and difference, and unequal opportunity. The singular use of apartheid as the all-encompassing trope for everything that was wrong with the past paradoxically closes off critical inquiry into enduring inequalities.[58]

The creeping culture of amnesia has worked to sever the "new South Africa" from its apartheid history. Conversely, the redemptive power of memory "refuses such historical abnegation, describing South Africa's contemporaneity as 'post-apartheid' and insistently hyphenating its present with its past." Framed in this way, South Africa's contemporaneity—that is, its located presence in historical time—is itself a site of unresolved tension and conflict where the promise of reconciliation and national unity has remained unfulfilled.[59]

With the end of apartheid and the transition to parliamentary democracy, many white South Africans warmly welcomed and openly embraced the challenges, opportunities, and possibilities that the "new South Africa" offered. Yet for the reluctant remainder of the white population, the dissolution of the unifying aesthetic and institutional framework of apartheid rule, along with the collapse of the animating myths of white superiority, came as a rude awakening. The long-standing canon of historical memory—what counted as the foundation of South Africa's heritage and why—lost its raison d'être. Where the national heritage was once carefully controlled for its pedagogic and aesthetic value, the recovery of collective memory in the "new South Africa" has opened a Pandora's box of uncertainty, anxiety, and fear.[60]

Many white South Africans born into privilege have constructed a sociocultural world for themselves that supports a fundamental misperception, misunderstanding, and denial of the grim socioeconomic realities of the "new South Africa," their place within it, and the situation of the black majority, who in the past they considered foreigners in their own land.[61] Like privileged social groups everywhere, these white South Africans fashioned an elaborate deception that acts to conceal the naked power of oppression and exploitation of others while preserving a sense of their own unsullied innocence and nourishing the mythical belief that their goodwill was the key ingredient in the negotiated settlement that paved the way for the end of apartheid.[62]

In the "new South Africa," the gulf between privileged and impoverished, powerful and marginal, and white and black has remained largely unchanged.[63] For many white South Africans, still physically and psychologically separated from their black fellow citizens, the image of black people still has retained much of its old stereotyped character: people enmeshed in poverty, ignorance, and disease; prone to violence and lawlessness; threatening proper standards in universities, efficiency in government and in the workplace, safety on the highways and in middle-class neighborhoods; and displacing the age-old institutions and culture of Europe with the chaos and degradation of Africa.[64]

Despite the anxieties, international isolation, and obvious moral failings of white minority rule, many whites actually preferred life in the old South Africa. Cocooned in their enclaves of affluence, many white South Africans have retreated into nostalgic sentimentality, yearning for a bygone era of order and stability. In the "new South Africa," the most visible and well-known monuments—upscale shopping malls, gambling casinos, high-rise luxury hotels—are iconic symbols of the global marketplace, the showcases not of cultural heritage but of consumer culture. The elasticity of image has undermined the power of monuments, memorials, and other commemorative sites to shape popular consciousness, privileging transience and ephemerality (appearance) over durability and stability, and visual display over monumental presence. The circulating power of the commodity has come to dominate the contemplative aura of sites of memory. The simulated space of the cathedrals of consumption has replaced the actual place of cultural heritage. There is little wonder that Bishop Desmond Tutu's heartfelt plea for some evidence of white generosity, reciprocity, or admission of any culpability for the impoverishment of a significant portion of black South Africa was barely acknowledged and largely ignored by corporate executives, mainstream opinion makers, and white power brokers. In the post-apartheid era, the ethos of the globalized marketplace has provided the propertied classes with a convenient discourse to justify their own standing in the socioeconomic order "while gratuitously urging the poor to take responsibility for their own upliftment" through the magical leaven of hard work and microentrepreneurship.[65] The steady stream of cautionary tales in the popular media warning against state-sponsored "quick-fix" solutions and urging negotiation and compromise has provided ample testimony to the banal extremes of denial, indifference, and lack of circumspection that has characterized much white psychic and communal life in the "new South Africa" after the end of apartheid.[66]

Amnesiacs have wanted to believe that the repeal of apartheid legislation, the adoption of the new constitution, and the transition to parliamentary democracy wiped the slate clean, allowing them to ignore the enduring legacies of structural inequalities and to start over *de novo,* unburdened by past inequities. The embrace of social amnesia in the "new South Africa" goes hand in hand with the desire to "cauterize history with the end of formal apartheid in April 1994 and to establish and promote the idea of radical discontinuity as a way of shrugging off the past and its shadows."[67]

The Heritage Industry and the Tourist Gaze: The Triumph of Happy Consciousness

Corporate South Africa has gone to great pains to break with a politicized past, to masquerade its own role in buttressing the white minority regime and benefiting from apartheid, and to substitute bland uplifting formulas for a genuine commitment to creating an even playing field. As large-scale-business leaders sought to define themselves as "honest brokers" during the political transition to "constructive partners" in the "new South Africa," they reinvented themselves, effectively distancing themselves from white minority rule and thereby erasing their hidden history of complicity with apartheid. Critics have charged that the unifying images of sport and advertising and the serial repetition of conciliatory gestures and slogans like "the rainbow nation" are trivial and empty.[68]

The power of the here-and-now consumer culture has threatened to overwhelm the aesthetics and politics of collective remembrance. In seeking what amounts to an alternative to ahistorical and mindless consumerism, Herbert Marcuse offers collective memory as a counterpoint to the return to normalcy. In his words, "Remembrance of the past may give rise to dangerous insights, and the established [order] seems to be apprehensive of the subversive contents of memory. Remembrance is a mode of dissociation from the facts, a mode of 'mediation' which breaks, for short moments, the omnipresent power of the facts."[69] Once an integral part of the living memory for those who actively participated in bringing about the end of white minority rule, the struggle against apartheid all too often has been repackaged in commodity form, transformed into cultural-heritage sites or recycled as tourist entertainment destinations. "Branding" functions as a kind of cultural capital in the system of signs that constitutes the neoliberal marketplace. With the transition to parliamentary democracy, global corporations were quick to exploit the new circumstances, rushing forward with advertising campaigns that constructed polished, prismatic images of the "new South Africa" as an exotic playground, a global tourist mecca, and a consumable "brand." In seeking to distance themselves from the history of apartheid oppression, business enterprises encouraged the newly enfranchised South African citizenry to embrace the future with reassuring clichés about consumer culture, upward mobility, and free markets. Advertising firms mimicked the language of political struggle, remolding and reshaping it to fit the needs of consumption. An advertisement for Bonnita milk inquired, "Why cry over spilt milk, when we can build a healthy nation? The past is just that . . . past." In offering its own credit cards, Forchini playfully suggested, "You've won your freedom. Now use it." In promoting hair-care products, Revlon promised a "special feeling" that is "revolutionary." While one company offered "freedom of choice," still another adopted the slogan "Seize the day!" As the familiar slogans of collective political struggle were increasingly linked to the privatized world of consumption, "selective amnesia" was able to gain a foothold. This strategic "un-remembering" has enabled such critical concepts as "freedom" and "equality" to be subsumed under the logic of the market and redefined in the interest of profit-making.[70]

This embrace of social amnesia is sometimes benign, the consequence of the inevitable passage of time that encourages forgetfulness. But sometimes it is also a calculated, deliberate effort to conceal complicity and evade responsibility. Those who wish others to forget often live in fear that others will remember.[71]

ACKNOWLEDGMENTS

The ideas that eventually led me to write this book began to take shape in the immediate post-1994 period, when the outcome of the negotiated settlement that brought an end to apartheid was far from certain. In earlier research and writing, I focused on the wars of maneuver and wars of position that accompanied the popular struggles against white minority rule and the final days of apartheid. The historical specificity of the end of apartheid and the transition to parliamentary democracy was that this political transformation was brought about by a negotiated settlement between two contending social forces that in neither case was able to keep its "side" in line with what each was willing to compromise in order to resolve the political impasse.

In writing this book, I wanted to move away from a more formulaic, conventional treatment of the political transition that would assess the strengths and weaknesses of the democratic turn in the "new South Africa." I decided instead to approach this highly volatile and unstable situation from a wholly different angle of vision. I was intrigued that political transitions typically mark a rather distinct break or rupture from the past, yet at the same time what came before is not so easily discarded, erased, and overcome. The spatial legacies of white minority rule remained deeply embedded in the social fabric of everyday life. I was also struck by the way that specific places (metaphorically, at least) seem to gather around themselves shared remembrances of events (and the persons who participated in them) drawn from the past. Put another way, I was fascinated by how sites of memory become vehicles for always remembering and never forgetting. Collective memories of the past seem to linger on, mutating and adapting to new circumstances.

This book was written in fits and starts over many years. I first began to visit the sites of memory that I describe in this book in 1998, when I held a temporary two-month position as senior lecturer at the University of the Witwatersrand in Johannesburg. Beginning in 1999, I helped to organize three Overseas Study Groups for Colgate University. The traveling associated with these Study Groups provided me with a great opportunity to visit, and revisit, various sites of memory scattered around South Africa.

During this time, I accumulated a great many debts to individuals and institutions. At every juncture, I was assisted by local scholars, curators, and friends whose generosity made this book possible. For sharing insights, knowledge, resources, and hospitality, I would like to thank many people. In Cape Town, Keith Sparks and Clive Newman were invaluable in arranging places to visit. Ciraj Rassool and Leslie Witz provided useful insights at early stages of writing. Curators at the District Six Museum stand out for their dedication and commitment to the shared memory of a place erased under apartheid rule. In Johannesburg, Philip Harrison, Alan Mabin, Cynthia Kros, Marie Huchzermeyer, Claire Bénit-Gbaffau, Mfaniseni (Fana) Sihlongonyane, Sarah Charlton, and Margot Rubin offered much-appreciated assistance and friendship. As always, Patrick Bond offered accommodation on numerous occasions. Loren Landau, Caroline Kihato, and Doug Tilton have been great traveling companions, who shared with humor and wit their insights into the curiosities of South Africa. I have benefited from the stimulating conversations with my colleagues at the University of Michigan, who are spread across such diverse fields as sociology, African studies, architecture, and urban planning.

From the start, I recognized the importance of photographs in helping to visualize the places that I have described in words. I thank Niel Chen, Liz Ogbu, Antoinette Engel, Pierre-Jean Durieu, Joe Levy, Edward Schonsett, William Cobane, Sabine Marschall, Nicolas Brulliard, Wilma Cruise, and Adam Cruise for allowing me to use their photographs. Yet I have not relied on photographic images alone. I personally visited every major site of memory that I write about in this book. I selected photographs that I believe both help the reader visualize what I present in the text and contribute to an understanding of how shared memories are inscribed in place.

I thank Pieter Martin, my editor at the University of Minnesota Press, who encouraged me to submit the manuscript and made very helpful suggestions for reshaping and revising it. I acknowledge those at the University of Minnesota Press who provided technical support. Kristian Tvedten, editorial assistant at the Press, was incredibly generous with his time and energy in taking charge (at literally the last minute) of locating and obtaining permission to reprint many of the photographs in the book. I also thank one anonymous reader for the Press and Christine Boyer, who both provided suggestions about much-needed revisions.

Colleagues at State University of New York at Binghamton, Colgate University, and the University of Michigan gave me helpful comments along this long journey from start to finish. I extend my appreciation to Albert Fu, Rick Baldoz, Jeff Howison, Eric Morier-Genoud, Sean Jacobs, Tony Samara, Andy Clarno, Cecil Madell, and Rosalind Fredericks for their friendship and intellectual conversations. Garth Myers, my collaborator on a number of projects, has always shared his ideas and good humor. I acknowledge the generous financial support from the Taubman College of Architecture and Urban Planning, Department of Afroamerican and African Studies (DAAS), and the Office of Vice President for Research, University of Michigan, for subvention funding to offset the costs of publication. With great sadness I acknowledge the passing of Neville Alexander and Heidi Holland, two South African friends who offered me inspiration and friendship during my trips to South Africa.

Writing this book would not have been possible without the love and patience of my wife, Anne Pitcher, and our daughter, Alida Pitcher-Murray. Observing her grow older with grace and dignity is a source of joy and wonder. She demonstrates remarkable patience with her often-distracted father. Though geographically removed, my two sons, Andrew and Jeremy, are always on my mind—if not in my line of sight. As they have moved into the post-childhood stages of their lives, I like talking with them about ideas and scholarly things. Each in his own way is proceeding along an unknown journey in search of creating separate lives, careers, and commitments.

I cannot fully express my gratitude for the support of my wife. Together we visited many of these sites of memory described in this book. My life is so enriched by her presence and her companionship.

NOTES

Preface

1. Lynn Meskell, "Trauma Culture: Remembering and Forgetting in the New South Africa," in *Memory, Trauma, and World Politics: Reflections on the Relationship between Past and Present*, ed. Duncan Bell (New York: Palgrave Macmillan, 2010), 157–75, esp. 158.

2. Andreas Huyssen, *Twilight Memories: Marking Time in a Culture of Amnesia* (New York: Routledge, 1995), 249.

3. Meskell, "Trauma Culture," 157–75, esp. 158. For a wider view, see Carina Perelli, "*Memoria de Sangre:* Fear, Hope, and Disenchantment in Argentina," in *Remapping Memory: The Politics of Timespace*, ed. Jonathan Boyarin (Minneapolis: University of Minnesota Press, 1994), 39, 49–50.

4. See Andreas Huyssen, *Present Pasts: Urban Palimpsests and the Politics of Memory* (Stanford: Stanford University Press, 2003), 95.

5. Melissa Tandiwe Myambo, "Capitalism Disguised as Democracy: A Theory of 'Belonging,' Not Belongings, in the New South Africa," *Comparative Literature* 63, no. 1 (2011): 63–85.

6. Iwona Irwin-Zarecka, *Frames of Remembrance: The Dynamics of Collective Memory* (New Brunswick, N.J.: Transaction Books, 1994), 7–8.

7. The literature is extensive, but see Meskell, "Trauma Culture," 157–75.

8. Svetlana Boym, *The Future of Nostalgia* (New York: Basic Books, 2001), xviii.

Introduction

1. Albie Sachs, "Preparing Ourselves for Freedom," in *Writing South Africa: Literature, Apartheid, and Democracy, 1970–1995*, ed. Derek Attridge and Rosemary Jolly (New York: Cambridge University Press, 1998), 239–48 (239).

2. Neville Alexander, *An Ordinary Country: Issues in the Transition from Apartheid to Democracy in South Africa* (Durban: University of Natal Press, 2002), 81–110.

3. John Gillis, "Introduction," in *Commemorations: The Politics of National Identity,* ed. Gillis (Princeton: Princeton University Press, 1994), 3. For the concept of "structure of feeling," see Raymond Williams, *The Long Revolution* (New York: Harper and Row, 1961).

4. Annie Coombes, *History after Apartheid: Visual Culture and Public Memory in a Democratic South Africa* (Durham: Duke University Press, 2003), 1–17, esp. 7; Martin Hall, "Social Archaeology and the Theaters of Memory," *Journal of Social Archaeology* 1, no. 1 (2001): 50–61; and JoAnn McGregor and Lyn Shoemaker, "Heritage in Southern Africa: Imagining and Marketing Public Culture and History," *Journal of Southern African Studies* 32, no. 4 (2006): 649–65.

5. Lynn Meskell and Collette Scheermeyer, "Heritage as Therapy: Set Pieces from the New South Africa," *Journal of Material Culture* 13, no. 2 (2008): 153–73, esp. 154.

6. See Omer Bartov, "Defining Enemies, Making Victims: Germans, Jews, and the Holocaust," *American Historical Review* 103, no. 3 (1998): 771–816, esp. 773.

7. Marita Sturken, *Tangled Memories: The Vietnam War, the AIDS Epidemic, and the Politics of Memory* (Berkeley and Los Angeles: University of California Press, 1997), 43.

8. For an excellent review of recent literature on memory studies, see Karen Till, "Memory Studies," *History Workshop Journal* 62 (2006): 325–41.

9. For the source of this phrase, see Bruce Braun, "Colonialism's Afterlife: Vision and Visuality on the Northwest Coast," *Cultural Geographies* 9 (2002): 202–47 (203).

10. Sturken, *Tangled Memories,* 43. See also Richard Terdiman, *Present Past: Modernity and the Memory Crisis* (Ithaca: Cornell University Press, 1993); and Huyssen, *Present Pasts,* 139.

11. See Carina Perelli, "The Power of Memory and the Memory of Power," in *Repression, Exile, and Democracy: Uruguayan Culture,* ed. Saúl Sosnowski and Louise Popkin (Durham: Duke University Press, 1993), 147–59, esp. 153.

12. David Berliner, "The Abuses of Memory: Reflections on the Memory Boom in Anthropology," *Anthropological Quarterly* 78, no. 1 (2005): 197–211; Wulf Kansteiner, "Finding Meaning in Memory: A Methodological Critique of Collective Memory Studies," *History and Theory* 41 (2002): 179–97; Kerwin Lee Klein, "On the Emergence of Memory in Historical Discourse," *Representations* 69, no. 1 (2000): 127–50; Johannes Fabin, "Remembering the Other: Knowledge and Recognition in the Exploration of Central Africa," *Critical Enquiry* 26 (1999): 49–69; Barbie Zelizer, "Reading the Past against the Grain: The Shape of Memory Studies," *Critical Studies in Mass Communication* 12 (1995): 214–39; and Susannah Radstone, *Memory and Methodology* (New York: Berg, 2000).

13. Duncan Bell, "Mythscapes: Memory, Mythology, and National Identity," *British Journal of Sociology* 54, no. 1 (2003): 63–81, esp. 65.

14. Klein, "On the Emergence of Memory in Historical Discourse," 128.

15. Kansteiner, "Finding Meaning in Memory," 179–97; Klein, "On the Emergence of Memory in Historical Discourse," 127–50; Jonathan Boyarin, *Remapping Memory: The Politics of Time Space* (Minneapolis: University of Minnesota Press, 1994), 23; Gillis, "Memory and Identity: The History of a Relationship," in *Commemorations*, ed. Gillis, 3–27; Allan Megill, "History, Memory, Identity," *History of the Human Sciences* 11, no. 3 (1998): 37–62.

16. Bell, "Mythscapes," 71.

17. Klein, "On the Emergence of Memory in Historical Discourse," esp. 145. See Bell, "Mythscapes," 71.

18. Bell, "Mythscapes," 64.

19. Pamuela Shurmer-Smith, "Review of *Casablanca: Movies and Memory,* by Marc Augé," *Cultural Geographies* 18, no. 4 (2001): 557–58.

20. Alon Confino, "Colletive Memory and Cultural History," in *Germany as a Culture of Remembrance* (Chapel Hill: University of North Carolina Press, 2006), 172.

21. See David Atkinson, "Enculturing Fascism? Towards Historical Geographies of Inter-war Italy," *Journal of Historical Geography* 25, no. 3 (1999): 393–400, esp. 394.

22. Colin Bundy, "New Nation, New History? Constructing the Past in Post-*Apartheid* South Africa," in *History Making and Present-Day Politics: The Meaning of Collective Memory in South Africa,* ed. Hans Erik Stolten (Uppsala: Nordiska Afrikainstitutet, 2007), 73–97.

23. Peyi Soyinka-Airewele, "Collective Memory and Selective Amnesia in a Transmutational Paradox," *Issue: A Journal of Opinion* 27, no. 1 (1999): 44–49.

24. Richard Werbner, "Introduction. Beyond Oblivion: Confronting Memory Crisis," in *Memory and the Postcolony: African Anthropology and the Critique of Power,* ed. Werbner (London: Zed Books, 1998), 1–17. See also Claudia Koonz, "Between Memory and Oblivion: Concentration Camps in German Memory," in *Commemorations,* ed. John Gillis, 258–80.

25. The term "vehicles of memory" is used by Yosef Haym Yerushalmi, *Zakhor: Jewish History and Jewish Memory* (Seattle: University of Washington Press, 1982), ix, xviii, xxix, 45, 73.

26. Huyssen, *Present Pasts,* 10, 28.

27. Ibid., 95–96.

28. Huyssen, *Twilight Memories,* 7.

29. For the source of some of these ideas, see Andreas Huyssen, "The Voids of Berlin," *Critical Inquiry* 24, no. 1 (1997): 57–81, esp. 57.

30. For the source of some of these ideas, see Deborah Cherry, "Statues in the Square: Hauntings at the Heart of Empire," *Art History* 29, no. 4 (2006): 660–97, esp. 665.

31. Sturken, *Tangled Memories,* 43. See also Huyssen, *Present Pasts,* 139. For an excellent review of recent literature on memory studies, see Till, "Memory Studies," 325–41.

32. The literature on collective memory is extensive. See, for example, Patrick H. Hutton, *History as an Art of Memory* (Hanover, N.H.: University Press of New England, 1993); David Thelan, *Memory and American History* (Bloomington: Indiana University Press, 1990); Jacques Le Goff, *History and Memory* (New York: Columbia University press, 1992); Patrick Geary, *Phantoms of Remembrance: Memory and Oblivion at the End of the First Millennium* (Princeton: Princeton University Press, 1994); Mark Masuda, *The Memory of the Modern* (New York: Oxford University Press, 1996); Susan Crane, *Museums and Memory* (Palo Alto: Stanford University Press, 2000); and Eviatar Zerubavel, *Time Maps: Collective Memory and the Social Shape of the Past* (Chicago: University of Chicago Press, 2003).

33. For some recent key works, see James E. Young, *The Texture of Memory: Holocaust Memorials and Meaning* (New Haven: Yale University Press, 1993); Chris Healy, *From the Ruins of Colonialism: History as Social Memory* (New York: Cambridge University Press, 1997); Joanne Rappaport, *The Politics of Memory: Native Historical Interpretation in the Colombian Andes* (New York: Cambridge University Press, 1990); and Jay Winter, *Sites of Memory, Sites of Mourning: The Great War in European Cultural History* (New York: Cambridge University Press, 1996).

34. See Jennifer Cole, "The Work of Memory in Madagascar," *American Anthropologist* 24, no. 4 (1998): 610–33; Debbora Battaglia, "The Body in the Gift: Memory and Forgetting in Sabari Mortuary Exchange," *American Ethnologist* 19, no. 1 (1992): 3–18; and Brad Weiss, "Forgetting Your Dead: Alienable and Inalienable Objects in Northwest Tanzania," *Anthropological Quarterly* 70, no. 4 (1997): 164–72.

35. Patti Waldmeir, *Anatomy of a Miracle: The End of Apartheid and the Birth of the New South Africa* (New York: W. W. Norton, 1997); Allister Sparks, *Tomorrow Is Another Country: The Inside Story of South Africa's Road to Change* (New York: Hill and Wang, 1995); and Steven Friedman and Doreen Atkinson, eds., *South African Review, 7: The Small Miracle: South Africa's Negotiated Settlement* (Johannesburg: Ravan Press, 1994). For a general survey of this literature, see David T. Jervis, "Miracle or Model? South Africa's Transition to Democracy," *International Third World Studies Journal and Review* 16 (2005): 37–45.

36. Myambo, "Capitalism Disguised as Democracy," 63–85.

37. James Statman, "Whites Are Living in Cloud-Cuckooland," *Sunday Independent,* July 5, 1998.

38. This phrase is borrowed from Huyssen, "The Voids of Berlin," 63.

39. Sarah Nuttall, "Stylizing the Self: The Y Generation in Rosebank, Johannesburg," *Public Culture* 16, no. 3 (2004): 430–52.

40. Ali Hlongwane, "Commemoration, Memory, and Monuments in the Contested Language of Black Liberation: The South African Experience," *Journal of Pan African Studies* 2, no. 4 (2008): 137–38.

41. Saskia Sassen, *Territory, Authority, Rights: From Medieval to Global Assemblages* (Princeton: Princeton University Press, 2006), 4.

42. See Yomi Durotoye and Robert Griffins, "Civilianizing Military Rule: Conditions and Processes of Political Transmutation in Ghana and Nigeria," *African Studies Review* 40 (1997): 133–60.

43. Soyinka-Airewele, "Collective Memory and Selective Amnesia," 44–49, esp. 44.

44. Ibid., 44–45.

45. Eve Bertelson, "Ads and Amnesia: Black Advertising in the New South Africa," in *Negotiating the Past: The Making of Memory in South Africa,* ed. Sarah Nuttall and Carli Coetzee (Cape Town: Oxford University Press, 1998), 221–48.

46. Melissa Tandiwe Myambo, "The Limits of Rainbow Nation Multiculturalism in the New South Africa: Spatial Configuration in Zakes Mda's *Ways of Dying* and Jonathan Morgan's *Finding Mr. Madini," Research in African Literatures* 41, no. 2 (2010): 93–120.

47. For a wider discussion, see Bell, "Mythscapes," 63–81.

48. Myambo, "The Limits of Rainbow Nation Multiculturalism," 93–95.

1. The Power of Collective Memory

1. David Lowenthal, "Past Time, Present Place: Landscapes and Memory," *Geographical Review* 65 (1975): 1–36 (32).

2. Salman Rushdie, *Midnight's Children* (London: Picador, 1981), 211.

3. William Graham Sumner, *Folkways* (New York: Arno Press, 1979 (1906), 636.

4. Barry Schwartz, "The Social Context of Commemoration: A Study in Collective Memory," *Social Forces* 61, no. 2 (1982): 374–402 (396).

5. Lowenthal, "Past Time, Present Place," 27.

6. See Charles Withers, "Place, Memory, Monument: Memorializing the Past in Contemporary Highland Scotland," *Ecumene* 3, no. 3 (1996): 325–44.

7. Jan Werner Müller, "Introduction: The Power of Memory, the Memory of Power, and the Power over Memory," in *Memory and Power in Post-war Europe,* ed. Müller (Cambridge: Cambridge University Press, 2002), 1–38.

8. Lowenthal, "Past Time, Present Place," 33.

9. For a critique of the oversaturated use of collective memory, see Berliner, "The Abuses of Memory," 197–211. See also Kansteiner, "Finding Meaning in Memory," 179–97.

10. See, for example, Neil Jarman, "Troubled Images," *Critique of Anthropology* 12, no. 2 (1992): 145–65; and Bill Rolston, "Politics, Painting, and Popular Culture: The Political Wall Murals of Northern Ireland," *Media, Culture & Society* 9 (1987): 5–28.

11. M. Christine Boyer, *The City of Collective Memory: Its Historical Imagery and Architectural Entertainments* (Cambridge, Mass.: MIT Press, 1994).

12. Annette Kuhn, *Family Secrets: Acts of Memory and Imagination* (London: Verso, 1995), 5–6.

13. Omer Bartov, "Intellectuals on Auschwitz: Memory, History, and Truth," *History and Memory* 5, no. 1 (1993): 87–123 (94).

14. See Alan Milward, "A Dubious Kind of Memory," *Times Literary Supplement*, October 10, 1997, 7. See also Ralph Rugoff, *Circus Americanus* (New York: Verso, 1997); Michel-Rolph Trouillot, "The Power in the Story," in *Silencing the Past: Power in the Production of History* (Boston: Beacon Press, 1994), 1–30; and Katharine Hodgkin and Susannah Radstone, "Introduction: Contested Pasts," in *Contested Pasts: The Politics of Memory*, ed. Hodgkin and Radstone (New York: Routledge, 2003), 1–28.

15. For the idea of "contact zones," see Mary Louise Pratt, *Imperial Eyes: Travel Writing and Transculturation* (New York: Routledge, 1992), esp. 1–15.

16. Lowenthal, "Past Time, Present Place," 1–36 (27).

17. Nuala Johnson, *Ireland, The Great War, and the Geography of Remembrance* (Cambridge: Cambridge University Press, 2003), 2–3.

18. Jonathan Boyarin, "Space, Time, and the Politics of Memory," in *Remapping Memory: The Politics of Timespace*, ed. Boyarin (Minneapolis: University of Minnesota Press, 1994), 22.

19. Zeynep Çelik, "Colonial/Postcolonial Intersections: *Lieux de mémoire* in Algiers," *Third Text* 49 (1999–2000): 63–72.

20. Tim Edensor, "National Identity and the Politics of Memory: Remembering Bruce and Wallace in Symbolic Space," *Environment and Planning D: Society and Space* 29 (1997): 175–94, esp. 175.

21. Peter Novick, *The Holocaust and Collective Memory* (London: Bloomsbury, 1999), 4; and Brian Osborne, "Constructing Landscapes of Power: The George Étienne Cartier Monument, Montreal," *Journal of Historical Geography* 24, no. 4 (1998): 431–58, esp. 432.

22. Edensor, "National Identity and the Politics of Memory," 176.

23. Francis Yates, *The Art of Memory* (London: Routledge, 1978).

24. Raphael Samuel, *Theatres of Memory*, vol. 1: *Past and Present in Contemporary Culture* (London: Verso, 1994), x–xi; David Lowenthal, *The Past Is a Foreign Country* (Cambridge: Cambridge University Press, 1985), 210–38; Nathan Wachtel, "Memory and History: An Introduction," *History and Anthropology* 2, no. 2 (1986): 207–24; and Gabrielle Spiegel, "Memory and History: Liturgical Time and Historical Time," *History and Theory* 41 (2002): 149–62.

25. Maurice Halbwachs, *On Collective Memory*, trans. Francis Ditter and Vida Yaz Ditter (New York: Harper and Row, 1980).

26. Ibid., 78–80, 140.

27. See Pierre Nora, ed., *Realms of Memory: Rethinking the French Past,* trans. Arthur Goldhammer, 3 vols. (New York: Columbia University Press, 1996–98). For an overview of these volumes and an exploration of the basic concepts, see Nancy Wood, "Memory's Remains: *Lieux de Mémoire,*" *History and Memory* 6 (1994): 123–54.

28. Pierre Nora, "Between Memory and History: *Les Lieux de Mémoire,*" trans. Marc Roudebush, *Representations* 26 (1989): 7–25.

29. Ibid., 7–9.

30. Ibid., 23–25.

31. Withers, "Place, Memory, Monument," 326.

32. Samuel, *Theatres of Memory,* 1:ix–x.

33. Boyarin, "Space, Time, and the Politics of Memory," 1–38, esp. 16.

34. Edensor, "National Identity and the Politics of Memory," 175.

35. Nuala Johnson, "Cast in Stone: Monuments, Geography, and Nationalism," *Environment and Planning D: Society and Space* 13 (1995): 51–66 (63).

36. Ibid., 51.

37. Karen Till, "Imagining National Identity: 'Chapters of Life' at the German Historical Museum," in *Textures of Place: Exploring Humanist Geographies,* ed. Paul Adams, Steven Hoelscher, and Karen Till (Minneapolis: University of Minnesota Press, 2001), 273–99 (273).

38. Benjamin Forest, Juliet Johnson, and Karen Till, "Post-Totalitarian National Identity: Public Memory in Germany and Russia," *Social and Cultural Geography* 5, no. 3 (2004): 357–80. See also Daniel Walkowitz and Lisa Maya Knauer, eds., *Memory and the Impact of Political Transformation in Public Space* (Durham: Duke University Press, 2004).

39. Kenneth Foote, Atilla Toth, and Anett Arvay, "Hungary after 1989: Inscribing a New Past on Place," *Geographical Review* 90, no. 3 (2000): 301–34; John Borneman, *After the Wall: East Meets West in the New Berlin* (New York: Basic Books, 1991); Hermine de Soto, "(Re)inventing Berlin: Dialectics of Power, Symbols, and Pasts, 1990–1995," *City and Society* 1 (1996): 29–49; Dario Gamboni, *The Destruction of Art* (London: Reaktion Books, 1997), 51–90; and Adrian Forty, "Introduction," in *The Art of Forgetting,* ed. Adrian Forty and Suzanne Küchler (Oxford: Berg, 2001), 1–18.

40. Benjamin Forest and Juliet Johnson, "Unraveling the Threads of History: Soviet-Era Monuments and Post-Soviet National Identity in Moscow," *Annals of the Association of American Geographers* 92, no. 3 (2002): 525–47; and Karen Till, "Staging the Past: Landscape Designs, Cultural Identity, and 'Erinnerungspolitik' at Berlin's Neue Wache," *Ecumene* 6 (1999): 251–83.

41. Hutton, *History as an Art of Memory.*

42. Benedict Anderson, *Imagined Communities: Reflections on the Origin and Spread of Nationalism* (London: Verso, 1983), 4–6.

43. Michael Ignatieff, *Blood and Belonging: Journeys into the New Nationalism* (New York: Farrar, Straus and Giroux, 1993).

44. Osborne, "Constructing Landscapes of Power," esp. 432. Saul Friedländer, for example, distinguishes between "mythic memory" of those with direct experience and the "rational understanding" of professional historians. Saul Friedländer, "History, Memory, and the Historian: Dilemmas and Responsibilities," *New German Critique* 80 (2000): 3–16, esp. 11.

45. For the source of these ideas, see Sikivu Hutchinson, *Imagining Transit: Race, Gender, and Transportation Politics in Los Angeles* (Bern: Peter Lang, 2003).

46. Nora, "Between History and Memory," 19.

47. Andrew Charlesworth, "Contesting Places of Memory: The Case of Auschwitz," *Environment and Planning D: Society and Space* 12 (1994): 579–93, esp. 579.

48. Karen Till, *The New Berlin: Memory, Politics, Place* (Minneapolis: University of Minnesota Press, 2005), 8–9. See also Brian Ladd, *The Ghosts of Berlin: Confronting German History in the Urban Landscape* (Chicago: University of Chicago Press, 1997); James E. Young, *At Memory's Edge: After-Images of the Holocaust in Contemporary Art and Architecture* (New Haven: Yale University Press, 2000); and Wulf Kansteiner, *In Pursuit of German Memory: Television, History, and Politics after Auschwitz* (Athens: Ohio University Press, 2006).

49. Charlesworth, "Contesting Places of Memory," 579, 581, 584, 591. For a similar case, see Maoz Azaryahu, "RePlacing Memory: The Reorientation of Buchenwald," *Cultural Geographies* 10 (2003): 1–20.

50. Lowenthal, *The Past Is a Foreign Country,* xxiii.

51. Jeremy Foster, *Washed with Sun: Landscape and the Making of White South Africa* (Pittsburgh: University of Pittsburgh Press, 2008), 17.

52. Ibid. 5.

53. Karen Till has argued that "most studies of public memory adopt a historical approach," what she calls "the biography of a site." See Till, "Memory Studies," 325–41 (327).

54. Huyssen, *Present Pasts,* 101.

55. Nuala Johnson, "Sculpting Heroic Histories: Celebrating the Centenary of the 1798 Rebellion in Ireland," *Transactions of the Institute of British Geographers* 19 [n.s.] (1994): 78–93.

56. Douglas Allen, "Memory and Place: Two Case Studies," *Paces* 21, no. 1 (2009): 56–61 (56).

57. Ibid., 59. See also Eva Hoffman, "The Balm of Recognition: Rectifying Wrong

through the Generations," in *Human Rights, Human Wrongs,* ed. Nicholas Owen (Oxford: Oxford University Press, 2003), 278–303.

58. Huyssen, *Present Pasts,* 101–2.

59. Julian Bonder, "On Memory, Trauma, Public Space, Monuments, and Memorials," *Places* 21, no. 1 (2009): 62–69, esp. 64.

60. Young, *The Texture of Memory,* 12.

61. See Mieke Bal, "Telling, Showing, Showing Off," *Critical Inquiry* 18, no. 4 (1992): 561. See also Donna Haraway, *Primate Visions: Gender, Race, and Nature in the World of Modern Science* (New York: Routledge, 1989), 26–58; and James Clifford, "On Collecting Art and Culture," in *The Predicament of Culture: Twentieth-Century Ethnography, Literature, and Art* (Cambridge, Mass.: Harvard University Press, 1988), 215–51.

62. Margaret Somers, "The Narrative Constitution of Identity: A Relational and Network Approach," *Theory and Society* 23 (1994): 605–49 (616).

63. Edward Casey, "Public Memory in the Making: Ethics and Place in the Wake of 9/11," in *Architecture, Ethics, and the Personhood of Place,* ed. Gregory Caicco (Lebanon, N.H.: University Press of New England, 2007), 69–90, esp. 69.

64. Nuala Johnson, "Mapping Monuments: The Shaping of Public Space and Cultural Identities," *Visual Communication* 1, no. 3 (2002): 293–98, esp. 293.

65. Boyer, *The City of Collective Memory,* 321.

66. Bonder, "On Memory, Trauma, Public Space, Monuments, and Memorials," 65.

67. Mark Crinson, "Urban Memory: An Introduction," in *Urban Memory: History and Amnesia in the Modern City,* ed. Crinson (New York: Routledge, 2005), xi–xx, esp. xii.

68. Winter, *Sites of Memory, Sites of Mourning.*

69. See Güven Arif Sargin, "Displaced Memories, or the Architecture of Forgetting and Remembrance," *Environment and Planning D: Society and Space* 22 (2004): 659–80.

70. Cherry, "Statues in the Square," 663, 664.

71. Jennifer Jordan, *Structures of Memory: Understanding Urban Change in Berlin and Beyond* (Stanford: Stanford University Press, 2006).

72. See, for example, David Atkinson and Denis Cosgrove, "Urban Rhetoric and Embodied Identities: City, Nation, and Empire at the Vittorio Emanuele II Monument in Rome, 1870–1945," *Annals of the Association of American Geographers* 88, no. 1 (1998): 28–49.

73. Cherry, "Statues in the Square," 665.

74. Daniel Herwitz, "Monument, Ruin, and Redress in South African Heritage," *Germanic Review* 86, no. 4 (2011): 235.

75. Marietta Kesting and Aljoscha Weskott, "Dream Machine—Introduction," in *Sun Tropes: Sun City and (Post-)Apartheid Culture in South Africa,* ed. Kesting and Weskott (Cologne: August Verlag, 2009), 13.

76. See James E. Young, "The Counter-Monument: Memory against Itself in Germany Today," *Critical Inquiry* 18, no. 2 (1992): 274.

77. Young, *The Texture of Memory*, 5.

78. Patricia Davison, "Museums and the Reshaping of Memory," in *Negotiating the Past*, ed. Nuttall and Coetzee, 143–60 (146).

79. Ibid., 145–46.

80. Till, "Reimagining National Identity," 274–75.

81. Masao Yamaguchi, "The Poetics of Exhibition in Japanese Culture," in *Exhibiting Cultures: The Poetics and Politics of Museum Display*, ed. Ivan Karp and Steven Lavine (Washington, D.C.: Smithsonian Institution Press, 1994), 57–67 (61).

82. Robert Foster, "Making National Cultures in the Global Ecumene," *Annual Review of Anthropology* 20 (1991): 235–60 (243).

83. Tony Bennett, "Civic Laboratories: Museums, Cultural Objecthood, and the Governance of the Social," *Cultural Studies* 19, no. 5 (2005): 521–47; Bennett, "Exhibition, Difference, and the Logic of Culture," in *Museum Frictions: Public Cultures/Global Transformation*, ed. Ivan Karp, Corinne A. Kratz, Lynn Szwaja, and Tomás Ybarra-Frausto (Durham: Duke University Press, 2006), 46–69; Barbara Kirshenblatt-Gimblet, "Exhibitionary Complexes," in *Museum Frictions*, ed. Karp et al., 35–45; and Mieke Bal, "Telling Objects: A Narrative Perspective on Collecting," in *The Cultures of Collecting*, ed. John Elsner and Roger Cardinal (London: Reaction Books, 1994), 97–115.

84. Sharon Macdonald, "Theorizing Museums: An Introduction," in *Theorizing Museums: Representing Identity and Diversity in a Changing World*, ed. Sharon Macdonald and Gordon Fyfe (Oxford: Blackwell, 1996), 1–20 (7).

85. Susan Crane, "Memory, Distortion, and History in the Museum," *History and Theory* 36, no. 4 (1997): 44–63, esp. 44.

86. Nuala Johnson, "The Spectacle of Memory: Ireland's Remembrance of the Great War, 1919," *Journal of Historical Geography* 25 (1999): 36–56, esp. 39.

87. Tony Bennett, "Civic Seeing: Museums and the Organisation of Vision," in *Companion to Museum Studies*, ed. Sharon Macdonald (Oxford: Blackwell, 2006), 263–81; and Bennett, "Stored Virtue: Memory, the Body, and the Evolutionary Museum," in *Regimes of Memory*, ed. Katharine Hodgkin and Susannah Radstone (New York: Routledge, 2002), 40–54.

88. Carl Grodach, "Museums as Urban Catalysts: The Role of Urban Design in Flagship Cultural Development," *Journal of Urban Design* 13, no. 2 (2008): 195–212 (196).

89. Irina Van Aalst and Inez Boogaarts, "From Museum to Mass Entertainment: The Evolution of the Role of Museums in Cities," *European Urban and Regional Studies*

9, no. 3 (2002): 195–209 (197). See also Elizabeth Wilson, "The Rhetoric of Public Space," *New Left Review* 209 (1995): 146–60.

90. Paul L. Knox, *Cities and Design* (London: Routledge, 2011), 192.

91. As the architectural historian Aldo Rossi famously put it, "We can say that the city itself is the collective memory of its people, and like the memory it is associated with objects and places. The city is the locus of the collective memory. The relationship between the locus and the citizenry then becomes the city's predominant image, both of architecture and of landscape, and as certain artifacts become part of its memory, new ones emerge. In this entirely positive sense great ideas flow through the history of the city and give shape to it" (Aldo Rossi, *The Architecture of the City* [Cambridge, Mass.: MIT Press, 1982], 130).

92. Anouk Bérlanger, "Urban Space and Collective Memory: Analysing the Various Dimensions of the Production of Memory," *Canadian Journal of Urban Research* 11, no. 1 (2002): 69–92, esp. 69–70.

93. Paul Stangl, "The Vernacular and the Monumental: Memory and Landscape in Post-war Berlin," *GeoJournal* 73 (2008): 245–53.

94. Michael Hebbert, "The Street as a Locus of Collective Memory," *Environment and Planning D* 23 (2005): 581–96.

95. Huyssen, *Present Pasts,* 49–50, 65.

96. Sam Appleby, "Crawley: A Space Mythology," *New Formations* 11 (1990): 19–44; Çelik, "Colonial/Postcolonial Intersections," 63–72; Maoz Azaryahu, "The Power of Commemorative Street Names," *Environment and Planning D: Society and Space* 14, no. 3 (1996): 311–30; Azarhayu, "German Reunification and the Politics of Street Names: The Case of East Berlin," *Political Geography* 16 (1997): 479–93; and Reuben Rose-Redwood, "From Number to Name: Symbolic Capital, Places of Memory, and the Politics of Street Renaming in New York City," *Social and Cultural Geography* 9, no. 4 (2008): 431–52.

97. Raphael Samuel, *Theatres of Memory,* vol. 2: *Island Stories, Unraveling Britain* (London: Verso, 1998), 354.

98. Spiro Kostof, *The City Assembled: The Elements of Urban Form through History* (London: Thames and Hudson, 1992), 243.

99. Hebbert, "The Street as a Locus of Collective Memory," 581–96, esp. 581.

100. Bérlanger, "Urban Space and Collective Memory," 71.

101. Till, *The New Berlin,* 8; Huyssen, *Present Pasts,* 32–33, 158–59; Charlesworth, "Contesting Places of Memory," 579–93; Adams, Hoelscher, and Till, eds., *The Textures of Place;* and Forest, Johnson, and Till, "Post-Totalitarian Identity," 357–80.

102. Doreen Massey, *Space, Place, and Gender* (Minneapolis: University of Minnesota Press, 1994), 121.

103. Hebbert, "The Street as a Locus of Collective Memory," 592.

104. Max Page, *The Creative Destruction of Manhattan, 1900–1940* (Chicago: University of Chicago Press, 1999), 251–52.

105. Bérlanger, "Urban Space and Collective Memory," 87; and Hebbert, "The Street as a Locus of Collective Memory," 582.

106. Rossi, *The Architecture of the City,* 131.

107. Boyer, *The City of Collective Memory,* 31.

108. Crinson, "Urban Memory," xi–xx, esp. xii.

109. Umberto Eco, "Architecture and Memory," *Via* 8 (1986): 88–94 (89).

110. For the source of this idea, see Rolf Goebel, "Urban Topography and Cultural Memory," *Anthropological Materialism* (2010), http://anthropologicalmaterialism.hypotheses.org/473. See also Goebel, "Berlin's Architectural Citations: Reconstruction, Simulation, and the Problem of Historical Authenticity," *PLMA* 118, no. 5 (2003): 1268–89, esp. 1281–82.

111. Walter Benjamin, *The Arcades Project,* trans. Howard Eiland and Kevin McNaughlin (Cambridge, Mass.: Belknap Press of Harvard University Press, 1999), 17, 21, 406.

112. On the connection between history and memory in Walter Benjamin, see Graeme Gilloch, *Myth and Metropolis: Walter Benjamin and the City* (Cambridge: Polity, 1996); and Sigrid Weigel, *Body- and Image-Space: Re-reading Walter Benjamin* (London: Routledge, 1996).

113. Crinson, "Urban Memory," 1–19.

114. Goebel, "Urban Topography and Cultural Memory."

115. Tim Edensor, "Building Stone in Manchester: Networks of Materiality, Circulating Matter, and the Ongoing Constitution of the City," in *Re-shaping Cities: How Global Mobility Transforms Architecture and Urban Form,* ed. Michael Guggenheim and Ola Söderström (New York: Routledge, 2010), 211–29, esp. 211.

116. John Urry, "Preface: Places and Performance," in *Travels in Paradox: Remapping Tourism,* ed. Claudio Minca and Tim Oakes (Boulder, Colo.: Rowman and Littlefield, 2006), vii–xi (ix).

117. Maria Kaika, *City of Flows: Modernity, Nature, and the City* (London: Routledge, 2005), 22.

118. Edensor, "Building Stone in Manchester," 211.

119. Mike Crang, "Urban Morphology and the Shaping of the Transmissible City," *City* 4, no. 3 (2004): 303–15, esp. 304.

120. Doreen Massey, "Power-Geometry and a Progressive Sense of Place," in *Mapping the Futures: Local Cultures, Global Change,* ed. Jon Bird, Barry Curtis, Tim Putnam, George Robertson, and Lisa Tickner (London: Routledge, 1993), 59–69.

121. Edensor, "Building Stone in Manchester," 213 (216).

122. Huyssen, *Past Presents,* 19, 71; and Lowenthal, "Past Time, Present Place," 1–36.

2. White Lies

1. Healy, *From the Ruins of Colonialism,* 5–7, 11–13.

2. Nora, "Between History and Memory," 7–25 (7).

3. For the popular use of this phrase, see Eric Wolf, *Europe and the People without History* (Berkeley and Los Angeles: University of California Press, 1982).

4. See Pippa Skotnes, "'Civilised off the Face of the Earth': Museum Display and the Silencing of the /Xam," *Poetics Today* 22, no. 2 (2001): 299–321; and Pippa Skotnes, "The Politics of Bushman Representations," in *Images and Empires: Visualities in Colonial and Post-Colonial Africa,* ed. Paul Landau and Deborah Kaspin (Berkeley and Los Angeles: University of California Press, 2002), 253–74.

5. For the source of these figures, see Franco Frescura, "National or Nationalist? A Critique of the National Monuments Council, 1936–1989," in *Proceedings of the National Urban Conservation Symposium Held at the University of the Witwatersrand, Johannesburg, 12–14 July 1990,* ed. Derek Japha and Vivienne Japha (Cape Town: Oakville Press, 1991), 15–26. See also Shane Moran, *Representing Bushmen: South Africa and the Origins of Language* (Rochester: University of Rochester Press, 2009).

6. Hans Pienaar, "After the Lion, Who'll Disappear Next?" *The Star,* June 11, 2001, 13.

7. Sabine Marschall, *Landscape of Memory: Commemorative Monuments, Memorials and Public Statuary in Post-Apartheid South-Africa* (Leiden: Brill, 2010), 2–7.

8. Young, "The Counter-Monument, 267–99, esp. 270.

9. Foster, *Washed with the Sun,* 17; and Jennifer Beningfield, *The Frightened Land: Land, Landscape, and Politics in Twentieth-Century South Africa* (London: Routledge, 2006).

10. Foster, *Washed with Sun,* 17.

11. Prasenjit Duara uses the phrase "narrative of descent" in "Historicizing National Identity, or Who Imagines What and When," in *Becoming National: A Reader,* ed. Geoff Ely and Ronald Suny (Oxford: Oxford University Press, 1996), 151–77, esp. 168.

12. Foster, *Washed with Sun,* 39.

13. Ibid., 3–4. See also David Bunn, "Whited Sepulchres: On the Reluctance of Monuments," in *Blank__: Architecture, Apartheid, and After,* ed. Hilton Judin and Ivan Vladislavić (Rotterdam: NAi Publishers, 1999), 92–117.

14. Foster, *Washed with Sun,* 3–4, 9–11.

15. This sentence is borrowed almost verbatim from Foster, *Washed with Sun,* 19.

16. Beningfield, *The Frightened Land,* 28, 30, 35 104–5.

17. William Beinart, *Twentieth-Century South Africa* (Oxford: Oxford University Press, 1994).

18. Jeremy Foster, "'Land of Contrasts' or 'Home We Have Always Known'? The SAR&H and the Imaginary Geography of White South African Nationhood, 1910–1930," *Journal of Southern African Studies* 29, no. 3 (2003): 657–80 (659).

19. Foster, *Washed with Sun,* 28. See also Saul Dubow, "Colonial Nationalism, the Milner Kindergarten and the Rise of 'South Africanism,'" *History Workshop Journal* 43 (Spring 1997): 53–86.

20. Foster, *Washed with Sun,* 28, 30.

21. Ibid., 33. See also Isabel Hofmeyr, "Building a Nation from Words: Afrikaans Language, Literature, and Ethnic Identity," in *The Politics of Race, Class, and Nationalism,* ed. Shula Marks and Stanley Trapido (London: Longman, 1987), 95–123; and Isabel Hofmeyr, "Popularizing History: The Case of Gustav Preller," *Journal of African History* 29, no. 3 (1988): 521–35, esp. 529.

22. Foster, *Washed with Sun,* 37.

23. The literature is voluminous, but see Foster, *Washed with the Sun,* 31–33, 262; Bunn, "Whited Sepulchres," 92–117; and Beningfield, *The Frightened Land,* 34–49, 272–83.

24. Eric Hobsbawm, "Introduction: Inventing Traditions," in *The Invention of Tradition,* ed. Eric Hobsbawm and Terence Ranger (New York: Cambridge University Press, 1983), 1–14.

25. Kaja Silverman, "Back to the Future," *Camera Obscura* 27 (1991): 109–32, esp. 120.

26. W. I. Thomas and D. S. Thomas, *The Child in America: Behavior Problems and Programs* (New York: Alfred A. Knopf, 1928), 571–72.

27. Herwitz, "Monument, Ruin, and Redress in South African Heritage," 232–48, esp. 235–36.

28. Ibid., 236.

29. Patrice Jeppson, "'Leveling the Playing Field' in the Contested Territory of the South African Past: A 'Public' versus a 'People's' Form of Historic Archaeology Outreach," *Historical Archaeology* 31, no. 3 (1997): 65–83.

30. See Leroy Vail, "Introduction: Ethnicity in Southern African History," in *The Creation of Tribalism in Southern Africa,* ed. Vail (Berkeley and Los Angeles: University of California Press, 1989), 10–19.

31. Foster, *Washed with Sun,* 34–38.

32. See Edward Said, "Invention, Memory, and Place," in *Landscape and Power,* ed. W. J. T. Mitchell (Chicago: University of Chicago Press, 1994), 261–90.

33. W. J. T. Mitchell, ed., "Introduction," *Landscape and Power,* 1–4, esp. 3.

34. Foster, *Washed with the Sun,* 262.

35. Bunn, "Whited Sepulchres," 98.

36. Foster, *Washed with Sun,* 47. See also Jeremy Foster, "Northward, Upward: Stories of Train Travel, and the Journey toward South African Nationhood, 1895–1950," *Journal of Historical Geography* 31 (2005) 296–215.

37. "The Great Trek was not an armed invasion into the vast open areas of South Africa, but was a trek in search of a new home, a Homeland of Promise, where they could enjoy the freedom from outside interference that they had always cherished. Neither was the Great Trek a casual and unorganized departure associated with grievances of a more or less materialist nature, it was a climax of gradual development toward national independence spreading over a period of more than a century. . . . [The Voortrekkers] helped in the opening up of Southern Africa to habitation by civilised peoples and by their combined efforts they opened up new areas of settlement, paving the way for the development of the land and the proper cultivation of the soil" (John Lees Small, *Monuments and Trails of the Voortrekkers* [Cape Town: Howard Timmons, 1968], n.p.).

38. See Foster, *Washed with Sun,* 52–55, 144–77, for the colonial architecture of Parktown Ridge, Johannesburg.

39. For a useful discussion, see Braun, "Colonialism's Afterlife," 202–47, esp. 203–4.

40. See Liz Gunner, "Remapping Land and Remaking Culture: Memory and Landscape in 20th-Century South Africa," *Journal of Historical Geography* 31 (2005): 281–95, esp. 282.

41. Simon Schama, *Landscape and Memory* (New York: Vintage, 1995), 14.

42. See, for example, Noëleen Murray, "Remaking Modernism: South African Architecture In and Out of Time," in *Desire Lines: Space, Memory, and Identity in the Post-apartheid City,* ed. Noëleen Murray, Nick Shepherd, and Martin Hall (New York: Routledge, 2007), 43–66.

43. Martin Hall, "The Archaeology of Colonial Settlement in Southern Africa," *Annual Review of Anthropology* 22 (1993): 177–2000.

44. Jo Noero, "Architecture and Memory," in *Global Cities: Cinema, Architecture, and Urbanism in a Digital Age,* ed. Linda Krause and Patrice Petro (New Brunswick, N.J.: Rutgers University Press, 2003), 185–94, esp. 186.

45. Vickie Leibowitz, "Making Memory Space: Recollection and Reconciliation in Post Apartheid South African Architecture" (master's thesis, School of Architecture and Design, RMIT University, 2008), 18–20 (19).

46. See Young, "The Counter-Monument," 270.

47. See Gary Baines, "The Politics of Public History in Post-*Apartheid* South Africa," in *History Making and Present-Day Politics: The Meaning of Collective Memory in South Africa,* ed. Hans Erik Stolten, 167–82.

48. See Ciraj Rassool and Leslie Witz, "The 1952 Jan van Riebeeck Tercentenary Festival: Constructing and Contesting Public National History in South Africa," *Journal of African History* 34 (1993): 447–68 (448).

49. Ibid., 457.

50. Jacqueline Maingard, "Imag(in)ing the South African Nation: Representations of Identity in the Rugby World Cup 1995," *Theatre Journal* 49, no. 1 (1997): 15–28, esp. 16.

51. Leslie Witz, *Apartheid's Festival: Contesting South Africa's National Pasts* (Bloomington: Indiana University Press, 2003), 66–70; and Nhlanhla Maake, "Inscribing Identity on the Landscape: National Symbols in South Africa," in *Text, Theory, Space,* ed. Kate Darian-Smith, Liz Gunner, and Sarah Nuttall (London: Routledge, 1996), 145–55.

52. For a wider discussion, see Bell, "Mythscapes," 63–81.

53. Young, "The Counter-Monument," 270; and Duncan Bell, "Introduction: Memory, Trauma, and World Politics," in *Memory, Trauma, and World Politics,* ed. Bell, 1–29.

54. See Atkinson, "Enculturing Fascism?," 393–400, esp. 394–95.

55. Janet Hall, "Museums, Myths, and Missionaries: Redressing the Past for a New South Africa," in *Museum, Media, Message,* ed. Eilean Hooper-Greenhill (New York: Routledge, 1995), 178–89; and Andrew Spiegel, "Struggling with Tradition in South Africa: The Multivocality of the Past," in *Social Construction of the Past: Representation as Power,* ed. George Bond and Angela Gilliam (New York: Routledge, 1994), 185–202.

56. Myambo, "The Limits of Rainbow Nation Multiculturalism in the New South Africa," 93–120.

57. Martin Hall, "Earth and Stone: Archaeology as Memory," in *Negotiating the Past,* ed. Nuttall and Coetzee, 180–200, esp. 197.

58. Martin J. Murray, "Building the 'New South Africa': Urban Space, Architectural Design, and the Disruption of Historical Memory," in *History Making and Present-Day Politics,* ed. Stolten, 227–47, esp. 228.

59. David Leary, "Naming and Knowing: Giving Forms to Things Unknown," *Social Research* 62, no. 2 (1995): 267–98, esp. 267–68, 270.

60. See Garth Myers, "Naming and Placing the Other," *Tijdschrift vour Economishe Sociale Geografie* 87, no. 3 (1996): 237–46; Lawrence Berg and Robin Kearns, "Naming as Norming: 'Race,' Gender, and the Identity Politics of Naming Places in Aotearoa/New Zealand," *Environment and Planning D: Society and Space* 14, no. 1 (1996): 99–122; and Reuben Rose-Redwood, Derek Alderman, and Maoz Azaryahu, "Geographies of Toponymic Inscription: New Directions in Critical Place-name Studies," *Progress in Human Geography* 34 (2010): 453–70.

61. Michele Tucci, Rocco Ronza, and Alberto Giodano, "Fragments from Many

Pasts: Layering the Toponymic Tapestry of Milan," *Journal of Historical Geography* 37 (2011): 370–84, esp. 370.

62. David Gross, "Critical Synthesis on Urban Knowledge: Remembering and Forgetting in the Modern City," *Social Epistemology* 4 (1990): 3–22; Steven Hoelscher and Derek Alderman, "Memory and Place: Geographies of a Critical Relationship," *Social and Cultural Geography* 5 (2004): 347–55; Brenda Yeoh, "Street-Naming and Nation-Building: Toponymic Inscriptions of Nationhood in Singapore," *Area* 28 (1996): 298–307; Maoz Azaryahu, "The Power of Commemorative Street Names," 311–30; and T. C. Chang and Shirlena Huang, "Recreating Place, Replacing Memory: Creative Destruction of Singapore River," *Asia Pacific Viewpoint* 46, no. 3 (2005): 267–80.

63. See also John Agnew, "The Impossible Capital: Monumental Rome under Liberal and Fascist Regimes, 1870–1943," *Geografiska Annaler* 80B (1998): 229–40; and Mia Swart, "Name Changes as Symbolic Reparation after Transition: The Examples of Germany and South Africa," *German Law Journal* 9, no. 2 (2008): 105–21.

64. For an extensive discussion, see contributions to Lawrence Berg and Jani Vuolteenaho, eds., *Critical Toponymies: The Contested Politics of Place Naming* (Burlington, Vt.: Ashgate, 2009).

65. Jeremy Cronin, "To Learn How to Speak . . . ," in *Inside* (Johannesburg: Ravan Press, 1983), 64.

66. Es'kia Mphanhlele, "The Tyranny of Place and Aesthetics: The South African Case," *Race and Literature* (1981): 48–59 (49).

67. Georgi Verbeeck, "Structure of Memory: *Apartheid* in the Museum," in *History Making and Present-Day Politics*, ed. Stolten, 217–26.

68. See Dunbar Moodie, *The Rise of Afrikanerdom: Power, Apartheid, and the Afrikaner Civil Religion* (Berkeley and Los Angeles: University of California Press, 1975), 150.

69. Alexander, *An Ordinary Country*, 103–4.

70. The literature is extensive. See, for example, Martin Hall, "Archaeology under Apartheid," *Archaeology* 41 (1998): 62–64; Hall, "Social Archaeology and the Theaters of Memory," *Journal of Social Archaeology* 1 (2001): 50–61; Nick Shepherd, "Disciplining Archaeology: The Invention of South African Prehistory, 1923–1953," *Kronos: Journal of Cape History* 28 (2002): 127–45; Shepherd, "The Politics of Archaeology in Africa," *Annual Review of Anthropology* 31 (2002): 189–209; Shepherd, "State of the Discipline: Science, Culture, and Identity in South African Archaeology, 187–2003," *Journal of Southern African Studies* 29 (2003): 823–44.

71. Saul Dubow, *Scientific Racism in Modern South Africa* (Cambridge: Cambridge University Press, 1995).

72. Milan Kundera, "Afterword: A Talk with the Author by Philip Roth," *The Book of Laughter and Forgetting* (New York: HarperCollins, 1994), 235.

73. Paul Connerton, "Seven Types of Forgetting," *Memory Studies* 1, no. 1 (2008): 59–71.

74. See Joshua Hagen, "Historical Preservation in Nazi Germany: Place, Memory, and Nationalism," *Journal of Historical Geography* 35 (2009): 690–715, 690.

75. Lynn Meskell, "Living in the Past: Historic Futures in Double Time," in *Desire Lines,* ed. Noëleen Murray, Nick Shepherd, and Martin Hall, 165–80.

76. See Adam Ashforth, *The Politics of Official Discourse in South Africa* (Oxford: Oxford University Press, 1990; Deborah Posel, *The Making of Apartheid* (Oxford: Oxford University Press, 1991); and Dubow, *Scientific Racism in Modern South Africa.*

77. Alexander, *An Ordinary Country,* 82–83, 106–8. See also Moodie, *The Rise of Afrikanerdom;* and Dan O'Meara, *Forty Lost Years: The Apartheid State and the Politics of the National Party, 1948–1994* (Athens: Ohio University Press, 1996).

78. Ivan Evans, *Bureaucracy and Race: Native Administration in South Africa* (Berkeley and Los Angeles: University of California Press, 1997).

79. Connerton, "Seven Types of Forgetting," 61.

80. Hermann Giliomee, *The Afrikaners: Biography of a People* (Charlottesville: University of Virginia Press, 2003); Moodie, *The Rise of Afrikanerdom,* 140–60; and Grundlingh, "Reframing Remembrance," in *History Making and Present-Day Politics,* ed. Stolten, 196–216.

81. Heribert Adam and Hermann Gilliomee, *Ethnic Power Mobilized: Can South Africa Change?* (New Haven: Yale University Press, 1979).

82. See Marschall, *Landscape of Memory,* 137–73.

83. T. R. H. Davenport, *South Africa: A Modern History,* 4th ed. (Toronto: University of Toronto Press, 1991), 342–43 (342).

84. Don Mattera, *Sophiatown: Coming of Age in South Africa* (Boston: Beacon Press, 1987); Trevor Huddleston, *Naught for Your Comfort* (London: Collins, 1956); and Davenport, *South Africa,* 343–44, 528.

85. The literature on both these places is extensive.

86. See, for example, Owen Dwyer and Derek Alderman, "Memorial Landscapes: Analytic Questions and Metaphors," *GeoJournal* 73 (2008): 165–78; Winter, *Sites of Memory, Sites of Mourning;* Forest and Johnson, "Unraveling the Threads of History," 524–47; and Forest, Johnson, and Till, "Post-Totalitarian National Identity," 357–80.

87. Katharine Hodgkin and Susannah Radstone, "Patterning the National Past: Introduction," in *Contested Pasts,* ed. Hodgkin and Radstone 169–74 (169).

88. Bill Nasson, *Abraham Essau's War: A Black South African War in the Cape, 1988–1902* (Cambridge: Cambridge University Press, 1991); *The South African War: The Anglo-Boer War, 1899–1902,* ed. Peter Warwick (London: Longman, 1980); B. E. Mongalo and Kobus du Pisani, "Victims of a White Man's War: Blacks in Concentration Camps

during the South African War (1899–1902)," *Historia* 44, no. 1 (1999): 148–82; Stowell Kessler, "The Black and Coloured Concentration Camps of the South African War, 1899–1902," in *Scorched Earth,* ed. Fransjohan Pretorius (Cape Town: Human and Rousseau, 2001), 132–53; and Kessler, "The Black and Coloured Concentration Camps of the Anglo-Boer War, 1899–1902: Shifting the Paradigm from Sole Martyrdom to Mutual Suffering" (Ph.D. diss., University of Cape Town, 2003).

89. Bunn, "Whited Sepulchres," 92–117.

90. Stephen Laufer, "Govt Wants to Lift the Veil off SA's History," *Business Day,* April 28, 1998. For the ideological construction of the landscape as "white space," see Foster, *Washed with Sun,* 14–44; and Beningfield, *The Frightened Land,* 34–54.

91. John Wright and Aron Mazel, "Bastions of Ideology: The Depiction of Precolonial History in the Museums of Natal and Kwazulu," *South African Museums Association Bulletin (SAMAB)* 17 (1987): 301–10.

92. Marschall, *Landscape of Memory,* 173–74.

93. Nora, "Between Memory and History," 7–25.

94. Charles Withers, "Place, Memory, Monument: Memorializing the Past in Contemporary Highland Scotland," *Ecumene* 3, no. 3 (1996): 340.

3. Facing Backward, Looking Forward

1. Theodor Adorno captured the core of this conundrum when he wrote: "'Coming to terms with the past' does not imply a serious working through of the past, the breaking of its spell through an act of clear consciousness. It suggests, rather, wishing to turn the page and, if possible, wiping it from memory. The attitude that it would be proper for everything to be forgiven and forgotten by those who were wronged is expressed by the party that committed the injustice." See Theodor Adorno, "What Does Coming to Terms with the Past Mean?" in *Bitburg in Moral and Political Perspective,* ed. Geoffrey Hartman (Bloomington: Indiana University Press, 1986), 114–29 (115).

2. Alexander, *An Ordinary Country,* 81–110.

3. Anderson, *Imagined Communities,* 187–206.

4. Paul Lansing and Julie King, "South Africa's Truth and Reconciliation Commission: The Conflict between Individual Justice and National Healing in the Post-apartheid Age," *Arizona Journal of International and Comparative Law* 15, no. 3 (1998): 753–89, esp. 773; and Mahmood Mamdani, "Amnesty or Impunity? A Preliminary Critique of the Report of the Truth and Reconciliation Commission of South Africa (TRC)," in *Repairing the Past? International Perspectives on Reparations for Gross Human Rights Abuses,* ed. Max du Plessis and Stephen Pete (Oxford: Intersentia, 2007), 83–118.

5. Timothy Garton Ash, *The File* (London: Flamingo, 1997), 201.

6. Anderson, *Imagined Communities,* 1–10.

7. Kundera, "Afterword," 235.

8. See Nora, "Between History and Memory," 12. See also Susan Crane, "Writing the Individual Back into Collective Memory," *American Historical Review* 102, no. 5 (1997): 1372–85; and Confino, "Collective Memory and Cultural History," 1386–403. For an excellent treatment of the underlying theoretical issues related to the collective memories of historical trauma and the process of nation-building, see Kiyoteru Tsutshui, "The Trajectory of Perpetrators' Trauma: Mnemonic Politics around the Asia-Pacific War in Japan," *Social Forces* 87, no. 3 (2009): 1389–422.

9. Huyssen, *Twilight Memories*, 7.

10. Sabine Marschall, "The Memory of Trauma and Resistance: Public Memorialization and Democracy in Post-Apartheid South Africa and Beyond," *Safundi: The Journal of South African and American Studies* 11, no. 4 (2010): 361–81.

11. Writing in another context, Salman Rushdie correctly identifies the dilemma of remembrance and forgetting when he suggests that "I, too, face the problem of history: what to retain, what to dump, how to hold on to what memory insists on relinquishing, and how to deal with change." See Salman Rushdie, *Shame* (New York: Alfred A. Knopf, 1983), 83.

12. Herwitz, "Monument, Ruin, and Redress in South African Heritage," 232–48; and Herwitz, "The Monument in Ruins," in *Ruins of Modernity*, ed. Julia Hell and Andreas Schönle (Durham: Duke University Press, 2010), 232–43.

13. Alison Landsberg, "Prosthetic Memory: *Total Recall* and *Blade Runner*," *Body & Society* 1, nos. 3–4 (1995): 175–89 (176).

14. Lowenthal, "Past Time, Present Place," 1–36 (27–28).

15. Koonz, "Between Memory and Oblivion," 258–80.

16. See Sabine Marschall, "The Heritage of Post-Colonial Societies," in *The Ashgate Research Companion to Heritage and Identity*, ed. Brian Graham and Peter Howard (Aldershot: Ashgate, 2008), 347–64, esp. 352.

17. See Sabine Marschall, "Articulating Cultural Pluralism through Public Art as Heritage in South Africa," *Visual Anthropology* 23, no. 2 (2010): 77–97.

18. For the source of these ideas, see Michelle Burns, "A Completion of Memory? Commemorating a Decade of Freedom in South Africa: 1994–2004," *Eras* 8 (2006): 15 pp., unpaginated online journal available at http://www.arts.monash.edju.au/eras.

19. Sabine Marschall, "How to Honour a Woman: Gendered Memorialisation in Post-*Apartheid* South Africa," *Critical Arts* 24, no. 2 (2010): 260–83 (260).

20. For comparative purposes, see Clive Kronenberg, "Culture, Nation, and Social Cohesion: A Scrutiny of Revolutionary Cuba," *Critical Arts* 22, no. 1 (2008): 49–68.

21. Marschall, *Landscape of Memory*; and Charmaine McEachern, *Narratives of Nation*

Media, Memory, and Representation in the Making of the New South Africa (New York: Nova Science Publishers, 2002).

22. Myambo, "The Limits of Rainbow Nation Multiculturalism in the New South Africa," 93–120.

23. Aletta Norval, "Memory, Identity, and the (Im)possibility of Reconciliation: The Work of the Truth and Reconciliation Commission in South Africa," *Constellations* 5, no. 2 (1998): 250–65; and Steven Robins, "'Can't Forget, Can't Remember': Reflections on the Cultural Afterlife of the TRC," *Critical Arts* 21, no. 1 (2007): 125–51.

24. For the source of some of these ideas, see Heidi Grunebaum-Ralph, "Re-Placing Pasts, Forgetting Presents: Narrative, Place, and Memory in the Time of the Truth and Reconciliation Commission," *Research in African Literatures* 32, no. 4 (2001): 198–212, esp. 198.

25. Hlongwane, "Commemoration, Memory, and Monuments," 135–70.

26. See Huyssen, *Twilight Memories*, 3.

27. Jill Liddington and Graham Smith, "Crossing Cultures: Oral History and Public History," *Oral History* 33, no. 1 (2005): 28–31.

28. Hlongwane, "Commemoration, Memory, and Monuments," 137.

29. Yonah Seleti (Heritage Manager), "December 16, Day of Reconciliation," *Cleansing and Healing Photographic Exhibition*, Freedom Park Trust (Pretoria).

30. Yvette Hutchison, "Memory and Desire: The Museum as Space for Performance?" in *Southern Africa: African Theatre*, ed. David Kerr (Bloomington: Indiana University Press, 2004), 51–67; and Andrew Crampton, "The Art of Nation-Building: (Re)presenting Political Transition at the South African National Gallery," *Cultural Geographies* 10 (2010): 218–42.

31. Marschall, *Landscape of Memory*, 1–3.

32. Bonder, "On Memory, Trauma, Public Space, Monuments, and Memorials," 62–69 (63).

33. See Cathy Caruth, *Unclaimed Experience: Trauma, Narrative, and History* (Baltimore: Johns Hopkins University Press, 1996).

34. Huyssen, *Present Pasts*, 28.

35. Chang and Huang, "Re-creating Place, Replacing Memory," 267–80 (269).

36. Herwitz, "Monument, Ruin, and Redress in South African Heritage," 235–36.

37. Helmut Puff, "Ruins as Models: Displaying Destruction in Postwar Germany," in *Ruins of Modernity*, ed. Julia Hell and Andreas Schönle (Durham: Duke University Press, 2010), 253–69, esp. 254.

38. For the source of some of these ideas, see Braun, "Colonialism's Afterlife," 202–47, esp. 203, 214, 237.

39. Murray, "Remaking Modernism," 43–66, esp. 57–58.

40. Georgi Verbeeck, "A New Past for a New Nation? Historiography and Politics in South Africa: A Comparative Approach," *Historia: Journal of the Historical Association of South Africa* 45, 2 (2000): 387–410.

41. Christopher Colvin, "'Brothers and Sisters, Do Not Be Afraid of Me': Trauma, History, and the Therapeutic Imagination in the New South Africa," in *Contested Pasts,* ed. Katharine Hodgkin and Susannah Radstone, 153–68.

42. Verbeeck, "A New Past for a New Nation?," 387–410.

43. See Stephen Legg, "Review Essay: Memory and Nostalgia," *Cultural Geographies* 11 (2004): 99–107.

44. Stephen Laufer, "Govt Wants to Lift the Veil off SA's History," *Business Day,* April 28, 1998. Information also derived from onsite visit, June 20, 2011.

45. Mia Swart, "Name Changes as Symbolic Representation after Transition: The Examples of Germany and South Africa," *German Law Journal* 9, no. 2 (2008): 105–21.

46. See Chang and Huang, "Re-creating Place, Replacing Memory," 268.

47. Jordan, *Structures of Memory,* 89.

48. Tucci, Ronza, and Giordano, "Fragments from Many Pasts," 370–84, esp. 370.

49. "Racist Stains Won't Fade Away," *Saturday Star,* April 11, 1998.

50. Azaryahu, "German Reunification and the Politics of Street Names," 479–83; Duncan Light, "Street Names in Bucharest: Exploring the Modern Historical Geographies of Post-Socialist Change," *Journal of Historical Geography* 30 (2004): 154–72; Graeme Gil, "Changing Symbols: The Renovation of Moscow Place Names," *Russian Review* 64, no. 4 (2005): 480–503; Dario Gamboni, "The Fall of the 'Communist Monuments,'" in *The Destruction of Art: Iconoclasm and Vandalism since the French Revolution* (London: Reaktion Books, 1997), 51–90; Emilia Palonen, "The City-Text in Post-Communist Bucharest: Street Names, Memorials, and the Politics of Commemoration," *GeoJournal* 73, no. 4 (2008): 219–30; Forest and Johnson, "Unraveling the Threads of History," 524–47; Beverly James, "Fencing in the Past: Budapest's Statue Park Museum," *Media, Culture & Society* 21, no. 4 (1999): 291–311; Paul Williams, "The Afterlife of Communist Statuary: Hungary's Szoborpark and Lithuania's Grutas Park," *Forum for Modern Language Studies* 44, no. 2 (2008): 185–98; and Božidar Jezernik, "Monuments in the Winds of Change," *International Journal of Urban and Regional Research* 22, no. 4 (1998): 582–88.

51. Maoz Azaryahu, "The Critical Turn and Beyond: The Case of Commemorative Street Naming," *ACME: An International E-Journal for Critical Geographies* 10, no. 1 (2011): 28–33, esp. 29.

52. Michael Wines, "Where the Road to Renaming Does Not Run Smooth," *New York Times,* May 25, 2007, A4; and Mahunele Thotse, "Contesting Names and Statues:

Battles over the Louis Trichardt/Makhado 'City-Text' in Limpopo Province, South Africa," *Kronos* 36, no. 1 (2010): 173–83.

53. See Marschall, *Landscape of Memory*, 140–46.

54. Azaryahu, "The Power of Commemorative Street Names," 311.

55. Sabine Marschall, "Commemorating the 'Trojan Horse' Massacre in Cape Town: The Tension between Vernacular and Official Expressions of Memory," *Visual Studies* 25, no. 2 (2010): 135–48.

56. Hans Erik Stolten, "History in the New South Africa: An Introduction," in *History Making and Present-Day Politics*, ed. Stolten, 5–50.

57. Sabine Marschall, "Visualizing Memories: The Hector Pieterson Memorial in Soweto," *Visual Anthropology* 19, no. 2 (2006): 145–69, esp. 146.

58. Marschall, *Landscape of Memory*, 140–46.

59. Marschall, "Visualizing Memories," 146.

60. Connerton, *How Societies Remember*, 6, 9.

61. Marschall, "Visualizing Memories," 147.

62. Roland Barthes, "Myth Today," in *Visual Culture: The Reader*, ed. Jessica Evans and Stuart Hall (Thousand Oaks, Calif.: Sage, 1999), 51–58, esp. 58.

63. Eric Hobsbawm, "Introduction: Inventing Traditions," in *The Invention of Tradition*, ed. Eric Hobsbawm and Terrence Ranger (Cambridge: Cambridge University Press, 1983), 1–14.

64. Ibid., 1.

65. Barthes, "Myth Today," 58.

66. Marschall, "Visualizing Memories," 148.

67. Ibid., 148.

68. Ibid.; Andrew Crampton, "The Voortrekker Monument, the Birth of *Apartheid*, and Beyond," *Political Geography* 20 (2001): 221–46; and Albert Grundlingh, "A Cultural Conundrum? Old Monuments and New Regimes: The Voortrekker Monument as Symbol of Afrikaner Power in Post-Apartheid South Africa," *Radical History Review* 81 (2001): 94–112.

69. Baines, "The Master Narrative of South Africa's Liberation Struggle," 298.

70. Marschall, "Articulating Cultural Pluralism," 77–97.

71. Marschall, "How to Honour a Woman," 262.

72. André Brink, "Stories of History: Reimagining the Past in Post-*Apartheid* Narrative," in *Negotiating the Past*, ed. Nuttall and Coetzee, 32, 33, 35.

73. Baines, "The Master Narrative of South Africa's Liberation Struggle," 284; and Marschall, "Visualizing Memories," 148.

74. Ibid., 146.

75. See Lindsay Bremner, "Reframing Township Space: The Kliptown Project," *Public Culture* 16, no. 4 (2004): 521–31; and Bremner, "Memory, Nation-Building, and the Post-*Apartheid* City: The *Apartheid* Museum in Johannesburg," in *Desire Lines*, ed. Murray, Shepherd, and Hall, 85–104.

76. See, for example, Paula Girshick, "Ncome Museum/Monument: From Reconciliation to Resistance," *Museum Anthropology* 27, nos. 1–2 (2004): 25–36; Sabine Marschall, "Canonizing New Heroes: The Proposed Heroes Monument in Durban," *South African Journal of Art History* 18 (2003): 80–93; Scott M. Schönfeldt-Aultman, "Monument(al) Meaning-Making: The Ncome Monument and Its Representation of Zulu Identity," *Journal of African Cultural Studies* 18, no. 2 (2006): 215–34; and Sabine Marschall, "Memory and Identity in South Africa: Contradictions and Ambiguities in the Process of Post-*Apartheid* Memorialization," *Visual Anthropology* 25, no. 4 (2012): 189–204.

77. Marschall, *Landscape of Memory*, 114–15.

78. Marschall, "Visualizing Memories," 149.

79. Marschall, *Landscape of Memory*, 62, 88–89, 93, 95, 99; and Marschall, "Commemorating the 'Trojan Horse' Massacre in Cape Town," 135–48.

80. Michael Lambek and Paul Antze, "Introduction: Forecasting Memory," in *Tense Past: Cultural Essays in Trauma and Memory*, ed. Paul Antze and Michael Lambek (New York: Routledge, 1996), xi–xxxviii, esp. xvii.

81. Marschall, *Landscape of Memory*, 317–21; Sabine Marschall, "Gestures of Compensation: Post-*Apartheid* Monuments and Memorials," *Transformation: Critical Perspectives on Southern Africa* 55 (2004): 78–95; and Marschall, "Symbols of Reconciliation or Instruments of Division? A Critical Look at New Monuments in South Africa," in *Culture and Belonging in Divided Societies: Contestation and Symbolic Landscapes*, ed. Marc Howard Ross (Philadelphia: University of Pennsylvania Press, 2009), 151–75.

82. Marschall, "Visual Memories," 156.

83. Ibid., 159. See James E. Young, "Memory/Monument," in *Critical Terms for Art History*, 2nd ed., ed. Robert Nelson and Richard Shiff (Chicago: University of Chicago Press, 2003), 234–47, esp. 238–40; Sergiusz Michalski, *Public Monuments: Art in Political Bondage, 1870–1997* (London: Reaktion Books, 1998); Johnson, "The Spectacle of Memory," 36–56; and Alex King, "Remembering and Forgetting in the Public Memorials of the Great War," in *The Art of Forgetting*, ed. Adrian Forty and Suzanne Küchler (New York: Berg, 1999), 147–65.

84. Marschall, "Visualizing Memories," 159.

85. See Huyssen, *Present Pasts*, 71.

86. Marschall, *Landscape of Memory*, 298–302.

87. See Helena Pohlandt-McCormick, *"I Saw a Nightmare . . ." Doing Violence to*

Memory: The Soweto Uprising, June 16, 1976 (New York: Guttenburg e-Books, published in conjunction with Columbia University Press, 2006), chap. 6.

88. Antjie Krog, *Country of My Skull: Guilt, Sorrow, and the Limits of Forgiveness in the New South Africa* (New York: Random House, 1998), publisher's note, viii.

89. Ibid., 1–10.

90. For the TRC in South Africa, see Charles Villa-Vincencio, "Part One: Around the Truth and Reconciliation Commission: Rhetoric and Public Good," *Quest: An African Journal of Philosophy* 16, nos. 1–2 (2002): 37–49. For a wider view, see Pradeep Jeganathan, "In the Ruins of Truth: The Work of Melancholia and Acts of Memory," *Inter-Asia Cultural Studies* 11, no. 1 (2010): 6–20.

91. Grunebaum-Ralph, "Re-Placing Pasts, Forgetting Presents," 198–212; and McEachern, *Narratives of Nation Media,* 19–37.

92. According to Colin Bundy, the aim of the TRC was "to close the door on the past to establish a version of the past that somehow transcends subjective and contesting views." He further argues that this impulse was derived from the TRC's commitment to reconciliation and nation-building. See Colin Bundy, "The Beast of the Past: History and the TRC," in *After the TRC: Reflections on Truth and Reconciliation in South Africa,* ed. Wilmot James and Linda van de Vijver (Cape Town: David Philip, 2000), 9–20 (15). On the filmic representation of the TRC, see Ashley Dawson, "Documenting the Trauma of *Apartheid: Long Day's Journey into Day* and South Africa's Truth and Reconciliation Commission," *Screen* 46, no. 4 (2005): 473–86.

93. Mark Sanders, *Ambiguities of Witnessing: Law and Literature in a Time of a Truth Commission* (Palo Alto: Stanford University Press, 2007), 3.

94. Jacques Derrida, *Demeure: Fiction and Testimony* (Palo Alto: Stanford University Press, 2000), 27.

95. Catherine Cole, *Performing South Africa's Truth Commission: Stages of Transition* (Bloomington: Indiana University Press, 2010). For a review of various positions, see Ed Charlton, "'Only Literature Can Perform the Miracle of Reconciliation': A Resurrection of the Logos of South Africa's Truth Commission?," *Research in African Literatures* 42, no. 4 (2011): 114–23.

96. McEachern, *Narratives of Nation Media,* 21; and Ingrid De Kok, "Cracked Heirlooms," in *Negotiating the Past,* ed. Nuttall and Coetzee, 57–71, esp. 57.

97. Alejandro Castillejo-Cuéllar, "Knowledge, Experience, and South Africa's Scenarios of Forgiveness," *Radical History Review* 97 (2007): 11–42, esp. 15, 23, 36–37.

98. Premesh Lalu and Brent Harris, "Journeys from the Horizons of History: Text, Trial, and the Tales in the Construction of Narratives of Pain," *Current Writing* 8, no. 2 (1996): 24–38.

99. Richard Wilson, *The Politics of Truth and Reconciliation in South Africa: Legitimizing the Post-Apartheid State* (Cambridge: Cambridge University Press, 2001), xvi–xvii; Lynn Graybill, *Truth and Reconciliation in South Africa: Miracle or Model?* (Boulder, Colo.: Lynne Rienner, 2002), x–xii; and Stephanie Marlin-Curiel, "A Little Too Close to the Truth: Anxieties of Testimony and Confession in Ubu and the Truth Commission and the Story I Am About to Tell," *South African Theatre Journal* 15 (2001): 77–103.

100. Clint van der Walt, Vijié Franchi, and Garth Stevens, "The South African Truth and Reconciliation Commission: 'Race,' Historical Compromise, and Transitional Democracy," *International Journal of Intercultural Relations* 27, no. 2 (2003): 251–67 (257).

101. Emmanuel Chukwudi Eze, "Transition and the Reasons of Memory," *South Atlantic Quarterly* 103, no. 4 (2004): 755–68.

102. Connerton, "Seven Types of Forgetting," 59–71 (62).

103. De Kok, "Cracked Heirlooms," in *Negotiating the Past,* ed. Nuttall and Coetzee, 57–71.

104. Charles Villa-Vincencio, "Learning to Live Together with Bad Memories," *Quest: An African Journal of Philosophy* 16, nos. 1–2 (2002): 37–49; Aletta Norval, "Memory, Identity, and the (Im)possibility of Reconciliation: The Work of the Truth and Reconciliation Commission in South Africa," *Constellations* 5, no. 2 (1998): 250–65; and Lynn Graybill, "Pardon, Punishment, and Amnesia: Three African Post-conflict Methods," *Third World Quarterly* 25, no. 6 (2004): 1117–30.

105. De Kok, "Cracked Heirlooms," in *Negotiating the Past,* ed. Nuttall and Coetzee, 59.

106. Huyssen, *Present Pasts,* 53–54.

107. David Coplan, "Popular History, Cultural Memory," *Critical Arts: A Journal of Cultural Studies* 14, no. 2 (2000): 122–44, esp. 138; and Suzan Vanzanten Gallagher, "'I Want to Say'/'Forgive Me': South African Discourse and Forgiveness," *PMLA* 117, no. 2 (2006): 303–6; and Shane Graham, "The Truth Commission and Post-*Apartheid* Literature in South Africa," *Research in African Literatures* 34, no. 1 (2003): 11–30.

108. Ulrich Baer, "The Hubris of Humility: Günter Grass, Peter Schneider, and German Guilt after 1989," *Germanic Review* 80, no. 1 (2005): 50–72 (52).

109. Crane, "Writing the Individual Back into Collective Memory," 1372–85.

110. Stephen Legg, "Contesting and Surviving Memory: Space, Nation, and Nostalgia in *Les Lieux de Mémoire,*" *Environment and Planning D* 23 (2005): 481–504. See also David Gross, *Lost Time: On Remembering and Forgetting in Late Modern Culture* (Amherst: University of Massachusetts Press, 2000), 151–52.

111. Norman Klein, *The History of Forgetting: Los Angeles and the Erasure of Memory* (London: Verso, 1997), 301.

112. Landsberg, *Prosthetic Memory,* 19–23.

113. Huyssen, *Twilight Memories,* 249.

114. Ibid., 253.

115. Ibid., 253–54.

116. Ibid. It should be noted that while I quote from Huyssen, he advances a different argument than mine.

117. For a useful discussion of these ideas, see Confino, "Collective Memory and Cultural History," 1387–403; John Gillis, "Heritage and History: Twins Separated at Birth," *Reviews in American History* 25 (1997): 375–78; Peter Bishop, "Memories Are Made of This," *Journal of Historical Geography* 22, no. 2 (1996): 214–20; and David Lowenthal, "Fabricating Heritage," *History & Memory* 10, no. 1 (1998): 5–24.

4. Collective Memory in Place

1. The literature is extensive, but see Katharyne Mitchell, "Monuments, Memorials, and the Politics of Memory," *Urban Geography* 24, no. 5 (2003): 442–59; Osborne, "Constructing Landscapes of Power," 431–58; W. J. T. Mitchell, ed., *Art and the Public Sphere* (Chicago: University of Chicago Press, 1990); Kirk Savage, "The Politics of Memory: Black Emancipation and the Civil War," in *Commemorations,* ed. Gillis, 127–49; Daniel Sherman, "Art, Commerce, and the Production of Memory in France after World War I," in *Commemorations,* ed. Gillis, 186–211; and Sanford Levinson, *Written in Stone: Public Monuments in Changing Societies* (Durham: Duke University Press, 1998).

2. See Young, "The Counter-Monument," 270.

3. Arthur Danto, "The Vietnam Veterans Memorial," *The Nation,* August 31, 1985, 152.

4. Ibid.

5. Charles Griswold and Stephen Griswold (photographer), "The Vietnam Veterans Memorial and the Washington Mall: Philosophical Thoughts on Political Iconography," *Critical Inquiry* 12, no. 4 (1986): 688–719 (689).

6. See Tony Judt, "A la Recherche du Temps Perdu," *New York Review of Books,* December 3, 1998, 51–58, esp. 51.

7. See Meskell and Sheermeyer, "Heritage as Therapy," 153–73.

8. Boym, *The Future of Nostalgia,* 79.

9. Rose-Redwood, "From Number to Name," 431–52 (431).

10. David Gross, "Critical Synthesis on Urban Knowledge: Remembering and Forgetting in the Modern City," *Social Epistemology* 4 (1990): 3–22.

11. Tucci, Ronza, and Giodano, "Fragments from Many Pasts," 370–84, esp. 371.

12. Boym, *The Future of Nostalgia,* 79.

13. Herwitz, "The Monument in Ruins," in *Ruins of Modernity,* ed. Julia Hell and Andreas Schönle, 232–43; and Andrew Crampton, "The Voortrekker Monument, the

Birth of *Apartheid,* and Beyond," *Political Geography* 20 (2001), 221–46. For comparative purposes, see James E. Young, "The Biography of a Memorial Icon: Nathan Rapoport's Warsaw Ghetto Monument," *Representations* 26 (1989): 69–106, esp. 69.

14. Coombes, *Visual Culture and Public Memory in a Democratic South Africa,* 22, 28.

15. Peter Carrier, *Holocaust Monuments and National Memory Cultures in France and Germany since 1989* (New York: Berghahn Books, 2005), 17.

16. Young, "The Biography of a Memorial Icon," 71.

17. Huyssen, *Present Pasts,* 3.

18. Huyssen, *Twilight Memories,* 250.

19. Robert Musil, "Monuments," in *Posthumous Papers of a Living Author,* trans. Peter Wortsman (Hygiene, Colo.: Eridanos Press, 1987), 61.

20. Young, "The Biography of a Memorial Icon," 70–71. See also Meskell, "Living in the Past," in *Desire Lines,* ed. Murray, Shepherd, and Hall, 165–80, esp. 170–71.

21. Young, "The Counter-Monument," 267–96 (294).

22. Kurt Forster, "Monument/Memory and the Mortality of Architecture," *Oppositions* 25 (1982): 2–19 (11).

23. Maria Tumarkin, *Traumascapes: The Fate and Power of Places Transformed by Tragedy* (Melbourne: Melbourne University Press, 2005). See also Jill Bennett, *Empathic Vision: Affect, Trauma, and Contemporary Art* (Stanford: Stanford University Press, 2005).

24. Cherry, "Statues in the Square," 664.

25. Meskell, "Trauma Culture," in *Memory, Trauma and World Politics,* ed. Bell, 157–74; and Lynn Meskell, "Sites of Violence: Terrorism, Tourism, and Heritage in the Archaeological Present," in *Embedding Ethics* (Oxford: Berg, 2005), 123–46; and Jenny Edkins, *Trauma and the Memory of Politics,* ed. Lynn Meskell and Peter Pels (Cambridge: Cambridge University Press, 2003).

26. Coombes, *Visual Culture and Public Memory in a Democratic South Africa,* 26.

27. See Grundlingh, "A Cultural Conundrum?," 95–112. For an account of aestheticization of politics and memory in Nazi Germany, see Robert Taylor, *The Word in Stone: The Role of Architecture in the National Socialist Ideology* (Berkeley and Los Angeles: University of California Press, 1974).

28. Herwitz, "Modernism at the Margins," 404–21, esp. 417–18; Coombes, *Visual Culture and Public Memory in a Democratic South Africa,* 26–27; and Bunn, "Whited Sepulchres," 93–115, esp. 104–5.

29. See Sampie Terreblanche, *A History of Inequality in South Africa, 1652–2002* (Pietermaritzburg: University of Natal Press, 2002), 219.

30. Leibowitz, "Making Memory Space," 39.

31. Albert Grundlingh and Hilary Safire, "From Feverish Festival to Repetitive Ritual?

The Changing Fortunes of Great Trek Mythology in an Industrializing South Africa, 1938–1998," *South African Historical Journal* 21 (1989): 19–37.

32. Herwitz, "Modernism at the Margins," 417.

33. Leibowitz, "Making Memory Space," 10.

34. Estelle Alma Mare, "A Critique of the Spoliation of the Ridges of the Capital City of South Africa," *South African Journal of Art History* 21, no. 1 (2006): 93–102.

35. For the source of this idea, see Bal, "Telling, Showing, Showing Off," 556–94, esp. 574.

36. Coombes, *Visual Culture and Public Memory in a Democratic South Africa,* 37; Leibowitz, "Making Memory Space," 40; Roger Charles Fisher, "Gerard Moerdik: Death and Memorializing in His Architecture for the Afrikaner Nationalist Project," *South African Journal of Art History* 25, no. 2 (2010): 151–60; and Alta Steenkamp, "Ambiguous Associations: Monuments Referred to in the Design of the Voortrekker Monument," *South African Journal of Art History* 26, no. 4 (2011): 79–89.

37. Herwitz, "The Monument in Ruins," 233–34; Herwitz, "Modernism at the Margins," 417–18; and Michael Leslie, "Bitter Monuments: Afrikaners and the New South Africa," *Black Scholar* 24, no. 4 (1994): 33–39.

38. Maoz Azaryahu and Kenneth Foote, "Historical Space as Narrative Medium: On the Configuration of Spatial Narratives of Time at Historical Sites," *GeoJournal* 73 (2008): 179–84, esp. 179.

39. Leibowitz, "Making Memory Space," 38.

40. Boyer, *The City of Collective Memory,* 33–34.

41. Alta Steenkamp, "*Apartheid* to Democracy: Representation and Politics in the Voortrekker Monument and the Red Location Museum," *arq: Architectural Research Quarterly* 10, no. 3–4 (2006): 249–54; and Cecilia Kruger and Marie van Heerden, "The Voortrekker Monument as Heritage Site: A New Statement of Significance," *Historia* 50, no. 2 (2005): 237–60.

42. Leibowitz, "Making Memory Space," 41.

43. Ibid., 41–42; and Coombes, *Visual Culture and Public Memory in a Democratic South Africa,* 28–29.

44. Herwitz, "Monument, Ruin, and Redress in South African Heritage," 232–48, esp. 236; and Kruger and van Heerden, "The Voortrekker Monument as Heritage Site," 237–60.

45. Leibowitz, "Making Memory Space," 42; and Coombes, *Visual Culture and Public Memory in a Democratic South Africa,* 28–29.

46. Ibid., 43.

47. Coombes, *Visual Culture and Public Memory in a Democratic South Africa,* 26–27;

and Elizabeth Delmont, "The Voortrekker Monument: From Monolith to Myth," *South African Historical Journal* 29 (1993): 76–101.

48. See Bal, "Telling, Showing, Showing Off," 573.

49. Edensor, "National Identity and the Politics of Memory," 179.

50. Bunn, "Whited Sepulchres," 92–117, esp. 103.

51. Herwitz, "Modernism at the Margins," 417–18. See also Estelle Alma Mare, "Monumental Complexity: Searching for Meaning in a Selection of South African Monuments," *South African Journal of Art History* 22, no. 2 (2007): 36–48.

52. Herwitz, "Modernism at the Margins," 418.

53. Ibid., 417–18.

54. Mitchell, "Monuments, Memorials, and the Politics of Memory," 443.

55. The first quotation is from Edensor, "National Identity and the Politics of Memory," 184. The second quotation is from Connerton, *How Societies Remember,* 37.

56. Connerton, *How Societies Remember,* 102.

57. Ibid., 43.

58. "We would underestimate the commemorative hold of the rite, we would minimize its mnemonic power, if we were to say that it *reminded* the participants of mythic events; we should say rather that the sacred event—was *re-presented;* the participants in the rite gave it ceremonially embodied form" (Connerton, *How Societies Remember,* 43).

59. See Till, "Staging the Past," 251–83, esp. 254.

60. Johnson, "Mapping Monuments," 293–98, esp. 293.

61. Connerton, *How Societies Remember,* 42.

62. Ibid., 42–43.

63. See Martin Broszat and Saul Friedländer, "A Controversy about the Historicization of National Socialism," *New German Critique* 44 (1988): 85–126.

64. Michael Walzer, "Public Space: Pleasures and the Costs of Urbanity," *Dissent* 33, no. 4 (1986): 470–75 (470).

65. Bunn, "Whited Sepulchres," 103–5.

66. See Savage, "The Politics of Memory," 131.

67. Young, *At Memory's Edge,* 13.

68. Young, "The Counter-Monument," 277–78.

69. Mare, "Monumental Complexity," 41–42.

70. Huyssen, *Present Pasts,* 1.

71. Coombes, *Visual Culture and Public Memory in a Democratic South Africa,* 50–52; and Meskell, "Trauma Culture," 157–74.

72. Young, "Memory/Monument," in *Critical Terms for Art History,* ed. Nelson and Shiff, 234–47, esp. 238–40; and Sergiusz Michalski, *Public Monuments: Art in Political Bondage, 1870–1997* (London: Reaktion Books, 1998).

73. Young, "The Biography of a Memorial Icon," 69, 99.

74. Bunn, "Whited Sepulchres," 109.

75. Alfredo González-Ruibal, "Time to Destroy: An Archaeology of Supermodernity," *Cultural Anthropology* 49, no. 2 (2008): 247–79.

76. Meskell, "Trauma Culture," 167.

77. Anne McClintock, *Imperial Leather: Race, Gender, and Sexuality in the Colonial Contest* (New York: Routledge, 1995), 40–41.

78. Neil Leach, "Erasing the Traces: The 'Denazification' of Post-*Apartheid* Johannesburg and Pretoria," in *The Hieroglyphics of Space: Reading and Experiencing the Modern Metropolis,* ed. Leach (New York: Routledge, 1995), 92–100.

79. Ibid., 80–91, esp. 81; and Michael Wise, *Capital Dilemma: Germany's Search for a New Architecture of Democracy* (New York: Princeton Architectural Press, 1998).

80. George Steinmetz, "Colonial Melancholy and Fordist Nostalgia: The Ruinscapes of Namibia and Detroit," in *Ruins of Modernity,* ed. Julia Hell and Andreas Schönle, 294–320. See Robert Nelson and Margaret Rose Olin, eds., *Monuments and Memory, Made and Unmade* (Chicago: University of Chicago Press, 2003).

81. Cherry, "Statues in the Square," 660–97, esp. 660.

82. See, for example, Laura Mulvey, "Disgraced Monuments," in *Architecture and Revolution,* ed. Neil Leach (London: Routledge, 1999), 219–27; Maria Todorova, "The Mausoleum of Georgi Dimitrov as *lieu de mémoire,*" *Journal of Modern History* 78, no. 2 (2006): 377–411; and Gavriel Rosenberg, *Munich and Memory: Architecture, Monuments, and the Legacy of the Third Reich* (Berkeley and Los Angeles: University of California Press, 2000), 1–4.

83. Cherry, "Statues in the Square," 664–65. See also Forest and Johnson, "Unraveling the Threads of History," 524–47.

84. See Mark Crinson, "Imperial Story-Lands: Architecture and Display at the Imperial and Commonwealth Institutes," *Art History* 22, no. 1 (1999): 99–123.

85. Lowenthal, "Fabricating Heritage," 13.

86. Grundlingh, "A Cultural Conundrum?" 109.

87. Didier Maleuvre, *Museum Memories: History, Technology, Art* (Stanford: Stanford University Press, 1999), 59.

88. Derek Hook, "Monumental Space and the Uncanny," *Geoforum* 36, no. 6 (2005): 688–704 (692).

89. H. Otto, "Strijdom Square's Future in Balance," *The Star,* June 1, 2001.

90. See Steven Cooke, "Negotiating Memory and Identity: The Hyde Park Holocaust Memorial, London," *Journal of Historical Geography* 26, no. 4 (2000): 449–65, esp. 449.

91. Jordan, *Structures of Memory,* 16.

92. Young, "The Counter-Monument," 270.

93. Sabine Marschall, "Symbols of Reconciliation or Instruments of Division?," in *Culture and Belonging in Divided Societies,* ed. Ross, 151–75; and Marschall, "Transforming the Landscape of Memory: The South African Commemorative Effort in International Perspective," *South African Historical Journal* 55 (2006): 165–85.

94. Meskell and Scheermeyer, "Heritage as Therapy," 153–73, esp. 158–59.

95. Marschall, *Landscape of Memory,* 209–10.

96. Ibid., 209.

97. Andreas Huyssen, "Monument and Memory in a Postmodern Age," *Yale Journal of Criticism* 6, no. 2 (1993): 249–61.

98. Marschall, *Landscape of Memory,* 209.

99. See Pieter Labuschagne, "Monument(al) Meaning Making in the 'New' South Africa: Freedom Park as a Symbol of a New Identity and Freedom?," *South African Journal of Art History* 25, no. 2 (2010): 112–24.

100. Marschall, *Landscape of Memory,* 270.

101. Ibid., 212–14.

102. Tal Alon-Mozes, Hadas Shadar, and Liat Vardi, "The Poetics and Politics of the Contemporary Sacred Place: Baba Sali's Grave Estate in Netivot, Israel," *Buildings and Landscapes* 16, no. 2 (2009): 73–85.

103. Meskell and Scheermeyer, "Heritage as Therapy," 159.

104. See Bremner, "Memory, Nation Building, and the Post-*Apartheid* City," 85–103 (85).

105. Marschall, *Landscape of Memory,* 212–38.

106. Young, "The Counter-Monument," 270.

107. Bremner, "Memory, Nation Building, and the Post-*Apartheid* City," 94. See also Rodney Warwick, "Freedom Park Is a Monumental Mess of History and Ideology," *Pretoria News,* January 5, 2007.

108. Carrier, *Holocaust Monuments and National Memory Cultures in France and Germany since 1989,* 215, 217.

109. "FF Plus Calls for Freedom Park Boycott," *South African Press Association (SAPA),* March 20, 2009; and Gary Baines, "Site of Struggle: The Freedom Park Fracas and the Divisive Legacy of South Africa's Border War/Liberation Struggle," *Social Dynamics* 35, no. 2 (2009): 330–44.

110. Marschall, *Landscape of Memory,* 212–38; Labuschagne, "Monument(al) Meaning Making in the 'New' South Africa," 112–24; and Mare, "Monumental Complexity," 36–48.

111. Gary Baines, "The Master Narrative of South Africa's Liberation Struggle: Remembering and Forgetting June 16, 1976," *International Journal of African Historical Studies* 40, no. 2 (2007): 283–302, esp. 283–85; and Ruth Kerkham Simbao, "The

Thirteenth Anniversary of the Soweto Uprisings: Reading in the Shadow of Sam Nzima's Iconic Photograph of Hector Pieterson," *African Arts* 40, no. 2 (2007): 52–69.

112. See Robert Hariman and John Lucaites, "Photographing the Vietnam War," in *American Visual Cultures,* ed. David Holloway and John Beck (New York: Continuum, 2005), 199–208, esp. 201.

113. Baines, "The Master Narrative of South Africa's Liberation Struggle," 287.

114. Lucille Davie, "June 16, 1976—Hastings Ndlovu's Day Too," *City of Johannesburg Official Website,* January 10, 2005.

115. See Sifiso Mxolisi Ndlovu, *The Soweto Uprisings: Counter-Memories of 1976* (Johannesburg: Ravan Press, 1998); Philip Bonner and Lauren Segal, *Soweto: A History* (London: Maskew Miller Longman, 1998); John Kane-Berman, *Soweto: Black Revolt, White Reaction* (Johannesburg: Ravan Press, 1978), and Baruch Hirson, *Year of Fire, Year of Ash* (London: Zed Press, 1979).

116. For comparative purposes, see Jeanine Centuori, "The Residual Landscape of Kent State, May 4th, 1970," *Landscape Journal* 18, no. 1 (1999): 1–10.

117. Lucille Davie, "The Day Hector Pieterson Died," *City of Johannesburg Official Website,* June 15, 2006.

118. Dolores Hayden, *The Power of Place: Urban Landscapes as Public History* (Cambridge, Mass.: MIT Press, 1997), 41.

119. Andreas Huyssen makes this point when discussing September 11 and the World Trade Center (*Present Pasts,* 158–60).

120. Simbao, "The Thirteenth Anniversary of the Soweto Uprisings," 61.

121. Marschall, "Visualizing Memories," 145–59.

122. For a wider discussion, see W. J. T. Mitchell, *Picture Theory* (Chicago: University of Chicago Press, 1994); and David Freedberg, *The Power of Images: Studies in the History and Theory of Response* (Chicago: University of Chicago Press, 1989).

123. Katharina Schramm, "Landscapes of Violence: Memory and Sacred Space," *History & Memory* 23, no. 1 (2011): 5–22, esp. 5.

124. See Healy, *From the Ruins of Colonialism,* 132.

125. See also Hlongwane, "Commemoration, Memory, and Monuments," 135–70.

126. Healy, *From the Ruins of Colonialism,* 131–32.

127. Louis Mink, "Philosophical Analysis and Historical Understanding," *Review of Metaphysics* 21, no. 4 (1968): 667–98 (688).

128. Sybil Milton, *In Fitting Memory: The Art and Politics of Holocaust Memorials* (Detroit: Wayne State University Press, 1981), 17.

129. Daniel Sherman, "Art, Commerce, and the Production of Memory in France after World War I," in *Commemorations,* ed. Gillis, 186–215, esp. 206–7.

130. Marschall, "Visual Memories," 161.

131. Davie, "The Day Hector Pieterson Died."

132. Boym, *The Future of Nostalgia*, 78. See also Alois Riegl, "The Cult of Monuments: Its Character and Origins," trans. Kurt Foster and Diane Ghirado, *Oppositions* 25 (1982): 21–50.

133. Davie, "The Day Hector Pieterson Died."

134. Marschall, "Visualizing Memories," 145–59; and Davie, "The Day Hector Pieterson Died."

135. Marschall, "Visualizing Memories," 145–59.

136. Fred Khumalo, "Deciding Whose Story Is History," *Sunday Times*, July 23, 2006.

137. Hlongwane, "Commemoration, Memory, and Monuments," 135–70; Kumalo, "Deciding Whose Story Is History"; and Baines, "The Master Narrative of South Africa's Liberation Struggle," 291.

138. Marschall, "Visualizing Memories," 145–46.

139. See Winter, *Sites of Memory, Sites of Mourning*, 93–96, esp. 93.

140. Crane, "Memory, Distortion, and History in the Museum," 44–63.

141. Marschall, "Visualizing Memories," 156.

142. Cornia Pretorius, "Beyond the Frame," *Sunday Times Lifestyle*, June 10, 2001, 10. See Barbie Zelizer, *Remembering to Forget: Holocaust Memory through the Camera's Eye* (Chicago: University of Chicago Press, 1998), 1–15, esp. 1.

143. Marianne Hirsch, "I Took Pictures: September 2001," in *Trauma at Home: After 9/11*, ed. Judith Greenberg (Lincoln: University of Nebraska Press, 2003), 69–87 (72).

144. Barbie Zelizer, "Photography, Journalism, Trauma," in *Journalism after September 11th*, ed. Barbie Zelizer and Stuart Allan (New York: Routledge, 2002), 55–74, esp. 57.

145. Marschall, "Visualizing Memories," 157–58; Baines, "The Master Narrative of South Africa's Liberation Struggle," 286; and Simbao, "The Thirteenth Anniversary of the Soweto Uprisings," 58.

146. See Victor Burgin, "Art, Common Sense, and Photography," in *Visual Culture: A Reader*, ed. Jessica Evans and Stuart Hall (Thousand Oaks, Calif.: Sage, 1999), 41–50; and Simbao, "The Thirteenth Anniversary of the Soweto Uprisings," 55, 58.

147. Marschall, "Visualizing Memories," 158.

148. Roland Barthes, *Camera Lucida: Reflections on Photography*, trans. Richard Howard (New York: Hill and Wang, 1981), 91.

149. For a useful treatment of landscape photography, see Ulrich Baer, "To Give Memory a Place: Holocaust Photography and the Landscape of Tradition," *Representations* 69 (2000): 38–62, esp. 41–42.

150. Max du Preez, "They Can Play, Because He Died," *Leading Architecture*, November–December 2002, 25–28; and Marschall, "Visualizing Memories," 152–53.

151. See Eeclo Runica, "Presence," *History and Theory* 45, no. 1 (2006): 1–29.

152. Marschall, "Visualizing Memories," 153.

153. Ibid., 160. For comparative purposes, see Oren Bauch Stier, "Performing Memory: Tourism, Pilgrimage, and the Ritual Appropriation of the Past," chap. 5 in *Committed to Memory: Cultural Mediations of the Holocaust* (Amherst: University of Massachusetts Press, 2003), 150–90.

154. Björn Krondorfer, Review of *Committed to Memory: Cultural Mediations of the Holocaust,* by Oren Baruch Stier," *Holocaust Genocide Studies* 19, no. 2 (2005): 290–92 (290).

155. Johnson, "The Spectacle of Memory, 36–56, esp. 37.

156. Healy, *From the Ruins of Colonialism,* 25.

157. See Till, *The New Berlin,* 14–15.

158. See Johnson, "The Spectacle of Memory," 37.

159. See Gillis, "Memory and Identity," in *Commemorations,* ed. Gillis, 3–26.

160. Young, *The Texture of Memory,* 5.

161. Ibid.

162. Marschall, "Visualizing Memories," 165.

163. Davie, "The Day Hector Pieterson Died." For a wider discussion, see Zoe Witcomb, "Shame and Identity: The Case of the Coloured in South Africa," in *Writing South Africa,* ed. Derek Attridge and Rosemary Jolly, 91–107.

164. Baines, "The Master Narrative of South Africa's Liberation Struggle," 293.

165. Ibid., 290.

166. Sturken, *Tangled Memories,* 9.

167. Douglas Booth, *The Field: Truth and Fiction in Sports History* (London: Routledge, 2005), 103.

168. Elizabeth Edwards, *Raw Histories: Photographs, Anthropology, and Museums* (Oxford: Berg, 2001), 9.

169. Simbao, "The Thirteenth Anniversary of the Soweto Uprisings," 66.

170. Murray Phillips, Mark O'Neil, and Gary Osmond, "Broadening Horizons in Sport History: Films, Photographs, and Monuments," *Journal of Sport History* 34, no. 2 (2007): 280.

171. Sturken, *Tangled Memories,* 21.

172. Edwards, *Raw Histories,* 13.

173. Simbao, "The Thirteenth Anniversary of the Soweto Uprisings," 55.

174. Phillips, O'Neil, and Osmond, "Broadening Horizons in Sport History," 271–93. A fashion-design company called Abasha Creations produced a T-shirt with a fictitious version of Hector Pieterson's report card depicting high marks in all subjects except for the hated *Afrikaans* (Simbao, "The Thirteenth Anniversary of the Soweto Uprisings," 67).

175. For the source of some of these ideas, see Michael Roth, "Remembering Forgetting: *Maladies de la Mémoire* in Nineteenth-Century France," *Representations* 26 (1989): 49–50.

176. Boym, *The Future of Nostalgia,* 53.

177. Hlongwane, "Commemoration, Memory, and Monuments," 135–70.

178. Mare, "Monumental Complexity," 42–43; and Chris van Vuuren, "Memories, Monuments, and Meanings: The Site of the Samora Machel Plane Crash," *South African Journal of Art History* 18 (2003): 222–32.

179. "Winnie Apagada da Historia," *Metical* (Mozambique) 399 (January 22, 1999). Special thanks to Eric Morier-Genoud for bringing this article to my attention, and to M. Anne Pitcher for translating it from the Portuguese.

5. Haunted Heritage

1. See Hayden, *The Power of Place,* 2–6; and Tim Edensor, *Industrial Ruins: Aesthetics, Materiality, and Memory* (London: Berg, 2005).

2. Till, *The New Berlin;* Tim Edensor, "The Ghosts of Industrial Ruins: Ordering and Disordering Memory in Excessive Space," *Environment and Planning D: Society and Space* 23, no. 2 (2005): 829–49; Edensor, "Waste Matter: The Debris of Industrial Ruins and the Disordering of the Material World," *Journal of Material Culture* 10, no. 4 (2005): 311–32; Sonja Kuftinec, "[Walking through a] Ghost Town: Cultural Hauntology in Mostar, Bosnia-Herzgovina, or Mostar: A Performance Review," *Text and Performance Quarterly* 18, no. 2 (1998): 81–95; Steve Pile, "Spectral Cities: Where the Repressed Returns and Other Short Stories," in *A Sense of Place,* ed. Jean Hillier and Emma Rooksby (Aldershot: Ashgate, 2002), 219–39; Pile, *Real Cities: Modernity, Space, and the Phantasmagorias of City Life* (London: Sage, 2005), 131–64; and Pile, "Ghosts and the City of Hope," in *The Emancipatory City?,* ed. Loretta Lees (London: Sage, 2004), 210–28.

3. Michel de Certeau, *The Practice of Everyday Life,* trans. Steve Rendall (Berkeley and Los Angeles: University of California Press, 1984), 108.

4. Michael Bell, "The Ghosts of Place," *Theory and Society* 26 (1997): 813–36 (813).

5. Till, *The New Berlin,* 8, 9.

6. Ibid., 8.

7. Cherry, "Statues in the Square," 660–97.

8. Till, *The New Berlin,* 14.

9. Avery Gordon, *Ghostly Matters: Haunting and the Sociological Imagination* (Minneapolis: University of Minnesota Press, 1997), 8–9.

10. Bell, "The Ghosts of Place," 813.

11. See Ladd, *The Ghosts of Berlin;* and Anthony Vidler, *The Architectural Uncanny: Essays in the Modern Unhomely* (Cambridge, Mass.: MIT Press, 1992).

12. Coombes, *Visual Culture and Public Memory in a Democratic South Africa,* 120.

13. Maria Tumarkin, *Traumascapes: The Power and Fate of Places Transformed by Tragedy* (Melbourne: Melbourne University Press, 2005), 14.

14. Ibid., 12, 13.

15. Boym, *The Future of Nostalgia,* 79.

16. Tumarkin, *Traumascapes,* 86.

17. Dylan Trigg, "The Place of Trauma: Memory, Hauntings, and the Temporality of Ruins," *Memory Studies* 2, no. 1 (2009): 87–101, esp. 99.

18. Ibid., 98.

19. Coombes, *Visual Culture and Public Memory in a Democratic South Africa,* 116.

20. Peggy Delport, "Signposts for Retrieval: A Visual Framework for Enabling Memory of Place and Time," in *Recalling Community in Cape Town: Creating and Curating the District Six Museum,* ed. Ciraj Rassool and Sandra Prosalendis (Cape Town: District Six Museum, 2001), 31–46.

21. Ciraj Rassool, "Memory and Politics of the History of the District Six Museum," in *Desire Lines,* ed. Murray, Shepherd, and Hall, 113–28. For an overview, see Kathleen Goodnow (with Jack Lowman and Jatti Bredekamp), *Challenge and Transformation: Museums in Cape Town and Sydney* (Paris: UNESCO—BPI/PUB, 2006), 113–43.

22. For comparable "lost space," see Catherine Switzer and Sara McDowell, "Redrawing Cognitive Maps of Conflict: Lost Spaces and Forgetting in the Centre of Belfast," *Memory Studies* 2, no. 4 (2009): 337–53.

23. Allessandro Angelini, "Spaces of Good Hope: Inscribing Memory, Territory, and Urbanity in District Six, Cape Town," Dark Roast Occasional Paper no. 13, Isandla Institute, 2003): 4. See also Karin Till, "Resilient Politics and Memory-Work in Wounded Cities: Rethinking the City through the District Six in Cape Town, South Africa," in *Collaborative Resilience: Moving from Crisis to Opportunity,* ed. Bruce E. Goldstein (Cambridge, Mass.: MIT Press), 283–307.

24. See Morgan Meyer, "Placing and Tracing Absence: A Material Culture in the Immaterial," *Journal of Material Culture* 17, no. 1 (2012): 103–10.

25. Tim Edensor, "Mundane Hauntings: Commuting through the Phantasmagoric Working-Class Spaces of Manchester, England," *Cultural Geographies* 15, no. 4 (2008): 313–33, esp. 315, 324.

26. Julian Jonker and Karen Till, "Mapping and Excavating Spectral Traces in Post-*Apartheid* Cape Town," *Memory Studies* 2, no. 4 (2009): 303–35 (306).

27. Chrischené Julius, "'Digging [D]eeper Than the Eye Approves': Oral Histories and Their Use in the *Digging Deeper* Exhibition of the District Six Museum," *Kronos* 34,

no. 1 (2008): 106–38, esp. 106; Angelini, "Spaces of Good Hope," 3–4; Judith Matloff, "Cape Town's Coloureds Remember Razed District," *Christian Science Monitor,* March 6, 1995, 10; and Donald McNeil, "Cape Town Honors Deciminated Neighborhood," *Cleveland Plain Dealer,* July 18, 1998, 14.

28. Paul Maylam, "The Rise and Decline of Urban *Apartheid* in South Africa," *African Affairs* 89, 354 (1990): 57–84; and Lauren Platsky and Cheryl Walker, eds., *The Surplus People: Forced Removals in South Africa* (Johannesburg: Ravan Press, 1985).

29. Geoffrey Baetchen, *Forget Me Not: Photography and Remembrance* (New York: Princeton Architectural Press, 2004); David Bate, *Photography after Postmodernism: Barthes, Stieglitz, and the Art of Memory* (London: I. B. Taurus, 2011); Barthes, *Camera Lucida;* and Elizabeth Edwards, "Photographs as Objects of Memory," in *Material Memories,* ed. Marius Kwint, Christopher Breward, and Jeremy Aynsley (Oxford: Berg, 1999), 221–36.

30. For a well-formulated history of District Six, see *The Struggle for District Six: Past and Present,* ed. Shamil Jeppie and Crain Soudien (Cape Town: Buchu Books, 1990). See also Rafael Marks and Marco Bezzoli, "The Urbanism of District Six, Cape Town," in *Africa's Urban Past,* ed. David Anderson and Richard Rathbone (Oxford: James Currey, 2000), 262–82.

31. The literature is extensive. See, for example, John Western, *Outcast Cape Town* (Berkeley and Los Angeles: University of California Press, 1997), 115–16, 120–25; Vivian Bickford-Smith, "The Origins and Early History of District Six to 1910," in *The Struggle for District Six,* ed. Shamil Jeppie and Crain Soudien, 35–43; Bickford-Smith, "South African Urban History, Racial Segregation, and the Unique Case of Cape Town?" *Journal of South African Studies* 21, no. 1 (1995): 63–78; and Deborah Hart, "Political Manipulation of Urban Space: The Razing of District Six, Cape Town," in *The Struggle for District Six,* ed. Jeppie and Soudien, 117–42.

32. Delport, "Signposts for Retrieval," 36–37.

33. McEachern, *Narratives of Nation Media, Memory, and Representation in the Making of the New South Africa,* 67–86, esp. 67–68; and Julius, "'Digging [D]eeper than the Eye Approves,'" 106.

34. Crain Soudien, "District Six: From Protest to Protest," in *The Struggle for District Six,* ed. Shamil Jeppie and Crain Soudien, 143–84.

35. Coombes, *Visual Culture and Public Memory in a Democratic South Africa,* 117; and Junker and Till, "Mapping and Excavating Spectral Traces in Post-*Apartheid* Cape Town," 303–35.

36. Julius, "'Digging [D]eeper Than the Eye Approves,'" 106.

37. "In this exhibition, we do not wish to recreate District Six as much as to repossess the history of the area as a place where people lived, loved, and struggled. It is an

attempt to take back our right to signpost our lives to those things we hold dear" (banner posted at the Opening of the District Six Museum). Anonymous author, quoted in Sandra Prosalendis, Jennifer Marot, Crain Soudien, and Anwah Naglia, "Punctuations: Periodic Impressions of a Museum," in *Recalling Community in Cape Town,* ed. Rassool and Prosalendis, 74–94 (82–83).

38. Davison, "Museums and the Reshaping of Memory," 143–60, esp. 148; Charmaine McEachern, "Mapping the Memories: Politics, Place, and Identity in the District Six Museum, Cape Town," in *Social Identities in the New South Africa: After Apartheid,* vol. 1, ed. Abebe Zegeye (Cape Town: Kwela, 2001), 499–522; and Tina Smith and Ciraj Rassool, "History in Photographs at the District Six Museum," in *Recalling Community in Cape Town,* ed. Rassool and Prosalendis, 131–45.

39. Rassool, "Memory and Politics of the History of the District Six Museum," 122–23.

40. Charmaine McEachern, "Working with Memory: The District Six Museum in the New South Africa," *Social Analysis* 42, no. 2 (1998): 47–72; and Ciraj Rassool, "Community Museums, Memory Politics, and Social Transformation in South Africa: Histories, Possibilities and Limits," in *Museum Frictions: Global Transformations/Public Cultures,* ed. Ivan Karp, Corinne Kratz, Lynn Szwaja, and Tomás Ybarra-Frausto, with Gustavo Buntinx, Barbara Kirshenblatt-Gimblett, and Ciraj Rassool (Durham: Duke University Press, 2006), 286–321.

41. Sean Field, "'I Dream of Our Old House, You See There Are Things That Can Never Go Away': Memory, Restitution, and Democracy," in *Lost Communities, Living Memories: Remembering Forced Removals in Cape Town,* ed. Sean Field (Cape Town: David Philip, 2001), 117–23. See also Field, "Imagining Communities: Memory, Loss, and Resilience in Post-*Apartheid* Cape Town," in *Oral History and Public Memories,* ed. Paula Hamilton and Linda Shopes (Philadelphia: Temple University Press, 2008), 107–24.

42. Angelini, "Spaces of Good Hope," 8.

43. Valmont Layne and Ciraj Rassool, "Memory Rooms: Oral History in the District Six Museum," in *Recalling Community in Cape Town,* 146–53.

44. Anna Bohlin, "The Politics of Locality: Memories of District Six in Cape Town," in *Locality and Belonging,* ed. Nadia Lovell (New York: Routledge, 1998), 168–88, esp. 177; and Peggy Delport, "Digging Deeper in District Six: Features and Interfaces in a Curatorial Landscape," in *Recalling Community in Cape Town,* ed. Rassoll and Prosalendis, 154–64.

45. Delport, "Signposts for Retrieval," 37.

46. McEachern, *Narratives of Nation Media,* 69–70; and Anna Bohlin, "The Politics of Locality: Memories of District Six in Cape Town," in *Locality and Belonging,* ed. Nadia Lovell (New York: Routledge, 1998), 168–88.

47. Martin Hall, "Cape Town's District Six and the Archaeology of Memory," in *Destruction and Conservation of Cultural Property,* ed. Robert Layton, Peter Stone, and Julian Thomas (New York: Routledge, 2001), 298–311 (308).

48. Tamera Leora Meets, "Deconstructing Museums and Memorials in Pre- and Post-Apartheid South Africa" (M.A. thesis, University of South Africa, 2009), 61, 34.

49. Rassool, "Memory and Politics of the History of the District Six Museum," 119.

50. Emma Bedford and Tracy Murinik, "Remembering That Place," in *The District Six Public Sculpture Project,* ed. Crain Soudien and Renate Meyer (Cape Town: District Six Museum Foundation, 1997), 12–22.

51. McEachern, "Mapping the Memories," 223–42 (233).

52. Ibid., 230, 233; and Rassool, "Memory and Politics of the History of the District Six Museum," 125–26.

53. Sofie Geschier, "'So There I Sit in a Catch-22 Situation: Remembering and Imagining Trauma in the District Six Museum," in *Imagining the City: Memories and Cultures in Cape Town,* ed. Sean Field, Renate Meyer, and Felicity Swanson (Cape Town: HSRC Press, 2007), 37–56.

54. Boym, *The Future of Nostalgia,* 42, 53, 75–76.

55. Meets, *Deconstructing Museums and Memorials in Pre- and Post-Apartheid South Africa,* 73–74.

56. Coombes, *Visual Culture and Public Memory in a Democratic South Africa,* 123; Sophie Geschier, "Beyond Experience: The Mediation of Traumatic Memories in South African History Museums," *Transformation* 59 (2005): 45–65; Field, "Imagining Communities," 107–24; and Julius, "'Digging [D]eeper Than the Eye Approves,'" 106–38.

57. Julius, "'Digging [D]eeper Than the Eye Approves,'" 112–15.

58. See Kirshenblatt-Gimblett, *Destination Culture,* 18–25.

59. Azaryahu and Foote, "Historical Space as Narrative Medium," 179–94.

60. Soudien, "District Six and Its Uses in the Discussion about Non-racialism," 125.

61. Bohlin, "The Politics of Locality," 168–88; and McEachern, "Mapping the Memories," 223–42.

62. Colin Miller, "Land Restitutions in District Six: Settling a Traumatic Landscape. Interview with Anwah Nagia," in *Recalling Community in Cape Town,* ed. Rassoll and Prosalendis, 166–79, esp. 177.

63. Sandra Prosalendis, "District Six—Kanaladorp," *Nordisk Museologi* 1 (1999): 135–46 (141).

64. Rassool, "Memory and Politics of the History of the District Six Museum," 125–26. See also Rassool, "Community Museums, Memory Politics, and Social Transformation," 286–321.

65. Crain Soudien, "District Six and Its Uses in the Discussion about Non-racialism,"

in *Coloured by History, Shaped by Place: New Perspectives on Coloured Identities in Cape Town,* ed. Zimitri Erasmus (Cape Town: Kwela, 2001), 114–30, esp. 116.

66. Prosalendis, "District Six—Kanaladorp," 141–42.

67. Boym, *The Future of Nostalgia,* xii.

68. McEachern, "Mapping the Memories," 235; Bohlin, "The Politics of Locality," 168–88; and Field, "'I Dream of Our Old House,'" 117–23.

69. Henry Trotter, "Trauma and Memory: The Impact of *Apartheid*-Era Forced Removals on Coloured Identity in Cape Town," in *Burdened by Race: Coloured Identities in South Africa,* ed. Mohamed Adhikar (Cape Town: University of Cape Town Press, 2009), 49–78 (56).

70. Henry Trotter ("Trauma and Memory," 56) uses this phrase, which he borrowed from Yael Zerubavel, "The Historic, the Legendary, and the Incredible: Invented Traditional and Collective Memory in Israel," in *Commemorations,* ed. Gillis, 105–23.

71. See Schwartz, "The Social Context of Commemoration," 374–402, esp. 377.

72. Boym, *The Future of Nostalgia,* 8.

73. Hall, "Cape Town's District Six and the Archaeology of Memory," 298–311; and Julius, "'Digging [D]eeper Than the Eye Approves,'" 106–38.

74. For a detailed and very helpful discussion, see Trotter, "Trauma and Memory," 49–78.

75. There are too many autobiographies to list here. See, for example, Linda Fortune, *The House in Tyne Street: Childhood Memories of District Six* (Cape Town: Kwela Books, 1996). See also Geschier, "'So There I Sit in a Catch-22 Situation,'" 37–56.

76. For a wider and more nuanced discussion, see Martin Hall, *Archaeology of the Modern World: Colonial Transcripts in South Africa and the Chesapeake* (New York: Routledge, 2000), 151–76; and Nasson, "Oral History and the Reconstruction of District Six," in *The Struggle for District Six,* ed. Jeppie and Soudein, 44–66.

77. Nasson, "Oral History and the Reconstruction of District Six," 48.

78. Hall, *Archaeology of the Modern World,* 151–76; and Soudien, "Holding on to the Past: Working with the 'Myths' of District Six," in *Recalling Community in Cape Town,* ed. Rassool and Prosalendis, 97–105.

79. *District Six—the Musical* played before packed audiences in Cape Town, Johannesburg, and Port Elizabeth from 1987 to 1990. See Hall, *Archaeology of the Modern World,* 165–66.

80. Arjun Appadurai, *Modernity at Large: Cultural Dimensions of Globalization* (Minneapolis: University of Minnesota Press, 1996), 77.

81. Julius, "'Digging [D]eeper Than the Eye Approves,'" 108–12.

82. Delport, "Digging Deeper in District Six," 154–64; Coombes, *History after Apartheid,* 139–41; and Rassool, "Memory and Politics of the District Six Museum," 121–22.

83. Rassool, "Memory and Politics of the History of the District Six Museum," 121–22 (122).

84. See Jennifer Bonnell and Roger Simon, "Difficult Exhibits and Intimate Encounters," *Museum and Society* 5, no. 2 (2007): 65–85, esp. 79–80.

85. Rustom Bharucha, "The Limits of the Beyond: Contemporary Art Practices, Intervention, and Collaboration in Public Spaces," *Third Text* 21, no. 4 (2007): 397–416 (401).

86. Bharucha, "The Limits of the Beyond," 404, 403. See also Till, "Resilient Politics and Memory-Work in Wounded Cities," 283–307.

87. Steve Robins, "No-Named People Who Kept the Cogs of *Apartheid* Oiled," *Cape Times,* August 6, 1997.

88. Ibid.

89. Trotter, "Trauma and Memory," 49–78; and Geschier, "Beyond Experience," 45–65. For a wider view, see Bonder, "On Memory, Trauma, Public Space, Monuments, and Memorials," 62–69, esp. 67.

90. Coombes, *Visual Culture and Public Memory in a Democratic South Africa,* 131–32.

91. Hall, *Archaeology of the Modern World,* 165–66; and Coombes, *Visual Culture and Public Memory in a Democratic South Africa,* 132, 134.

92. Rassool, "Memory and Politics of the History of the District Six Museum," 119.

93. Martin Hall and Pia Bombardella, "Paths of Nostalgia and Desire through Heritage Destinations at the Cape of Good Hope," in *Desire Lines,* ed. Murray, Shepard, and Hall, 245–58, esp. 256.

94. Bohlin, "The Politics of Locality," 172.

95. Angelini, "Spaces of Good Hope," 22.

96. See Kerstin Barndt, "'Memory Tracers of an Abandoned Set of Futures': Industrial Ruins in the Postindustrial Landscapes of Germany," in *Ruins of Modernity,* ed. Hell and Schönle, 270–93, esp. 270–71.

97. Boym, *The Future of Nostalgia,* 49.

98. Huyssen, *Present Pasts,* 28.

99. Boym, *The Future of Nostalgia,* 53.

100. Antonia Malan and Crain Soudien, "Managing Heritage in District Six, Cape Town: Conflicts Past and Present," in *The Archaeology of Twentieth-Century Conflict,* ed. John Schofield (London: Routledge, 2002), 249–65.

101. Italo Calvino, *Invisible Cities,* trans. William Weaver (New York: Harvest Books, 1982), 33.

102. Huyssen, *Present Pasts,* 17.

103. Angelini, "Spaces of Good Hope," 35.

104. Steven Robins, "Global Warnings: Urban Governance at the Cape of Storms," in

Ambiguous Restructurings in Post-Apartheid Cape Town: The Spatial Form of Socio-Political Change, ed. Christoph Haferburg and Jürgen Oßenbrügge (London: Lit Verlag, 2003), 87–114, esp. 89.

105. Myra Shackley, "Potential Futures for Robben Island: Shrine, Museum, or Theme Park?" *International Journal of Heritage Studies* 7, no. 4 (2001): 355–63, esp. 355.

106. Keyan Tomaselli, Maureen Eke, and Patricia Davison, "Transcending Prison as a Metaphor for *Apartheid,*" *Visual Anthropology* 9, no. 3–4 (1997): 285–300, esp. 286.

107. Arthur Davey, "Robben Island and the Military, 1931–1960," in *The Island: A History of Robben Island, 1488–1990,* ed. Harriet Deacon (Cape Town: Mayibuye Books and David Philip, 1996), 76–92.

108. Moses Dlamini, *Hell-Hole Robben Island: Reminiscences of a Political Prisoner in South Africa* (Trenton, N.J.: Africa World Press, 1984); and J. U. Jacobs, "Discourses of Detention," *Current Writing* 3, no. 1 (1991): 193–99.

109. See contributions to *The Island: A History of Robben Island, 1488–1990,* ed. Deacon.

110. Oliver Tambo, *Preparing Ourselves for Power: Oliver Tambo Speaks* (London: Heinemann Educational, 1987), 199.

111. Caroline Strange and Michael Kempa, "Shades of Dark Tourism: Alcatraz and Robben Island," *Annals of Tourism Research* 30, no. 2 (203): 386–405.

112. Liz Westby-Nunn, South African Tourism Board, quoted in *Cape Argus,* June 7, 1993.

113. Davison, "Museums and the Reshaping of Memory," 143–60, esp. 154–55; Harriet Deacon, "Remembering Tragedy, Constructing Modernity: Robben Island as a National Monument," in *Negotiating the Past,* ed. Nuttall and Coetzee, 161–79; Coombes, *Visual Culture and Public Memory in a Democratic South Africa,* 58–59; and Veronique Rioufol, "Behind Telling: Post-*Apartheid* Representations of Robben Island's Past," *Kronos* 26 (2000): 22–41.

114. The examples are extensive. See Govan Mbeki, *Learning from Robben Island: The Prison Writings of Govan Mbeki* (Cape Town: David Philip, 1991); Frank Anthony, *Robbeneiland My Kruis My Huis* (Genadenda: Kampen, 1983); Mosiuoa Patrick Lekota, *Prison Letters to a Daughter* (Johannesburg: Taurus, 1991); Indres Naidoo, *Island in Chains: Ten Years on Robben Island as Told by Indres Naidoo to Albie Sachs* (Harmondsworth: Penguin, 1982); Eddie Daniels, *There and Back: Robben Island, 1964–1979* (Cape Town: Mayibuye Books, 1998); Neville Alexander, *Robben Island Dossier, 1964–1974* (Cape Town: University of Cape Town, 1994); and D. M. Zwelonke, *Robben Island* (London: Heinemann, 1973). For a survey of autobiographical writing, see J. H. Jacobs, "Narrating the Island: Robben Island in South African Literature," *Current Writing* 4 (1992): 73–84.

115. Paul Gready, "Autobiography and the 'Power of Writing': Political Prison Writing in the *Apartheid* Era," *Journal of Southern African Studies* 19, no. 4 (1993): 515–23. See also Fran Buntman, "Categorical and Strategic Resistance and the Making of Political Prisoner Identity in *Apartheid's* Robben Island Prison," *Social Identitites* 4, no. 4 (1998): 417–41.

116. Lindy Wilson, producer and director, *Robben Island: Our University,* VHS Video, Charlottesville, Va., 1988. For an analysis of the film, see Tomaselli, Eke, and Davison, "Transcending Prison as a Metaphor of *Apartheid,*" 285–300.

117. See Fran Buntman, "From Hell-Hole to Blessing in Disguise: A Study of Politics on Robben Island, 1963–1987" (honours diss., University of the Witwatersrand, 1988); and Buntman, *Robben Island and Prisoner Resistance to Apartheid* (Cambridge: Cambridge University Press, 2003).

118. Deacon, "Intangible Heritage in Conservation Management Planning," 310–11.

119. Deacon, "Remembering Tragedy, Construction Modernity," 161–62. See also Lynne Duke, "*Apartheid* Era Jail Restored as Monument," *Washington Post,* January 27, 1997, 7.

120. "Robben Island Now a National Monument," *The Star,* December 21, 1995; Deacon, "Remembering Tragedy, Constructing Modernity," 161–79; and "Grim Tour of the Island Is a Living History Lesson," *The Star,* January 26, 1997. See also Clifford Shearing and Michael Kempa, "A Museum of Hope: A Story of Robben Island," *Annals of the American Academy of Political and Social Science* 592, no. 1 (2004): 62–78.

121. "Robben Island Now a National Monument," *The Star,* December 21, 1995; Deacon, "Remembering Tragedy, Constructing Modernity," 161–79; and "Grim Tour of the Island Is a Living History Lesson," *The Star,* January 26, 1997. See also Clifford Shearing and Michael Kempa, "A Museum of Hope: A Story of Robben Island," *Annals of the American Academy of Political and Social Science* 592, no. 1 (2004): 62–78.

122. Harriet Deacon, "Intangible Heritage in Conservation Management Planning: The Case of Robben Island," *International Journal of Heritage Studies* 10, no. 4 (2004): 309–19, esp. 309.

123. Gerrie Lubbe, "The Early Years of Muslim Resistance," *Kronos* 12 (1987): 49–56 (49).

124. Johnson, "Mapping Monuments," 293–98, esp. 293.

125. Deacon, "Intangible Heritage in Conservation Management Planning," 313–14.

126. Rioufol, "Behind Telling," 21–44.

127. Tim Edensor, *Tourists at the Taj Mahal: Performance and Meaning at a Symbolic Site* (New York: Routledge, 1998), 8–15; and Shalini Singh, "Secular Pilgrimages and Sacred Tourism in the Indian Himalayas," *GeoJournal* 64, no. 4 (2005): 215–23.

128. Dierdre Boden and Harvey Molotch, "Compulsion to Proximity," in *Now/*

Here: Time, Space, and Modernity, ed. Roger Friedland and Dierdre Boden (Berkeley and Los Angeles: University of California Press, 1994), 257–86.

129. Harry Garuba, "Museums, Mimesis, and the Narratives of the Tour Guides of Robben Island," in *Desire Lines,* ed. Murray, Shepard, and Hall, 129–44, esp. 134.

130. Pau Obrador and Sean Carter, "Art, Politics, Memory: Tactical Tourism and the Route of Anarchism in Barcelona," *Cultural Geographies* 17, no. 4 (2010): 525–31;

131. Garuba, "Museums, Mimesis, and the Narratives," 133.

132. Ibid., 132–33.

133. Deacon, "Remembering Tragedy, Constructing Modernity," 177.

134. Shackley, "Potential Futures for Robben Island," 357.

135. Garuba, "Museums, Mimesis, and the Narratives," 136.

136. Coombes, *Visual Culture and Public Memory in a Democratic South Africa,* 100–101.

137. Ibid.

138. Edensor, "National Identity and the Politics of Memory," 181.

139. Marita Sturken, *Tourists of History: Memory, Kitsch, and Consumerism from Oklahoma City to Ground Zero* (Durham: Duke University Press, 2007), 20–25.

140. Shackley, "Potential Futures of Robben Island," 355–63.

141. "Letter to Editor," *Weekly Mail & Guardian,* October 17–29, 1997.

142. Davison, "Museums and the Reshaping of Memory," 157–58; and "Corruption Surfaces on Robben Island," *Sunday Independent,* May 24, 1998.

143. Rooksana Omar, "Meeting the Challenges of Diversity in South African Museums," *Museums International* 57, no. 4 (2005): 52–59.

144. Janet Hall, "Museums, Myths, and Missionaries: Redressing the Past for a New South Africa," in *Museum, Media, Message,* ed. Eilean Hooper-Greenhill (New York: Routledge, 1995), 175.

145. Amareswar Galla, "Transformation in South Africa: A Legacy Challenged," *Museum International* 51, no. 2 (1999): 38–43 (38).

146. C. Grieg Crysler, "Violence and Empathy: National Museums and the Spectacle of Society," *Traditional Dwellings and Settlements Review* 17, no. 2 (2006): 19–38, esp. 20.

147. Liebowitz, "Making Memory Space," 62.

148. Lisa Findley, *Building Change: Architecture, Politics, and Cultural Agency* (New York: Routledge, 2005), 123.

149. Liebowitz, "Making Memory Space," 55–57. In this and the following paragraphs, I draw on sources that Vickie Liebowitz provides.

150. Ulrich Baer, "To Give Memory a Place: Holocaust Photography and the Landscape of Tradition," *Representations* 69 (2000): 50, 56.

151. See Hilde Hein, *The Museum in Transition: A Philosophical Perspective* (Washington, D.C.: Smithsonian Institution Press, 2000), 8 (first quotation); and Tony Bennett, *The Birth of the Museum* (New York: Routledge, 1995), 59–88 (second quotation).

152. Liebowitz, "Making Memory Space," 64.

153. John Matshikiza, "History in the Making," *Mail & Guardian,* November 30–December 6, 2001, 19.

154. Bremner, "Memory, Nation-Building, and the Post-*Apartheid* City," 85–103 (89).

155. Liebowitz, "Making Memory Space," 64–67.

156. Bremner, "Memory, Nation-Building, and the Post-*Apartheid* City." 94.

157. Liebowitz, "Making Memory Space," 66.

158. This information is derived from Coombes, *Visual Culture and Public Memory in a Democratic South Africa,* 105.

159. Coombes, *Visual Culture and Public Memory in a Democratic South Africa,* 108; and see Sabine Marschall, "Serving Male Agendas: Two National Women's Monuments in South Africa," *Women's Studies* 33, no. 8 (2004): 1009–33.

160. Rayda Becker, "The New Monument to the Women of South Africa," *African Arts* 33 (2000): 1–3.

161. For comparative purposes, see James Schmidt, "Cenotaphs in Sound: Catastrophe, Memory, and Musical Memorials," *Proceedings of the European Society for Aesthetics* 2 (2010): 454–78.

162. Coombes, *Visual Culture and Public Memory in a Democratic South Africa,* 108.

163. Jean-Michel Rabaté, *The Ghosts of Modernity* (Gainesville: University Press of Florida, 1996), xvi.

164. Marschall, "Serving Male Agendas," 1009–33 (1019).

165. Ibid., 1020, 1022.

166. See Serguisz Michalski, *Public Monuments: Art in Political Bondage, 1870–1997* (London: Reaction Books, 1998).

167. Becker, "The New Monument to the Women of South Africa," 3–4.

168. See John Gillis, "Introduction—Memory and Identity, in *Commemorations,* ed. Gillis, 3–24; and Sara McDowell, "Commemorating 'Dead Men': Gendering the Past and Present in Northern Ireland," *Gender, Place, and Culture* 15, no. 4 (2008): 335–54.

169. Marschall, "How to Honour a Woman," 260–83 (263).

170. Ibid., 263.

171. Marschall, "Serving Male Agendas," 1023; and Becker, "The New Monument to the Women of South Africa," 8.

172. Gayatri Spivak and Sonia Gunew, "Questions of Multiculturalism," in *The*

Cultural Studies Reader, ed. Simon During (London: Routledge, 1993), 193–202 (193). The last quotation is from Marschall, "Serving Male Agendas," 1025.

173. Marschall, "Serving Male Agendas," 1028, 1030.

6. Makeshift Memorials

1. Meskell and Scheermeyer, "Heritage as Therapy," 153–55; and Hlongwane, "Commemoration, Memory, and Monuments," 135–70.

2. Mattera, *Sophiatown,* 151.

3. See Crane, "Writing the Individual Back into Collective Memory," 1379–80.

4. See Daniel James, "Meatpackers, Peronists, and Collective Memory: A View from the South," *American Historical Review* 102, no. 5 (1997): 1404–12, esp. 1411–12.

5. Edensor, "National Identity and the Politics of Memory," 181–82 (182).

6. Erin Mosely, "'Visualizing *Apartheid:* Contemporary Art and Collective Memory during South Africa's Transition to Democracy," *Antípoda: Revista de Antropología y Arqueología* 5 (2007): 97–119 (99).

7. John Bodnar, *Remaking America: Public Memory, Commemoration, and Patriotism in the Twentieth Century* (Princeton: Princeton University Press, 1992).

8. Stangl, "The Vernacular and the Monumental," 245–53.

9. Ekaterina Haskins and Justin DeRose, "Memory, Visibility, and Public Space: Reflections on Commemoration(s) of 9/11," *Space & Culture* 6, no. 4, (2003): 377–93.

10. Nora, "Between Memory and History," 7.

11. See Haskins and DeRose, "Memory, Visibility, and Public Space," 377–93. See also contributions to *Spontaneous Shrines and the Public Memorialization of Death,* ed. Jack Santino (New York: Palgrave Macmillan, 2006).

12. Marschall, "Commemorating the 'Trojan Horse' Massacre in Cape Town," 135–48.

13. Kenneth Doka, "Memorial, Ritual, and Public Tragedy," in *Living with Grief: Coping with Public Tragedy,* ed. Marcia Lattanzi-Light and Kenneth Doka (New York: Brunner-Routledge, 2003), 179–90.

14. Holly Everett, *Roadside Crosses in Contemporary Memorial Culture* (Denton: University of North Texas Press, 2002), 82; Peter Jan Margry and Cristina Sanchez-Carretero, "Rethinking Memorialization: The Concept of Grassroots Memorials," in *Grassroots Memorials: The Politics of Memorializing Traumatic Death,* ed. Peter Jan Margry and Cristina Sanchez-Carretero, 1–49; and Jack Santino, "Performative Commemoratives: Spontaneous Shrines and the Public Memorialization of Death," in *Spontaneous Shrines and the Public Memorialization of Death,* ed. Santino (New York: Palgrave Macmillan, 2006), 5–15.

15. Robert Dobler, "Alternative Memorials: Death and Memory in Contemporary America" (M.A. thesis, University of Oregon, 2010), 70–71.

16. Marschall, "Commemorating the 'Trojan Horse' Massacre," 142 (146).

17. Philip Stone and Richard Sharpley, "Consuming Dark Tourism: A Thanatological Perspective," *Annals of Tourism Research* 35, no. 2 (2008): 574–95.

18. Amy Biehl arrived in South Africa in 1993 as an exchange student on a Fulbright Fellowship and was continuing her Ph.D. studies in political science at the University of the Western Cape. While in Cape Town, she spent much of her time registering black voters in South Africa's historic April 1994 elections.

19. Quotations from Dobler, *Alternative Memorials,* 1.

20. Jordan, *Structures of Memory,* 1.

21. Dobler, *Alternative Memorials,* 71–72.

22. See Malcolm Foley and John Lennon, "JFK and Dark Tourism: A Fascination with Assassination," *International Journal of Heritage Studies* 2 (1996): 198–211; Lennon and Foley, *Dark Tourism: The Attraction of Death and Disaster* (London: Continuum, 2000); A. V. Seaton, "Guided by the Dark: From Thanatopsis to Thanatourism," *International Journal of Heritage Studies* 2, no. 4 (1996): 234–44; Rachel Hughes, "The Abject Artifacts of Memory: Photographs from Cambodia's Genocide," *Media, Culture & Society* 25 (2003): 23–44; A. Craig Wright and John Lennon, "Selective Interpretation and Eclectic Human Heritage in Lithuania," *Tourism Management* 28, no. 2 (2007): 519–29; and see also Erik Cohen, "Educational Dark Tourism at an *In Populo* Site: The Holocaust Museum in Jerusalem," *Annals of Tourism Research* 38, no. 1 (2001): 193–209.

23. For comparative purposes, see J. E. Tunbridge and Gregory Ashworth, *Dissonant Heritage: The Management of the Past as a Resource in Conflict* (Chichester: John Wiley, 1996); and Caroline Strange, "The Port Arthur Massacre: Tragedy and Public Memory in Australia," *Studies in Law, Politics, and Society* 20 (2000): 159–82.

24. Avishai Margalit, *The Ethics of Memory* (Cambridge, Mass.: Harvard University Press, 2002), 158–59.

25. Schmidt, "Cenotaphs in Sound," 454–78 (478).

26. Marschall, "How to Honour a Woman," 262.

27. See Young, "The Counter-Monument, 267–96, esp. 271–72.

28. Marschall, "Commemorating the 'Trojan Horse' Massacre in Cape Town," 142; Cassie Wu, "Transformations of the Home in Zwelethu Mthethwa's Portrait Photographs," *African Arts* 43, no. 2 (2010): 68–77; and Jessica Dubow and Ruth Rosengarten, "History as the Main Complaint: William Kentridge and the Making of Post-*Apartheid* South Africa," *Art History* 27, no. 4 (2004): 671–90.

29. For a critical review of many contributors to the world of visual art, see Leora Farber, "The Address of the Other: The Body and the Senses in Contemporary South

African Visual Art," *Critical Arts: A South-North Journal of Cultural and Media Studies* 24, no. 4 (2010): 303–20. See also Stephanie Marlin-Curiel, "Rave New World: Trance-Mission, Trance-Nationalism, and Trance-Scendence in the 'New' South Africa," *TDR: The Drama Review* 45, no. 4 (2001): 149–68; Hanelile Marx, "Archetypes of Memory and Amnesia in South African Soap Opera," *Tydskrif Vir Letterkunde* 42, no. 1 (2004): 113–26; and Lynn Brinkman, *From Apartheid to HIV/AIDS: The Construction of Memory, Identity, and Communication through Public Murals in South Africa* (master's thesis, Bowling Green State University, 2007).

30. See Marc Howard Ross, "Strategies for Transforming and Enlarging South Africa's Post-*Apartheid* Symbolic Landscape," in *Culture and Belonging in Divided Societies: Contestation and Symbolic Landscapes,* ed. Ross (Philadelphia: University of Pennsylvania Press, 2009), 193–215.

31. Young, "The Counter-Monument," 270.

32. Steven Sack, "Where Walls Are the Fabric of Freedom," *Mail & Guardian,* November 26–December 2, 1993. See also Sabine Marschall, "Transforming Symbolic Identity: Wall Art and the South African City," *African Arts* 41, no. 2 (2008): 12–23.

33. Sabine Marschall, "A Critical Investigation into the Impact of Community Mural Art," *Transformation* 40 (1999): 55–86; and Marschall, "Affirming Africa: Recovering Cultural Heritage and Representing Ordinary People's Lives in South African Community Mural Art," *Mots Pluriels* 16 (2000), http://wwwarts.uwa.edu.au/MotsPluriels/MP1600sm.html.

34. "A Post-*Apartheid* Tribute: Art Leading the People," *New York Times,* January 12, 1999.

35. For South Africa, see Loren Kruger, "Fault Lines, Cape Town Castle," *Public Culture* 10, no. 1 (1997): 209–10. For a wider view, see, for example, Steven Hoelscher, "Angels of Memory: Photography and Haunting in Guatemala City," *GeoJournal* 73 (2008): 195–217; Neil Jarman, "Troubled Images," *Critique of Anthropology* 12, no. 2 (1992): 145–65; and Rolston, "Politics, Painting, and Popular Culture," 5–28.

36. For a treatment of painting as theatrical performance, see Johannes Fabian, *Remembering the Present: Painting and Popular History in Zaire* (Berkeley and Los Angeles: University of California Press, 1996), 261–64.

37. See Tenley Bick, "Horror Stories: *Apartheid* and the Abject Body in Jane Alexander," *African Arts* 43, no. 4 (2010): 30–41.

38. See Coombes, *Visual Culture and Public Memory in a Democratic South Africa,* 60, 64, 84, 86, 160; Andre Odendaal, "Let It Return: Work of the Mayibuye Center," *Museums Journal* 94 (1994): 24–26; and Carolyn Mooney, "A South African Center Seeks to Preserve a Painful Memory of the *Apartheid* Era," *Chronicle of Higher Education,* July 3, 1998, 16.

39. See Till, "Staging the Past," 251–83, esp. 254.

40. For the source of some of these ideas in this paragraph, see Michael Woods, "Performing Power: Local Politics and the Tounton Pageant of 1928," *Journal of Historical Geography* 25, no. 1 (1999): 57–59.

41. Ruth Teer-Tomaselli, "Moving toward Democracy: The South African Broadcasting Corporation and the 1994 Election," *Media, Culture & Society* 17, no. 4 (1995): 577–601.

42. See Jeffrey Broxmeyer, "Of Politicians, Populism, and Plates: Marketing the Body Politic," *Women's Studies Quarterly* 38, no. 4–4 (2010): 138–52.

43. Grunebaum-Ralph, "Re-Placing Pasts, Forgetting Presents, 198–212; and McEachern, *Narratives of Nation Media, Memory, and Representation,* 87–109.

44. Rachel Swarns, "Destination Soweto," *Saturday Argus,* May 26–27, 2001. For a wider view, see Obrador and Carter, "Art, Politics, Memory," 525–31.

45. De Certeau, *The Practice of Everyday Life*, 36–37. See also David Pinder, "Ghostly Footsteps: Voices, Memories, and Walks in the City," *Cultural Geographies* 8 (2001): 1–19; and Pinder, "Arts of Urban Exploration," *Cultural Geographies* 12 (2005): 383–411.

46. See Yazir Henry, "Where Healing Begins," in *Looking Back Reaching Forward: Reflections on the Truth and Reconciliation Commission in South Africa,* ed. Charles Villa-Vincencio and Wilhelm Verwoerd (Cape Town: University of Cape Town Press, 2000), 166–73.

47. John Urry, *The Tourist Gaze: Leisure and Travel in Contemporary Societies* (London: Sage, 1990).

48. Bianca Freire-Medeiros, "The Favela and Its Touristic Transits," *Geoforum* 40 (2009): 580–88.

49. Till, "Construction Sites and Showcases," 51–78.

50. G. Ashworth, "Tourism and the Heritage of Atrocity: Managing the Heritage of South African *Apartheid* for Entertainment," in *New Horizons in Tourism: Strange Experiences and Stranger Practices,* ed. T. V. Singh (Lucknow, India: CAB International, 2004), 95–108; and Rita Barnard, "Oprah's Paton, or South Africa and the Globalization of Suffering," *Safundi: The Journal of South African and American Studies* 7, no. 4 (2006): 1–21.

51. Christian Rogerson, "Shared Growth in Urban Tourism: Evidence from Soweto, South Africa," *Urban Forum* 19, no. 4 (2008): 395–411.

52. Jonathan Noble, "Memorialising the Freedom Charter: Contested Imaginations for the Development of Freedom Square at Kliptown, 1991–2006," *South African Journal of Art History* 23, no. 1 (2008): 13–32; and Bremner, "Reframing Township Spaces," 521–31.

53. Charlene Smith, "Shebeen Route Is a Tourist Magnet," *Saturday Star,* March 7,

1998. See also Achille Mbembe, Nsizwa Dlamini, and Grace Khunou, "Soweto Now," *Public Culture* 16, no. 4 (2004): 499–506.

54. S. S. Goudie, Firoz Kahn, and Darryll Killian, "Transforming Tourism: Black Empowerment, Heritage, and Identity beyond *Apartheid,*" *South African Geographical Journal* 81, no. 1 (1999): 23–31; and Scarlett Cornelissen, "Tourism Impact, Distribution, and Development: The Spatial Structure of Tourism in the Western Cape Province of South Africa," *Development Southern Africa* 22, no. 2 (2005): 163–85.

55. Quotation from *Cape Argus,* April 29, 1998. See also Shelley Ruth Butler, "Should I Stay or Should I Go? Negotiating Township Tours in Post-*Apartheid* South Africa," *Journal of Tourism and Cultural Change* 8, nos. 1–2 (2010): 15–29.

56. Lowenthal, "Fabricating Heritage," 5–24 (7).

57. Samuel, *Theatres of Memory,* 1:205.

58. Lowenthal, "Fabricating Heritage," 7–8.

59. "Shebeen Route Is a Tourist Magnet," *Saturday Star,* March 7, 1998.

60. Philippa Garson, "The Mandela Family Museum," *City of Johannesburg Official Website,* October 26, 2004, available at http//www.cityofjohannesburg.org.html.

61. "Mandela Wants Winnie Evicted from House," *Saturday Star,* February 28, 1998; and "Shebeen Route Is a Tourist Magnet," *Saturday Star,* March 7, 1998.

62. Huyssen, *Present Pasts,* 109.

63. Lucille Davie, "Madiba's Soweto Home Being Restored," *City of Johannesburg Official Website,* December 18, 2008; and Davie, "Mandela House Opens in Soweto," *City of Johannesburg Official Website,* March 9, 2009.

7. Textual Memories

1. Athol Fugard, quoted in Mel Gussow, "From a Discarded Novel to Fugard's New Play," *New York Times,* January 5, 1999, B3.

2. See James E. Young, "Interpreting Literary Testimony: A Preface to Reading Holocaust Diaries and Memoirs," *New Literary History* 18, no. 2 (1987): 403–23, esp. 403.

3. Elizabeth Mittman, "Shifting Limits, Enduring Paradoxes: On Autobiography and Cultural Memory," *Monatshefte* 102, no. 2 (2010): 208–22, esp. 213.

4. Paul John Eakin, *Fictions in Autobiography: Studies in the Art of Self-Definition* (Princeton: Princeton University Press, 1985), 226.

5. There are countless examples. See André Brink, "Interrogating Silence: New Possibilities Facing South African Literature," in *Writing South Africa,* ed. Derek Attridge and Rosemary Jolly, 14–28; Judith Lüghe Couille, "New Life Stories in the New South Africa," in *Economies of Representation: Colonialism and Commerce,* ed. Leigh Dale and Helen Gilbert (Burlington, Vt.: Ashgate, 2007), 183–92; and Lynn Meskell and Lindsay

Weiss, "Coetzee on South Africa's Past: Remembering at a Time of Forgetting," *American Anthropologist* 108, no. 1 (2006): 88–99.

6. Jacqueline Maingard, "South African Cinema: Histories and Futures," *Screen* 48, no. 4 (2007): 511–15.

7. Boym, *The Future of Nostalgia,* 80.

8. See Katarzyna Pieprzak, "Nostalgia and the New Cosmopolitan: Literary and Artistic Interventions in the City of Casablanca," *Studies in Twentieth and Twenty-First Century Literature* 33, no. 1 (2009): 47–69.

9. Allan Megill, "History, Memory, Identity," *History of the Human Sciences* 11, no. 4 (1998): 37–62, esp. 44.

10. Mittman, "Shifting Limits, Enduring Paradoxes," 209.

11. See Paul John Eakin, *How Our Lives Become Stories: Making Selves* (Ithaca: Cornell University Press, 1999), 93–98; and Eakin, *Living Autobiographically: How We Create Identity in Narrative* (Ithaca: Cornell University Press, 2008).

12. Mieke Bal, "Introduction," in *Acts of Memory: Cultural Recall in the Present,* ed. Mieke Bal, Jonathan Crewe, and Leo Spitzer (Hanover, N.H.: University Press of New England 1999), vii–xvii, esp. xiii.

13. Sturken, *Tangled Memories,* 5 (italics in the original).

14. Landsberg, *Prosthetic Memory,* 19.

15. Elleke Boehmer, "Endings and New Beginning: South African Fiction in Transition," in *Writing South Africa,* ed. Attridge and Jolly, 43–56 (46). See also Martin Trump, "Introduction," in *Rendering Things Visible: Essays on South African Literary Culture,* ed. Trump (Johannesburg: Ravan Press, 1990), x–xii; and Elleke Boehmer, Laura Chrisman, and Kenneth Parker, eds., *Altered State? Writing and South Africa* (Hebden Bridge: Dangaroo Press, 1994).

16. See Stephen Clingman, "Revolution and Reality: South African Fiction in the 1980s," in *Rendering Things Visible,* ed. Trump, 41–60; Gready, "Autobiography and the 'Power of Writing,'" 489–523; and Thomas Thale, "Paradigms Lost? Paradigms Regained: Working-Class Autobiography in South Africa," *Journal of Southern African Studies* 21, no. 4 (1995): 613–22.

17. Boehmer, "Endings and New Beginning," 52.

18. Ibid., 46–53. See also Elleke Boehmer, Liz Gunner, and Nhlanhla Maake, "Introduction: New Representations out of Neglected Spaces: Changing Paradigms in South African Writing and Film," *Journal of Southern African Studies* 21, no. 4 (1995): 557–60.

19. Shaun Irlam, "Unraveling the Rainbow: The Remission of Nation in Postapartheid Literature," *South Atlantic Quarterly* 103, no. 4 (2004): 695–717.

20. Njabulo Ndebele, *South African Literature and Culture: Rediscovery of the Ordinary* (Manchester: Manchester University Press, 1991), vii.

21. Boehmer, "Endings and New Beginning," in *Writing South Africa,* ed. Attridge and Jolly, 44. See also Isabel Hofmeyr, "Popular Literature in Africa: Post-Resistance Perspectives," *Social Dynamics* 30, no. 2 (2005): 128–14.

22. Lewis Nkosi, "Postmodernism and Black Writing in South Africa," in *Writing South Africa,* ed. Attridge and Jolly, 75–90 (75).

23. Njabulo Ndebele, "The Rediscovery of the Ordinary: Some New Writings in South Africa," *Journal of Southern African Studies* 12, no. 2 (1986): 143–57 (143).

24. Njabulo Ndebele, "Beyond 'Protest': New Directions in South African Literature," in *Criticism and Ideology: 2nd African Writers Conference Stockholm,* ed. Kirsten Holst Petersen (Uppsala: Scandinavian Institute of African Studies and Nordiska Afrikainstitutet, 1988), 205–16 (205).

25. The ideas for this paragraph are taken from Ndebele, "The Rediscovery of the Ordinary," 143–46; and Njabulo Ndebele, "Redefining Relevance," *Pretexts* 1, no. 1 (1989): 40–51. See also David Chioni Moore, "Of Transitions Fast and Slow: Writing South Africa at the Turn of the Millennium," *Macalester International* 9 (2000): 279–90.

26. "We were shown in this [protest] literature the predictable drama between ruthless oppressors and their pitiful victims; ruthless policemen and their cowed, bewildered prisoners; brutal farmers and their exploited farm hands; cruel administrative officials in a horribly impersonal bureaucracy, and the bewildered residents of the township, victims of that bureaucracy; crowded trains and the terrible violence that goes on in them among the oppressed; and a variety of similar situations" (Ndebele, "Redefining Relevance," 43–44).

27. Ndebele, "The Rediscovery of the Ordinary," 149.

28. Loren Kruger, "The Uses of Nostalgia: Drama, History, and Liminal Moments in South Africa," *Modern Drama* 38 (1995): 60–70 (62); Jacqueline Maingard, *South African National Cinema* (New York: Routledge, 2008); Ian Steadman, "Towards Popular Theatre in South Africa," *Journal of Southern African Studies* 16, no. 2 (1990): 208–28; and Steadman, "Theatre beyond *Apartheid,*" *Research in African Literatures* 22, no. 4 (1991): 77–90.

29. Ndebele, "Redefining Relevance," 43–44. See also Edward Barnaby, "The Realist Novel as Meta-Spectacle," *JNT: Journal of Narrative Theory* 38, no. 1 (2008): 37–59.

30. See Miriam Tlali, "Interview," in *Writing South Africa,* ed. Attridge and Jolly, 141–48 (141).

31. Boehmer, "Endings and New Beginning," 53.

32. Brink, "Interrogating Silence: New Possibilities Facing South African Literature," 21–22.

33. Mark Devenny, "Left Behind: Marxism and Aesthetics in South African Literary Debate," *Africa Perspective* 2, no. 1 (1993): 92–103.

34. See Brink, "Interrogating Silence," 14–17.

35. Ndebele, "Redefining Relevance," 42–43; and Robert Plummer, "SA Writers in the 'In Between' Zone," *Weekly Mail & Guardian,* March 6–12, 1998.

36. Albie Sachs, "Preparing Ourselves for Freedom," in *Writing South Africa,* ed. Attridge and Jolly, 239–48 (239).

37. Ndebele, "The Rediscovery of the Ordinary," 143–57; and Njabulo Ndebele, "Turkish Tales and Some Thoughts on South African Fiction," *Ten Years of Staffrider, 1978–1988,* 7, no. 3–4 (1989): 318–40.

38. Ndebele, "Beyond 'Protest,'" 205–16; Nadine Gordimer, "Living in the Interregnum," in *The Essential Gesture: Writing, Politics, and Places,* ed. Stephen Clingman (London: Penguin, 1989), 261–84; Gordimer, *Writing and Being* (Cambridge, Mass.: Harvard University Press, 1996); André Brink, "An Uneasy Freedom: Dangers of Political 'Management of Culture' in South Africa," *Times Literary Supplement,* September 24, 1993, 13; Graham Pechey, "The Post-*Apartheid* Sublime: Rediscovering the Extraordinary," in *Writing South Africa,* ed. Attridge and Jolly, 57; J. M. Coetzee, *Doubling the Point: Essays and Interviews,* edited by David Attwell (Cambridge, Mass.: Harvard University Press, 1992), 7–9, 66–67, 383–84; and Michael Green, *Novel Histories: Past, Present, and Future in South African Fiction* (Johannesburg: Witwatersrand University Press, 1998).

39. On this issue, my views depart somewhat from David Medalie, "Old Scars, Old Bones, Old Secrets: Three Recent South African Novels," *Journal of Southern African Studies* 23, no. 4 (1997): 507–8.

40. James Berger, *After the End: Representations of Post-Apocalypse* (Minneapolis: University of Minnesota Press, 1999), 5.

41. See Jay Winter, "Notes on the Memory Boom: War, Remembrance, and the Uses of the Past," in *Memory, Trauma, and World Politics,* ed. Bell, 54–73; and Sidonie Smith and Julia Watson, *Reading Autobiography: A Guide to Interpreting Personal Narratives* (Minneapolis: University of Minnesota Press, 2001).

42. For the source of some of these ideas, see Richard Delgado, "Storytelling for Oppositionalists and Others: A Plea for Narrative," *Michigan Law Review* 87, no. 8 (1989): 2411–13.

43. Gordimer, "Living in the Interregnum," 261–84 (269–70).

44. See Jonathan Crush, "Gazing on *Apartheid:* Post-Colonial Travel Narratives of the Golden City," in *Writing the City: Eden, Babylon, and the New Jerusalem,* ed. Peter Preston and Paul Simpson-Housley (New York: Routledge, 1996), 257–84.

45. Shameem Black, "Commemoration from a Distance: On Metamemorial Fiction," *History & Memory* 23, no. 2 (2011): 40–65, esp. 41; Cathy Caruth, ed., *Trauma: Explorations in Memory* (Baltimore: Johns Hopkins University Press, 1995); Caruth, *Unclaimed Experience: Trauma, Narrative, and History* (Baltimore: Johns Hopkins

University Press, 1996); Bal, Crewe, and Spitzer, eds., *Acts of Memory;* and Antze and Lambek, eds., *Tense Past.*

46. Claire Hackett and Bill Rolston, "The Burden of Memory: Victims, Storytelling, and Resistance in Northern Ireland," *Memory Studies* 2, no. 4 (2009): 355–76, esp. 355, 362.

47. Fiona Ross, "On Having Voice and Being Heard: Some After-Effects of Testifying before the South African Truth and Reconciliation Commission," *Anthropological Theory* 3, no. 4 (2003): 325–41.

48. Crane, "Memory, Distortion, and History in the Museum," 44–63 (46).

49. See Silke Horshkotte, "Recollective Processes and the 'Topography of Memory' in W. G. Sebald's *Austerlitz,*" in *Diaspora and Memory: Figures of Displacement in Contemporary Literature, Arts, and Politics,* ed. Marie-Aude Baronian, Stephan Besser, and Yolande Jansen (Amsterdam: Rodopi, 2006), 193–202, esp. 200.

50. Young, "Interpreting Literary Testimony," 403–23, esp. 403, 420.

51. Bernadine Doge, "Re-imag(in)ing the Past," *Rethinking History* 10, no. 4 (2006): 345–67, esp. 346.

52. Elizabeth Tonkin, *Narrating Our Pasts: The Social Construction of Oral History* (Cambridge: Cambridge University Press, 1992), 97–112; and Judith Okely, "Anthropology and Autobiography: Participatory Experience and Embodied Knowledge," in *Anthropology and Autobiography,* ed. Judith Okely and Helen Calloway (New York: Routledge, 1992), 1–28.

53. Gready, "Autobiography and the 'Power of Writing,'" 489–523.

54. Roger Luckhurst, "Reflections on Joan Didion's *The Year of Magical Thinking,*" *New Formations* 67 (2009): 91–100 (91).

55. Barry Unsworth, *Sugar and Rum* (Harmondsworth: Penguin, 1990), 106.

56. J. Lutge Coullie, "'Not Quite Fiction': The Challenges of Post-Structuralism to the Reading of Contemporary South African Autobiography," *Current Writing* 3, no. 1 (1991): 1–23 (1); and David Attwell, "On the Question of Autobiography: Interview with J. M. Coetzee," *Current Writing* 3, no. 1 (1991): 117–22.

57. Jane Starfield, "'Not Quite History': The Autobiographies of H. Selby Msimang and R. V. Selope Thema and the Writing of South African History," *Social Dynamics* 14, no. 2 (1988): 16–35 (16).

58. Gready, "Autobiography and the 'Power of Writing,'" 490–91; and J. M. Coetzee, "Interview," *Doubling the Point,* ed. Attwell, 17–18.

59. For the source of some of these ideas, see Jonathan Crush, "Imagining the South African City," *Social Dynamics* 19, no. 2 (1993): 128–48.

60. Marc Bloch, *The Historian's Craft,* trans. Peter Putnam (New York: Vintage Books, 1953), 61, 62.

61. Georg Lukács, *The Historical Novel,* trans. Hannah Mitchell and Stanley Mitchell (Lincoln: University of Nebraska Press, 1983), 341.

62. Young, "Interpreting Literary Testimony," 403–4, 406.

63. See Marc Dolan, "The (Hi)story of Their Lives: Mythic Autobiography and the 'Lost Generation,'" *Journal of American Studies* 27, no. 1 (1993): 35–56, esp. 39–40.

64. See Lisa Lowe, *Critical Terrains: French and British Orientalisms* (Ithaca: Cornell University Press, 1991), 8.

65. Paul Ricoeur, *Time and Narrative,* trans. Kathleen McLaughlin and David Pellauer, 2 vols. (Chicago: University of Chicago Press, 1985).

66. See, for example, Saskia Lourens, "The Politics of Remembering and Forgetting in Present-day South Africa: André Brink's *On the Contrary,*" in *Diaspora and Memory,* ed. Marie-Aude Baronian, Stephan Besser, and Yolande Jansen, 175–84.

67. Some of the ideas presented here are taken from Tom Lodge, "The Last Hero," *Times Literary Supplement,* December 26, 1997, 11.

68. Commonwealth Eminent Persons Group, *Mission to South Africa: The Commonwealth Report* (Harmonsworth: Penguin, 1986), 66.

69. Lodge, "The Last Hero," 11. For a wider view, see Fatima Meer, *Higher Than Hope: The Authorized Biography of Nelson Mandela* (New York: Harper and Row, 1988); and Mary Benson, *Nelson Mandela* (Harmondsworth: Penguin, 1986).

70. Raymond Williams, *The English Novel from Dickens to Lawrence* (London: Hogarth Press, 1970), 192.

71. Nelson Mandela, *Long Walk to Freedom: An Autobiography of Nelson Mandela* (Boston: Little, Brown, 1994).

72. Martin Legassick, "Review Article: Myth and Reality in the Struggle against Apartheid," *Journal of Southern African Studies* 24, no. 2 (1998): 443–58, esp. 444.

73. Martin Meredith, *Nelson Mandela: A Biography* (New York: St. Martin's Press, 1997).

74. Legassick, "Review Article," 443–44.

75. Sarah Nutthall, "Telling 'Free' Stories? Memory and Democracy in South African Autobiography since 1994," in *Negotiating the Past,* ed. Nuttall and Coetzee, 75–88, esp. 76–78 (77).

76. Legassick, "Review Article," 444–45.

77. F. W. de Klerk, *The Last Trek—A New Beginning: The Autobiography* (New York: St. Martin's Press, 1999).

78. Suzanne Daley, "Book by De Klerk Shatters Any Illusions about His Feelings toward Mandela," *New York Times,* January 16, 1999.

79. Suzanne Daley, "Architect of His Own Undoing," *New York Times,* July 4, 1999.

80. See Nellie McKay, "The Narrative Self: Race, Politics, and Culture in Black

American Woman's Autobiography," in *Feminisms in the Academy,* ed. Donna Stanton and Abigail Stewart (Ann Arbor: University of Michigan Press, 1995), 74–94 (75), for some of the ideas expressed in the following paragraphs.

81. Mamphela Ramphele, *Crossing Boundaries* (New York: Feminist Press, 1997).

82. Ibid., 3, 21–22, 45–46.

83. For the source of some of these ideas, see Dolan, "The (Hi)story of Their Lives," 35–56.

84. See Young, "Interpreting Literary Testimony," 403–4.

85. Ramphele, *Crossing Boundaries,* 183–84.

86. See Thale, "Paradigms Lost? Paradigms Regained," 613–22, esp. 621–22.

87. See Boehmer, Gunner, and Maake, "Introduction: New Representations out of Neglected Spaces," 558–59.

88. See Barbara Harlow, *Resistance Literature* (London: Methuen, 1987).

89. Ezekiel Mphahlele, *Down Second Avenue* (London: Faber and Faber, 1959); and Peter Abrahams, *Tell Freedom* (London: Faber and Faber, 1954).

90. Thale, "Paradigms Lost? Paradigms Regained," 621–22.

91. Albie Sachs, *Soft Vengeance of a Freedom Fighter,* revised and updated (London: Souvenir Press, 2011); and Raymond Suttner, *Inside Apartheid's Prison* (New York: Ocean Press, 2001).

92. Umkhonto we Sizwe (MK) [Spear of the Nation] was the armed wing of the African National Congress. Ronnie Kasrils, *"Armed and Dangerous": My Undercover Struggle against Apartheid* (Oxford: Heinemann, 1993). For another example of this kind of writing, see Carl Niehaus, *Fighting for Hope* (Cape Town: Human and Rousseau, 1994).

93. "[Kasrils] tells his story—except for the final chapters—on the model of a popular adventure novel or a Hitchcock movie, and somehow, by making it entertaining, makes it seem less testimonial rather than more literary." Nadine Gordimer, *Writing and Being: The Charles Eliot Norton Lectures, 1994* (Cambridge, Mass.: Harvard University Press, 1995), 26.

94. Kasrils, *"Armed and Dangerous,"* 4–5, 16–18, 36–38, 97–98.

95. Gordimer, *Writing and Being,* 25.

96. See Thale, "Paradigms Lost? Paradigms Regained," 614–15.

97. See Crush, "Gazing on *Apartheid,*" in *Writing the City,* ed. Preston and Simpson-Housley, 262.

98. J. M. Coetzee, "Confession and Double Thoughts," in *Doubling the Point,* 252.

99. Francis Hart, "Notes for an Anatomy of Modern Autobiography," *New Literary History* 1, no. 3 (1970): 485–511 (491).

100. Richard Terdiman, "The Mnemonics of Musset's *Confession,*" *Representations* 26 (1989): 26–48, esp. 26.

101. Young, "Interpreting Literary Testimony," 406, 407, 409.

102. Terdiman, "The Mnemonics of Musset's *Confession,*" 26.

103. Ibid., 27.

104. Loren Kruger, "The Uses of Nostalgia: Drama, History, and Liminal Moments in South Africa," *Modern Drama* 38, no. 1 (1995): 60–71.

105. "Confession is one component in a sequence of transgression, confession, penitence, and absolution. Absolution means the end of the episode, the closing of the chapter, liberation from the oppression of memory. Absolution in this sense is therefore the indispensable goal of all confession, sacramental or secular" (J. M. Coetzee, "Confession and Double Thoughts: Tolstoy, Rousseau, Dostoevsky," in *Doubling the Point,* ed. Attwell, 251–95, esp. 251–52.

106. Georg Lukács, *The Theory of the Novel,* trans. Anna Bostock (Cambridge, Mass.: MIT Press, 1971), 48.

107. See Nuttall, "Telling 'Free' Stories?" in *Negotiating the Past,* ed. Nuttall and Coetzee, 79–80 (79).

108. See Thale, "Paradigms Lost? Paradigms Regained," 622.

109. Ross Chambers, *Untimely Interventions: AIDS Writing, Testimonial, and the Rhetoric of Haunting* (Ann Arbor: University of Michigan Press, 2004), xxxi–xxxii. For the source of these ideas, see Luckhurst, "Reflections on Joan Didion's *The Year of Magical Thinking,*" 92.

110. See Luckhurst, "Reflections on Joan Didion's *The Year of Magical Thinking,*" 100. By combining journalistic investigation, philosophical inquiry (especially around the notion of white guilt), and truth-telling, Jonny Steinburg, *Midlands* (Johannesburg: Jonathan Ball Publishers, 2002), also falls into this confessional style of writing.

111. Wilhelm Verwoerd, *My Winds of Change* (Johannesburg: Ravan Press, 1998).

112. Ibid., 5, 170–71.

113. J. M. Coetzee, "Confession and Double Thoughts," *Doubling the Point,* 252.

114. See Rita Felski, "On Confession," *Beyond Feminist Aesthetics: Feminist Literature and Social Change* (Cambridge, Mass.: Harvard University Press, 1989), 86–121.

115. See, for example, Mark Sanders, "Truth, Telling, Questioning: The Truth and Reconciliation Commission, Antjie Krog's *Country of My Skull,* and Literature after Apartheid," *Modern Fiction Studies* 46, no. 1 (2000): 13–41.

116. James Gregory, *Goodbye Bafana: Nelson Mandela, My Prisoner, My Friend* (London: Headline, 1995).

117. Ibid., 56–57, 104–5.

118. Michiel Heyns makes this point when discussing the well-known fiction writer Mark Behr, who publicly confessed at a writer's conference to serving as an informer for the apartheid state. See Michiel Heyns, "The Whole Country's Truth:

Confession and Narrative in Recent White South African Writing," *MFS: Modern Fiction Studies* 46, no. 1 (2000): 42–60; and Rita Barnard, "*The Smell of Apples, Moby-Dick,* and Apartheid Ideology," *Modern Fiction Studies* 46, no. 1 (2000): 207–26.

119. Some of the ideas for the following paragraphs are taken from John Kenneth Noyes, "Departing, Returning, and Longing for Home: Narration and the Pathos of Nation," *JLS/TLW* 13, nos. 1–2 (1997): 21–37. However, the way that I employ these ideas departs significantly from the way Noyes uses them.

120. Ibid., 26.

121. Luckhurst, "Reflections on Joan Didion's *The Year of Magical Thinking,*" 91.

122. Arthur Frank, *The Wounded Storyteller: Body, Illness, and Ethics* (Chicago: University of Chicago Press, 1995), 55.

123. Luckhurst, "Reflections on Joan Didion's *The Year of Magical Thinking,*" 91.

124. Noyes, "Departing, Returning, and Longing for Home," 25.

125. Boym, *The Future of Nostalgia,* xviii.

126. Ibid., 49.

127. Cloete Breytenbach, *The Spirit of District Six* (Cape Town: Human and Rousseau, 1997); Yousuf Rassool, *District Six—Lest We Forget: Recapturing Subjugated Cultural Histories of Cape Town, 1897–1956* (Bellville: University of the Western Cape, 2000); and Linda Fortune, *The House in Tyne Street: Childhood Memories of District Six* (Cape Town: Kwela, 1996).

128. William "Bloke" Modisane, *Blame Me on History* (London: Thames and Hudson, 1963), 5.

129. Boym, *The Future of Nostalgia,* 49.

130. Ibid., 49.

131. V. S. Naipaul, *The Enigma of Arrival* (New York: Random House, 1988), 130.

132. Boym, *The Future of Nostalgia,* xviii.

133. Gérard Genette, *Narrative Discourse: An Essay in Method,* trans. Jane Lewin (Cambridge: Cambridge University Press, 1997), 142–50.

134. Annemarie Wolpe, *A Long Way Home* (London: Virago, 1994).

135. For a discussion of this kind of narrative strategy, see David Danow, *Models of Narrative: Theory and Practice* (New York: St. Martin's, 1997), 27–29.

136. Wolpe, *A Long Way Home,* 150–65.

137. Noyes, "Departing, Returning, and Longing for Home," 26, 31–32.

138. Wolpe, *A Long Way Home,* 175–86.

139. Noyes, "Departing, Returning, and Longing for Home," 29.

140. Breytenbach, *Return to Paradise.*

141. In *A Season in Paradise* (New York: Persea Books, 1980), Breytenbach recounts his three-month visit to South Africa with his French-born Vietnamese wife, Yonande,

in 1972–73, after living in Paris in self-imposed exile since 1959. In *The True Confessions of an Albino Terrorist* (Johannesburg: Taurus, 1984), he narrates the story of his clandestine return to South Africa, under the sponsorship of Okhela, an erstwhile revolutionary organization comprised of exiled white South Africans; his capture, well-publicized "show trial," and subsequent conviction under the terms of the draconian antiterrorism statues; and his seven-year prison term.

142. Boym, *The Future of Nostalgia,* 49, 50.

143. See Lawrence Joffe, "A New Future," *New Statesman & Society,* December 10, 1993, 39.

144. Neil Lazarus, "Longing, Radicalism, Sentimentality: Reflections on Breyten Breytenbach's *A Season in Paradise,*" *Journal of Southern African Studies* 12, no. 2 (1986): 18–182, esp. 161.

145. See, for example, Simon Lewis, "Tradurre e Tradire: The Treason and Translation of Breyten Breytenbach," *Poetics Today* 22, no. 2 (2001): 435–52.

146. "High-sounding phrases occasionally convey neither superlative insight nor great sensitivity, but the rather precious posturing of an intellectual who takes himself very seriously indeed" (Lazarus, "Longing, Radicalism, Sentimentality," 170).

147. Gillian Slovo, *Every Secret Thing: My Family, My Country* (Boston: Little, Brown, 1997). See also Marian MacCurdy, "Truth, Trauma, and Justice in Gillian Slovo's Every Secret Thing," *Literature and Medicine* 19, no. 1 (2000): 115–32.

148. Boym, *The Future of Nostalgia,* 49.

149. Robert Hewison, *The Heritage Industry: Britain in a Climate of Decline* (London: Methuen, 1987), 134.

150. Boym, *The Future of Nostalgia,* 8.

151. Ibid., 3- 5.

152. Genette, *Narrative Discourse,* 36–40, 50–54.

153. Boehmer, "Endings and New Beginning," 45.

154. Rian Malan, *My Traitor's Heart: A South African Exile Returns to Face His Country, His Tribe, and His Conscience* (New York: Random House, 1990); Graham Boynton, *Last Days in Cloud Cuckooland: Dispatches from White Africa* (New York: Random House, 1997); and Lester Venter, *When Mandela Goes: The Coming of South Africa's Second Revolution* (Johannesburg: Transworld, 1997).

155. For a positive response to the book, see Irene Visser, "How to Live? Guilt and Goodness in Rian Malan's *My Traitor's Heart,*" *Research in African Literature* 39, no. 3 (2008): 149–63.

156. Malan, *My Traitor's Heart,* 272–425.

157. Ibid., 276.

158. Ibid., 69.

159. Ibid., 421.

160. "A White African Writes Hauntingly of His Own Land," *The Star,* April 1, 1998.

161. Personal e-mail communication with Lester Venter, December 2, 1997.

162. James Atlas, "What Is Fukuyama Saying? And to Whom Is He Saying It?" *New York Times Magazine,* October 22, 1989, 38.

163. David Lowenthal, "Dilemmas of Preservation," in *Our Past before Us: Why Do We Save It?,* ed. David Lowenthal and Marcus Binney (London: T. Smith, 1981), 213–37; and Christopher Shaw and Malcolm Chase, "The Dimensions of Nostalgia," in *The Imagined Past: History and Nostalgia,* ed. Christopher Shaw and Malcolm Chase (Manchester: Manchester University Press, 1989), 1–17.

164. Hewison, *The Heritage Industry,* 54–58.

165. See Samuel, *Theatres of Memory: Volume 1,* 261.

Epilogue

1. John Gillis, "Heritage and History," 375–79, esp. 377; and David Lowenthal, *Possessed by the Past: The Heritage Crusade and the Spoils of History* (New York: Free Press, 1996), 121–22.

2. Johnson, "Framing the Past," 187–207, esp. 187.

3. Kirshenblatt-Gimblett, *Destination Culture,* xxv.

4. See Robert Hewison, "Commerce and Culture," in *Enterprise and Heritage: Crosscurrents of National Culture,* ed. John Corner and Sylvia Harvey (London: Routledge, 1991), 162–77.

5. Richard Evans, *In Defense of History* (New York: W. W. Norton, 1999).

6. Johnson, "Framing the Past," 187–207.

7. See Gillis, "Heritage and History," 375–79, esp. 377.

8. David Lowenthal, "Identity, Heritage, and History," in *Commemorations,* ed. Gillis, 41–57 (43).

9. Lowenthal, *The Heritage Crusade and the Spoils of History,* 120.

10. Johnson, "Framing the Past," 189. See also Nuala Johnson, "Where Geography and History Meet: Heritage Tourism and the Big House in Ireland," *Annals of the Association of American Geographers* 86 (1996): 551–66.

11. Mike Crang and Penny Travlou, "The City and Topologies of Memory," *Environment and Planning D: Society and Space* 19, no. 2 (2001): 161–77 (161).

12. A. Joan Saab, "Historical Amnesia: New Urbanism and the City of Tomorrow," *Journal of Planning History* 6, no. 3 (2007): 191–213, esp. 192.

13. Nuala Johnson, "Framing the Past," 189.

14. Leslie Witz, Ciraj Rassool, and Gary Minkley, "Repackaging the Past for South African Tourism," *Daedalus* 130, no. 1 (2001): 277–96.

15. Kirschenblatt-Gimblett, *Destination Culture,* 151.

16. Birgitta Svensson, "The Nature of Cultural Heritage Sites," *Ethnologia Europaea* 28, no. 1 (1998): 5–16, esp. 5.

17. Dean McCannell, "Staged Authenticity: Arrangements of Social Space in Tourist Settings," *American Journal of Sociology* 79 (1973): 589–603; McCannell, *Empty Meeting Grounds* (New York: Routledge, 1992); Erik Cohen, "Authenticity and Commodification in Tourism," *Annals of Tourism Research* 15 (1988): 371–86; Nesar AlSayyad, "Global Norms and Urban Forms in the Age of Tourism: Manufacturing Heritage, Consuming Tradition," in *Consuming Tradition, Manufacturing Heritage: Global Norms and Urban Forms in an Age of Tourism,* ed. AlSayyad (New York: Routledge, 2001), 1–33; and David Howes, "Introduction: Commodities and Cultural Borders," in *Cross-Cultural Consumption: Global Markets, Local Realities,* ed. Howes (New York: Routledge, 1996), 1–16.

18. Robert David Sack, *Place, Modernity, and the Consumer's World: A Relational Framework for Geographical Analysis* (Baltimore: Johns Hopkins University Press, 1992), 161–62; Erik Cohen, "Contemporary Tourism—Trends and Challenges: Sustainable Authenticity or Contrived Post-Modernity?" in *Change in Tourism: People, Places, Processes,* ed. R. Butler and D. Pearce (New York: Routledge, 1995), 12–29.

19. George Ritzer, *The Globalization of Nothing* (New York: Pine Forge Press, 2004), 105.

20. Connerton, *How Societies Remember,* 14, 61.

21. Huxtable, *The Unreal America,* 92–107.

22. Bérlanger, "Urban Space and Collective Memory," 69–92, esp. 69–70.

23. Ibid., 74.

24. Ibid.

25. See Christian Rogerson, "Urban Tourism in the Developing World: The Case of Johannesburg," *Development Southern Africa* 19, no. 1 (2002): 169–90.

26. JoAnn McGregor and Lyn Schumaker, "Heritage in Southern Africa: Imagining and Marketing Public Culture and History," *Journal of Southern African Studies* 32, no. 4 (2006): 649–65.

27. Bérlanger, "Urban Space and Collective Memory," 79.

28. Huxtable, *The Unreal America,* 88.

29. See Herbert Marcuse, *One-Dimensional Man: Studies in the Ideology of Advanced Industrial Society* (Boston: Beacon Press, 1964), 76. For the "predisposition to amnesia" in the "new South Africa," see Bryan Rostron, "Welcome to Our Torture Chamber: Tourist Attractions in South Africa," *New Statesman,* September 17, 2001, 32–38.

30. Sheryl Ozinsky, "Prejudice Has No Place in Selling the City," *Cape Times,* March 16, 2001; Khadija Magardie, "Amateurs' Threat to Township Tours," *Mail & Guardian,*

March 16–22, 2001; and "Adventure Tourism Takes Off in SA," *Pretoria News* (Winter Holiday Travel Destinations Supplement), May 25, 2001. For a wider view, see Christopher Steiner, "Authenticity, Repetition, and the Aesthetics of Seriality: The Work of Tourist Art in the Age of Mechanical Reproduction," in *Unpacking Culture: Art and Commodity in Colonial and Postcolonial Worlds,* ed. Ruth Phillips and Christopher Steiner (Berkeley and Los Angeles: University of California Press, 1999), 87–103.

31. Rogerson, "Urban Tourism in the Developing World," 178–79.

32. Scarlett Cornelissen, "Producing and Imaging 'Place' and 'People': The Political Economy of South African International Tourist Representation," *Review of International Political Economy* 12, no. 4 (2005): 674–99.

33. For the history of this approach to heritage, see Foster, *Washed with the Sun.*

34. Timothy Mitchell, "The World as Exhibition," *Comparative Studies in Society and History* 31, no. 2 (1989): 217–36 (220).

35. See Garth Allen and Frank Brennan, *Tourism in the New South Africa: Social Responsibility and the Tourist Experience* (London: I. B. Tauris, 2004), 18–46, 207–20; Phumzile Ngwenya, "New 'Veza' Will Make SA Travel Fun for Tourism," *Business Day,* May 29, 2001.

36. Kirshenblatt-Gimblett, *Destination Culture,* 194.

37. See Catherine Cameron, "The Marketing of Heritage: From the Western World to the Global Stage," *City & Society* 20, no. 2 (2008): 160–68; AlSayyad, "Global Norms and Urban Forms in the Age of Tourism, 1–33; and Catherine Cameron, "Emergent Industrial Heritage: The Politics of Selection," *Museum Anthropology* 23, no. 3 (1999): 58–72.

38. Allen and Brennan, *Tourism in the New South Africa,* 18–46.

39. Sturken, *Tourists of History,* 21–26.

40. Ulrich Baer, "To Give Memory a Place: Holocaust Photography and the Landscape of Tradition," *Representations* 69 (2000): 50.

41. Jan Baumgartner, "Deep in Africa, a Most Civilized Discovery," *New York Times,* January 3, 1999.

42. Peter Hain, *Sing the Beloved Country: The Struggle for the New South Africa* (London: Pluto, 1996), 211.

43. Kenneth Little, "On Safari: The Visual Politics of a Tourist Representation," in *The Varieties of Sensory Experience: A Sourcebook in the Anthropology of the Senses,* ed. David Howes (Toronto: University of Toronto Press, 1991), 148–66, esp. 150, 153–54.

44. See Edward Bruner and Barbara Kirshenblatt-Gimblett, "Maasai on the Lawn: Tourist Realism in East Africa," *Cultural Anthropology* 9, no. 2 (1994): 435–70.

45. Little, "On Safari," 156–57; and Edward Bruner, "The Maasai and the Lion King: Authenticity, Nationalism, and Globalization in African Tourism," *American Ethnologist* 28, no. 4 (2001): 881–908.

46. W. J. T. Mitchell, "Showing Seeing: A Critique of Visual Culture," *Journal of Visual Culture* 1, no. 2 (2002): 165–81 (179).

47. Susan Sontag, *On Photography* (New York: Farrar, Straus and Giroux, 1979), 15.

48. Little, "On Safari," 150.

49. Mitchell, "The World as Exhibition," 217–36.

50. Little, "On Safari," 150, 153–56.

51. See Jane Carruthers, *The Kruger National Park: A Social and Political History* (Pietermaritzburg: University of Natal Press, 1995).

52. See Allen and Brennan, *Tourism in the New South Africa,* 104–33.

53. Little, "On Safari," 150, 153–56.

54. See Mitchell, "The World as Exhibition," 217–36.

55. Boyer, *The City of Collective Memory,"* 6.

56. Michel de Certeau, *The Writing of History,* trans. Tom Conley (New York: Columbia University Press, 1988), vii, 3–5.

57. Statement of Deputy President Thabo Mbeki on the Occasion of the Debate on the Budget Vote of the Office of the Deputy President (National Assembly, June 3, 1998).

58. Wilson, *The Politics of Truth and Reconciliation in South Africa,* 15–16, 153–55; Lynn Graybill, *Truth and Reconciliation in South Africa,* x–xii; and Meskell, "Trauma Culture," 157–75.

59. Bick, "Horror Stories," 30–41, esp. 30, 40. See also Okwui Enwesor, "Reframing the Black Subject: Ideology and Fantasy in Contemporary South African Representation," in *Reading the Contemporary: African Art from Theory to the Marketplace,* ed. Okwui Enwezor and Olu Oguibe (Cambridge, Mass.: MIT Press, 1999), 376–99; and Enwesor, "The Enigma of the Rainbow Nation: Contemporary South African Art at the Crossroads of History," in *Personal Effects: Power and Poetics in South African Contemporary Art,* vol. 1, ed. Sophie Perryer (New York: Museum of African Art in association with Spier [Cape Town], 2004), 23–43.

60. Raymond Ngcobo, "*Apartheid* and Alienation in the Work of Art," in *Grey Areas: Representation, Identity, and Politics in Contemporary South African Art,* ed. Brenda Atkinson and Candice Breitz (Johannesburg: Chalkham Hill Press, 1999), 153–55.

61. See Foster, *Washed with Sun,*1–13; Beningfield, *The Frightened Land,* 207–26; and John Peffer, *Art and the End of Apartheid* (Minneapolis: University of Minnesota Press, 2007).

62. Statman, "Whites Are Living in Cloud-Cuckooland."

63. See Nicolas Pons-Vignon and Ward Anseeuw, "Great Expectations: Working Conditions in South Africa since the End of *Apartheid,*" *Journal of Southern African Studies* 35, no. 4 (2009): 883–99.

64. Enwesor, "Reframing the Black Subject," 376–99.

65. Statman, "Whites Are Living in Cloud-Cuckooland."

66. Ibid.; and Richard Ballard, "Assimilation, Emigration, Semigration, and Integration: 'White' Peoples' Strategies for Finding a Comfort Zone in Post-Apartheid South Africa," in *Under Construction: "Race" and Identity in South Africa Today,* ed. Natasha Distiller and Melissa Steyn (Pietermaritzburg: Heinemann, 2004), 51–66.

67. Medalie, "Old Scars, Old Bones, and Old Secrets," 507–14 (507).

68. Myambo, "The Limits of Rainbow Nation Multiculturalism," 93–120.

69. Marcuse, *One-Dimensional Man,* 98.

70. Bertelson, "Ads and Amnesia," 228, 231, 233, 235, 239–41.

71. Grunebaum-Ralph, "Re-placing Past, Forgetting Presents," 198–202; and Meskell, "Trauma Culture," 157–75.

INDEX

MARTIN J. MURRAY is professor of urban planning in the Taubman College of Architecture and Urban Planning and adjunct professor in the Department of Afroamerican and African Studies at the University of Michigan. He is the author of *City of Extremes: The Spatial Politics of Johannesburg, Taming the Disorderly City: The Spatial Landscape of Johannesburg after Apartheid, The Revolution Deferred: The Painful Birth of Post-Apartheid South Africa,* and *South Africa: Time of Agony, Time of Destiny,* and coeditor, with Garth Myers, of *Cities in Contemporary Africa: Place, Politics, and Livelihood.*